D0858615

FORTY YEARS BEHIND THE WALL

Fr. M. Raymond, O.C.S.O.

Our Sunday Visitor, Inc.
Huntington, Indiana 46750

Scripture texts used in this work are taken from the Douay-Rheims and Kleist-Lilly editions. Additional texts are taken from *The New American Bible*, copyright © 1970, by the Confraternity of Christian Doctrine, Washington, D.C. and *The Jerusalem Bible*, copyright © 1966 Darton, Longman & Todd, Ltd. and Doubleday & Co., Inc. All rights reserved. The excerpt from the poem, "The Road Not Taken" is from *The Poetry of Robert Frost*, ed. Edward C. Latham, copyright © 1916, 1930, 1939, © 1969 by Holt, Rinehart and Winston, copyright © 1944, © 1958 by Robert Frost, copyright © 1964, 1967 by Lesley Frost Ballantine.

Copyright © 1979 Our Sunday Visitor, Inc.

All rights reserved. No part of this book may be reproduced or copied in any form or by any means — graphic, electronic, or mechanical, including photocopying, recording, taping, or information storage and retrieval systems — without written permission of the publisher.

ISBN: 0-87973-644-5
Library of Congress Catalog Card Number: 79-83875

Cover design by James E. McIlrath. The aerial photograph of the Abbey of Gethsemani used on the cover is used courtesy of the Gethsemani Abbey Archives.

Published, printed and bound in the United States of America

to
Mary Immaculate
Mother of all Priests in Gratitude for Her
Mothering of me

and to
One of Her special daughters
Lady Anne Lane Dearinger
in appreciation of her many years of true
friendship

and finally to
the late and greatly loved
Father John P. Flanagan, S.J.
for his inspiring life of love —
for God — and of me!

Contents

✝

Foreword

†

Hi! Do you want to read a book that is different? You do? Well, read on; for this book is going to be different — very different; not only for you, but also for me. Further, I promise to make it shockingly different — and differently shocking. First of all, there will be no sex in it. Then there will be no theological sensationalism — no new theories, no new explanations of age-old truths, no new insights or intuitions about Scriptural passages we accepted from earliest youth without any "demythologizations!" It seems I'm bypassing those seemingly surefire paths to best-seller lists, doesn't it? Well, I would not be the least bit chagrined if this does make one of those lists, but I would be very chagrined, not only with myself, but also with you, if I did have to use those overused things to sell this "revelation."

Yes, this is going to be a very revealing book, but without a semblance of anything even remotely related to what is technically known as "private revelations." Yet I am about to reveal many things that have been strictly private for some forty years, and that is enough to put me into a state of shock! I have been pestered for years by well-meaning people to write about myself, but have always refused.

I will never forget the first time this matter came up. I had obtained a very reluctantly given permission to speak

7

with Tom Merton. In those happy days we never broke silence here at Gethsemani. We belonged to the Strict Observance then, and we still do. But there have been changes. At any rate, it was shortly after Tom's *Exile Ends in Glory* had been published. His "exile" has ended since, and I am sure it ended "in glory." This was one of Tom's earliest books. I read with avidity, for I had been through his *Thirty Poems*, his first publication as a Trappist, and I saw that God had sent us rare talent. His title for this account of Mother Berchman intrigued me. Tom always had excellent titles for his work. Before I had gotten very deeply into the book I saw what Tom meant by "exile." Mother Berchman had gone from France with the pioneer group of nuns to found the first Cistercian convent of Trappistines in Japan. That was exile. That it ended in "glory" was most evident from Tom's lengthy account. But the account disappointed me; it even angered me a bit. I had read his *Thirty Poems* in 1944. *Exile Ends in Glory* came out in 1947. Tom had been with us six years by that time. Hence, I had come to know him quite well. With my deepening knowledge of him came a heightening of my admiration for him as a monk and as a writer. Further, I knew I could speak openly, and I did.

In my usually gentle manner I blurted out: "Tom, this stinks! You can do much better than this. Why don't you let yourself go?"

Tom smiled. He was a happy monk who never took himself too seriously. Here, he was a very honest youngster. To me, he always was a "youngster," although he was thirty-three, while I was more than ten years older. Further, I had ten years advantage over him in publishing as a Trappist, but I knew there was mutual trust and admiration.

He took my breath away by agreeing with me. "You're right, Raymond. It does stink. But wait until my next one appears. It will be out shortly. You'll see that I really let myself go in this one."

"What's it about, Tom?"

"It's my autobiography."

I was speechless. I just stared. Only the week previous to our session, I had read somewhere that no one should ever write his autobiography until he was seventy, and then only if he had contributed something worthwhile to culture or civilization. I agreed heartily with that statement. Yet, here was Thomas Merton, at thirty-three, not only writing, but having published, his autobiography!

Well, he gave me the first copy of *Seven Storey Mountain* which came off the press. I devoured it, and got permission to speak with him again. This time I clasped his hand vigorously, and enthusiastically greeted him, "Congratulations, Tom! This is great! Truly yourself. You let yourself go, all right. Believe me, boy, this will turn out to be a great seller; for it is a great book. I mean *great!*"

He was not so sure. In typical Merton fashion he murmured, "I don't know about that. We'll wait and see. I can say I enjoyed writing it."

I could not let it go at that and added, "That last chapter, though, calls for comment — and, on your part, caution."

"What are you talking about, Raymond?"

"Contemplation, Tom. You make it sound too easy. Believe me, boy, you have a lot to learn about it. Let me tell you that, before you ever become a mystic, you have, first, to have been an ascetic, and one for a long, long time. Tom, you are still new at this business, so *festina lente* — make haste slowly. But, *do* keep a'going."

That was the beginning of years of hassle about contemplation between me and Tom. He did keep going, managed eventually to do what he had not done at that time. He contributed much to culture and, I hope, to civilization by the veritable volume of publications that poured from his pen. His autobiography turned out to be what I had prognosticated: a great book and a tremendous seller.

9

It was at this time that Tom asked me what I was writing. I had to confess that, at that moment, I was writing nothing.

"Why don't you write about yourself?" he asked.

"Never!" I thundered instantaneously.

"Why not?" he came back. "It's easy."

"Maybe for you, Tom. But not for me. I couldn't do it."

I am over seventy now. But what have I contributed to culture or civilization that could possibly justify this departure? Nothing. Yet I am going to write an autobiography, although covering only my forty years behind these walls of Gethsemani, the Trappist monastery hidden among the hills that cloister us here in Nelson County, Kentucky, U.S.A.

It was the number *forty* that set me off, in my ruby jubilee year as a Trappist, to tell you something about those years. Forty is a scriptural number, a mystical number, and a rather popular number, which many use as an excuse and an explanation. Who hasn't heard of "the foolish forties"? Well, in my fortieth year as a Trappist, in what many refer to as "the desert," let me be foolish enough to be scriptural — and maybe a bit mystical. I will show you that this "desert" has been anything but dry. I may be a fool for making the attempt. But I don't mind being a fool, so long as I am being a "fool for Christ."

He was in the desert, a real desert, for forty days and forty nights — fasting. I have done some fasting, too, in my forty years, but there ends the similarity between Christ in His desert and this Christian in his. Mark tells us that during His sojourn Christ lived amid wild beasts and that angels waited on Him. I have not been amongst wild beasts, and I have never actually seen an angel, though I hesitate to say they have not been around, or that they have never waited on me. Luke states that Christ ate nothing in all that time. Again, that marks a difference between Christ and this Christian. I have eaten — nothing very fancy, nothing to tickle that palate. But I have eaten — something.

What I have always found humorous is that Matthew and Luke state that after that He was hungry. Well, what human being — and never forget that Jesus was fully human — would not be hungry after forty days and forty nights of fasting? I know I have been hungry, ravenously hungry, after a single day of fasting. During the forty days of Lent, in the first thirty years of my sojourn here, we had only one meal a day. Believe me, just before that one meal, I was hungry.

From Genesis to the Acts of the Apostles Holy Scripture has reference after reference to forty days, forty nights, and even forty years. In the sixth chapter of Genesis we read how God, the Unchangeable, seems to have changed His mind about men. He saw that "the wickedness of men was great upon the earth, and all the thought of their hearts was bent upon evil at all times." Quite an indictment. So "it repented Him (God) that He had made man on earth." He told Noah that He would send "rain upon the earth forty days and forty nights" to destroy "all the substance that was upon the earth, from man even to beast, and the creeping things and fowls of the air."

The next forty days and forty nights we read about involved Moses and Mount Sinai. We have read much about the Sinai Peninsula these last few years, but not too much about those Ten Commandments Moses received from God centuries ago. If these had been observed "down the nights and down the days," not to mention "down the arches of the years," we would not be reading so much about that peninsula these days and these years. But we can be grateful to Moses for obtaining those two tablets up there on the mountain, for all the good, all the beauty, and all the truth mankind has known since then, can be traced back to those Commandments.

Next, we have a long walk of forty days and forty

nights. Elijah made this, and on very little food. He went into the desert, and ended up on a mountain, too — Mount Horeb, called "the mountain of God." There always seems to be a correlation between deserts, mountains, God, and His Glory. I strike that note here for we monks are supposed to be in a "desert," supposed to be climbing "the mountain of God," and supposed to be ever seeking Him and promoting His Glory.

But I guess the Chosen People of God in the desert for forty years is the most precise parallel for me to use. They were headed for the Promised Land. We are chosen, too, and we are headed for paradise. Some even call the cloister paradise. But there was trouble in paradise — the first and real paradise — and in our *Paradisus Claustralis*, too. One reason I do not insist too much on the parallel between the original Chosen People and their Promised Land and us and our paradise is that so few of them ever made it! I hope, indeed, I know the percentage of those who make it from this paradise is much higher.

That remark brings me to say that the final reference in Scripture to the number "forty" is the one that, I hope, will characterize this effort. Luke tells us in the first chapter of the Acts that Jesus "showed Himself alive to them after His Passion by many demonstrations: for forty days He had continued to appear to them and tell them about the kingdom of God."

That, truly, is the purpose for breaking my silence. I am going to share some secrets with you about this place and this life. It was Chesterton who once said that "the secret of Christianity is *joy*." He found fault with us for having kept that secret to ourselves. Let me rid myself of that one fault.

I cannot give you a detailed account of the days and nights that make up the forty years. Were I to attempt that I would be outdoing St. John who felt forced to end his Gospel with "There were many other things that Jesus did; if all were written down, the world itself, I suppose, would not hold all the books that would have to be written." I plan to write one book, and that, I trust, will not be too lengthy a volume. But I also hope it will be good news.

You know that "gospel" means just that: good news. Listening to our newscasters you would never be led to believe that Christ had been sent by the Father to give us good news. Reading our leading magazines or scanning the headlines of our daily papers you are made to wonder what happened to that last command of Christ: "Proclaim the Good News to all creation." What is good about the news we hear and read: murders, robberies, rapes, kidnappings, hijackings, civil wars, commando raids, earthquakes, tidal waves, destruction and death, death, death. Yet Christ came to give life!

That is why I insist this book is going to be different and because of that difference, it is going to be shocking. I am going to give you much good news and much life; for I am a Christian — and have been for forty years behind these walls.

I do owe great thanks to one individual: my brother, Fr. Jack Flanagan, S.J. You see, I had started to say that I have had a lot of fun and never a day of frustration during my forty years when I grew very conscious of my amnesia and my "selective memory." Then I learned that Fr. Jack had saved every one of my letters I had written him since 1936. Further, he had a carbon of every letter he had written me. What a mine I had found! Wait until you read my early letters from behind the walls. You will be asking: "Where's the fun amidst all these frustrations?" I *have* had a lot of fun, and I have had comparatively *few* frustrations. See if you agree.

1

I Arrive . . .

and Almost Depart

†

It was dark as I left the Watterson Hotel and headed for Union Station that rather dreary morning of November 14, 1936. I was something like the morning — dark and dreary — or to be more exact, ambivalent. I was of two minds about Louisville. I had arrived in the dusk of evening. I was leaving it in the dusk of early morning. I had not seen much of the city the night before. In fact, I was asking myself whether it was a city, or just an overgrown town. Most certainly it was little like New York, Boston, Philadelphia, or Washington, cities quite well known to me in my early years. Nor was it anything like Seattle, Portland, San Francisco, or Los Angeles, cities I had been working in during the past year, giving missions and retreats. It was something like Worcester, Massachusetts, a bit bigger than Eugene, Oregon and Great Falls, Montana, where I had functioned for a while quite recently. Well, what difference did it make? I was leaving it for Gethsemani — wherever that was. I was starting a new adventure, and that should have had me "high." But I had just left Boston and my family, and that always gave me a "low."

Soon I was on the local of the Louisville-Nashville Railroad. This train nearly had me sneering. All I could liken it to was the local I used to take for Boston when I was employed by the New York, New Haven and Hartford Railroad during my last few years in high school. Well, this *was* a local, as evident from the condition of the cars, which were anything but new, and certainly not too comfortable. As we jolted out of the yards, I got my first glimpse of the Kentucky countryside. I was not favorably impressed.

It was early morning. A haze hung over the hills, or knobs as they were called in this part of the world. The trees on those hills, all save the oaks and the evergreens, were bare. Houses were rare, once we left the city, and I concluded that the state was sparsely settled. I knew very little about the Blue Grass State. I had heard about the Kentucky Derby, had read about Daniel Boone, and knew it was a border state during the Civil War, the birthplace of Abraham Lincoln. I had sung Stephen Foster's song "My Old Kentucky Home." That was about it. I knew then that I had some boning up to do, to clear away my ignorance concerning the state I was contemplating making my home.

I soon tired of looking out on the bleak countryside. So I turned inside to my travelling companions. They were not many, nor were they any more impressive than the countryside. I did catch the "twang" as snatches of conversations came to my ears. I noted it was different, not exactly a southern drawl, but nothing like the clipped speech of the Yankee. I concluded I was travelling with what some books and TV shows snobbishly called "hillbillies." Unconsciously (I hope), the Yankee supposed-superiority was at work as I settled back to read some of my Office.

I had not read much before I closed my breviary and began to wonder just what lay immediately ahead. I chuckled as I recalled the answer I had given to a fellow Jesuit: "To live in the society of Jesus," was my reply. He laughed, but I knew it was in appreciation of the paranomasia, and not in gratitude for the explanation. I knew then, as I know now, that the motivating force could be summed up in the one word: *reparation*.

15

I had loved life in the Society of Jesus. As I looked back now, I recognized those years as crowded, yet exhilarating. My first two years had been happily spent as a novice on the old Lillienthal Estate on the Hudson River, just above Yonkers, New York, and not too far away from New York City. The mansion on that estate had been designed for anything but a novitiate. Yet, in it we managed to have all the established places of a traditional novitiate: chapel, chapter room, ascetories, dormitories, refectory, guest parlors, separate rooms for the master of novices, minister of the community, confessors, and a retired missionary. Then, in the basement, we had shoe-room, shower room, scullery, and kitchen. We dignified that area by calling it the sub-cloister. It was "sub" all right, but anything but a cloister.

The grounds of the estate had been cut up — and how! The former front lawn had become a "farm." Actually, it was only a vegetable garden, and I, at sixteen, had been named head farmer. Imagine that — a city slicker learning how to harness up horses, to drive them and make a straight furrow; how to plant, cultivate, harvest, and store; how to care for pigs and chickens. I even built a silo! It was then and there that I awoke to the fact that I loved the outdoors and loved to work, to really labor.

In my "primi-year" — 1920-1921, we cut out a tennis court and erected a handball court. They were well used every Thursday, which was the one day every week we called a free day. In the summer months those Thursdays saw us rowing across the Hudson for swimming just below the Palisades. Once a month we would picnic over there for a whole day.

It was a happy two years, well balanced between work and play. All the work, however, was not manual. No, indeed! We tyros had to learn all about the spiritual life. And were we taught! Yet, here I was in 1936 heading for a second novitiate — really a third, for I had completed the entire Jesuit course, and followed with a tertianship in which

16

one repeated all the exercises of the first novitiate — from the "long retreat" of thirty days to the various "trials" in hospitals, homes, parishes to the ordinary routine of work, play, prayer, and study.

What would my third novitiate be like? I did not know then. I was certain of only one thing: they would be nothing like the fourteen that had followed my years at Yonkers. How right I was!

I mentally ran down the sixteen busy and ever noisy years of my Jesuit life as the train clicked me toward silence that November morning in 1936. As we neared Gethsemani, I increasingly felt a tingling sense of expectation, tinged with anxiety. I had been talking, and talking, and talking for sixteen years — as student, professor, and retreat master and giver of parish missions over the entire Pacific slope from Vancouver to San Diego. Yet, here I was, heading for a cloister hidden among the knobs of Nelson County, Kentucky, and toward absolute silence.

Was I crazy? That query never entered my head during that train ride. It did afterwards! I recall a keen curiosity I had about the life I was about to enter. I knew something about myself after thirty-two years of living with myself, but I knew practically nothing about the Trappist way of life, except that it was cloistered and penitential. There was the rub. Could I, who had been ever on the go as a Jesuit, be cloistered? Could I, who had always plunged deep into life and into living, be penitential? It was the challenge these two aspects presented that had attracted me in the first place. Since I always loved and most always accepted a challenge, I was in eager anticipation to enter the life.

The sun was just above the knobs as the train chugged to a stop at Gethsemane Station. I grinned as I looked at the tiny, box-like affair and was reminded of similar stations I had seen as I crossed from Montreal to Vancouver in the summer of '34 with my brother, Father Eddie, an Oblate of Mary Immaculate.

I was somewhat puzzled and felt a bit lost. I, alone, detrained. A tiny pouch of mail was dropped with me. I saw no station master, nor anyone else around. Except for some large warehouses, there was nothing to be seen in that dreary and desolate spot. I moved toward the station. As I did so I espied a strange form coming down the dirt road. All I could think of, as I looked at that approaching form, was Rip Van Winkle and the "brownies" who roamed the Catskill Mountains back in New York State. Coming toward me was a white-bearded man in a brown robe which was tucked up and tied at his knees, and with a hood attached to it pulled over his head. He was a strange apparition.

He came closer, then quietly asked, "Are you the postulant?" Now the Jesuits do not have a postulancy. They take you right in, give you a short, intensive retreat, then clothe you in the black cassock. I had come across the term in my study of canon law, had heard references made to it by nuns, but to be asked personally was somewhat startling and disconcerting. Groping for a moment, I finally gasped, "I guess I am."

"Come," this figure said, and he led me toward a tiny black buggy. Not another word was spoken as the bony, white horse pulled us up a hilly, gravel road, jogged around a few bends between hills, and brought us to a more heavily forested section. I saw no humans or human habitations and was thinking that I was truly in the backwoods, when a final turn brought us in view of a huge, grey-white building standing stark under the now risen sun. I concluded this was the Abbey of Our Lady of Gethsemani.

Thank God the sun was shining that morning, else I would have to describe my arrival at Gethsemani as eerie. During my years as a Jesuit, I travelled much, and practically always there were friends or acquaintances awaiting my arrival. Such meetings were always warm, and often boisterous. Never did I have to board a buggy or a carry-all. Most always a limousine, or at least a huge passenger car, transported me from the station or airport to a Jesuit residence or a parish rectory, where more warmth and noisy welcomes were given me. This morning in November of 1936 I had an absolutely silent companion with me. He did not even speak to the horse he was driving. Before, my destination was almost always in a huge metropolis. This day I was in the country — and I mean country. I did not glimpse a single human being as we drove those two miles or so from Gethsemane Station to Gethsemani Abbey.

But let me add one detail which kept my arrival from being truly eerie. I looked into the eyes of my "reception committee" when he greeted me at the station. They were burning, bright, blue eyes. They belonged to Brother Paul, as I later learned to name him, and in those eyes I saw "heaven." There was peace there. There was purity. There was quiet joy and clarity. There was a tranquillity about his whole person, yet activity to be sensed in his absolute silence. This man was busy, very busy internally. He was busy with God. Here was someone — and something — that was different, very, very different. I was more than curious. I was intrigued. What was the secret?

We were driving down a silent, tree-shaded lane, toward the gate house. I had lived in big houses before. St. Andrew-on-the-Hudson was a massive structure. It had to be, for it was novitiate, juniorate, and tertianship for the entire Maryland-New York Province, which at that time numbered over a thousand Jesuits. The monastery building of Gethsemani loomed as gigantic to my inquiring eyes.

Then the fun began, although, at the time, I thought it all quite queer. I began to suspect that I had made a huge mistake. For once Brother Paul had reined in his horse, he simply pointed to some double doors, over which ran a Roman arch of poured concrete. Above that arch, in a niche stood a statue of Our Lady with Child. I recognized it as that of Our Lady of Victories, whose original shrine is in Paris, France. As I looked at her I did not feel very victorious. Across the arch, in big, bold, black letters ran the words: PAX INTRANTIBUS. It meant: "Peace to those who enter," but how does one enter? Brother Paul had driven away as soon as he had dropped me off, and I was all alone before those silent, closed doors.

I saw no knob on the doors, nor could I find any latch. But I did see, about eye-level, what looked like a grate, not very large; maybe a foot square. "This is great!" I thought. Then I espied a tiny wooden cross suspended from a thin chain that obviously ran through the roof just below that massive arch. I grabbed the cross, pulled the chain, and heard a bell ring within those walls. Nothing happened, so I pulled again. Again the bell rang. How lonely it sounded! Soon I heard faltering steps, something of a shuffle, behind those doors. A panel behind that foot-square grate was drawn back, and I was gazing at a busy beard topped by a pair of quiet eyes. That was all I could see. I said nothing. I was awaiting a greeting or a query. Neither came. The panel closed. I was left standing before those doors, still alone. Talk about queer! Then I heard a very large key being clumsily inserted into a lock. A rattle, then a loud click, and half of those double doors opened. I bent and grabbed my bag and took a step toward the opening, only to have a brown-clad figure, identical in every detail to the brown-robed Brother Paul, fall on his knees before me, but with never a word to me. I looked at him for a moment, and concluded that this strange kneeling figure must have wanted a blessing. I was right. I traced a hurried sign of the cross over him; he arose and simply pointed to another door that stood two steps above us.

I nodded my gratitude to the silent doorkeeper, and opened the door to which he had pointed. It led me into a large, primitive room. The floor was of wide planks, very roughly planed, unpainted, unvarnished, crudely laid with quite wide spaces between them. Over to one side stood a black, pot-bellied stove, while across from it a much larger

20

pot-bellied monk, in black and white this time, spreading a white cloth over a very crude-looking table. It was Father Oddo, the guest master. In a heavy German accent he exclaimed: "Oh, you must be the postulant we are expecting. I am setting a dining table for the families of two monks who will make their solemn professions tomorrow. You must be Father Flanagan."

I admitted I was, and then said, "Let me help you, Father." Those were the first words I spoke since leaving Louisville. His were the first I heard since leaving Gethsemane Station. I was happy to learn they were not mutes in this monastery.

"I will tell Father Abbot that you will make a great monk. You are willing to work."

Here was a monk growing ecstatic over an offer of help for a trifling job. I began to wonder more seriously whether I had made a colossal mistake by coming here.

We set the table. Then Father Oddo led me across a rather unkempt garden to the main building. Again I was impressed by its size. Once we had entered the massive, arched doors, I was met with another bold, black, large-lettered sign which read: GOD ALONE. Strange as it seems now, I found that greeting a bit chilling. Through another set of huge doors we went and I was led down a dark corridor that seemed anything but inviting.

Even in the dimness of that lengthy corridor I was able to read the inscription that ran along the high border. It read: "Leave your body at the door. There is room here only for your soul." It was signed, "St. Bernard." Before I had time to digest that message Fr. Oddo was knocking on a door which held the sign "Rev. Abbas." It opened. I entered, rather chilled by this time, only to be warmly greeted by a thin-faced, very emaciated looking man who said, "Welcome! I am Father Frederic." Again two sparkling eyes held my vision, and again, as with Brother Paul, I saw "heaven." But this time there was a difference. These blue

21

eyes snapped. They twinkled. They were alive. They glittered — and even danced.

I was in the presence of Dom Mary Frederic Dunne, fifth abbot of the Abbey of Our Lady of Gethsemani. And what a presence that was! It radiated alertness, energy, interest, kindness, and comfort.

He very soon led me out of that office, but not before I had taken in its condition. It was crowded — almost cluttered. A huge roll-topped desk occupied most of the floor space. Under that roll-top one glimpsed many pigeonholes, each crammed with letters, notes, contracts, and memoranda. The few chairs in the room were piled high with books. No wonder he did not ask me to be seated. Against the front wall stood a glass-enclosed library with shelves jammed with books. On the rear wall hung an old-fashioned telephone. I had taken the room in with a few darting glances, and concluded that its occupant was a very busy man, but I wondered how orderly.

Dom Frederic led me into a small room, almost as cluttered as his office. Immediately he began plying me with questions about certain documents I was supposed to have in my possession. It soon appeared that I had not carried along all the documents necessary for a canonical transfer. I was surprised at myself, and a bit ashamed. But Dom Frederic put me at my ease immediately by saying there was no cause for concern whatsoever, and that he himself would expedite the matter.

Very shortly thereafter I was escorted upstairs to what the Trappists called "the hotel." Father Oddo showed me to what was to be my room until those documents arrived. What a room! The ceiling was sixteen to eighteen feet above the floor. The walls were painted a sickly dark green, and that paint was peeling. A few dim prints, in heavy frames, depicted the Madonna on one wall and the Crucifixion on the other. They were no great works of art by anyone's calculations. In one corner was an ancient washstand with a chipped enamel basin, with a chipped enamel pitcher, a single towel, and a single face cloth. I was told the washroom was down the other end of the corridor. There was a single rocking chair in the center of the room which looked as old or older than the monastery itself. A few throw rugs were lying here and there on the floor, while over to one side stood a huge bed. It looked to me like a bed one would find in a second- or even third-class hotel.

Little did I know then, but in that "hotel" room I would stay for five very long weeks because of those missing documents. Still, they were anything but idle weeks. The next day I asked Father Oddo if there was something I could do. He was then working in the library — not on books, but painting the blinds or shutters, which were taken down every fall from the many windows around the huge inside cloister to be scraped and painted for use the following spring and summer. I scraped and painted every morning and afternoon of those five weeks.

I was not entirely alone during those weeks, for, in what the monks called time for "lectio divina," time for spiritual reading, and what, as a Jesuit, I called free time, I had daily visits from a Father Augustine.

This man can be characterized as my life-saver. He was a monsignor, in fact a prothonotary apostolic, who held three doctorates, one in philosophy, one in theology, and a third in canon law. He had come to Gethsemani from Three Rivers, Canada, where he had been Vicar General of the diocese, rector of the seminary, and professor of theology. When I first met him I summed him up as an "old man." He was seventy-two years of age at the time. Now that I have passed that, I see how relative age really is! Today I would label him as anything but an old man.

What impressed me immediately was his simplicity, humility, kindness, intelligence, and honesty. He had been at Gethsemani twenty years when I first met him, and was director of studies, professor of both philosophy and theology, dean of the faculty, president of all the conferences, and sub-cantor of the choir. To me he was a delightful daily visitor, the oasis in my otherwise dry day, the only one with whom I could enjoy an exchange of ideas, and from whom I could obtain direct and profound answers to the many questions I had about the life I was contemplating entering.

Almost immediately he advised me to make a retreat of election. I thought I had made my election long before I had left Boston, and wondered if the old man had any idea of the kind of a man they were calling a postulant. Then came the real bomb. He told me to make it on my own. He told me he would visit me daily to check on my progress. I have often thanked God that dear old Father Augustine suggested I follow the Spiritual Exercises of St. Ignatius. I knew those Exercises, for I made them every year of my life as a Jesuit. Further, I had given them to college and high school students. But this would be the first time I had ever attempted them on my own. What an experience! But first, I must share another experience I had while in the hotel.

In those days I had only the second floor of that hotel as my entire world. There was located my room, the refectory, washroom, work room (the library and those shutters), and the church. From the gallery, I would look down the longest, narrowest, strangest stretch of a church I had ever seen. I had been in cathedrals, parish churches of all sizes, modest chapels, and simple "halls" on army posts and in C.C.C. camps, from coast to coast and border to border. But never had I been in a monastic church. My first glimpse of the one at Our Lady of Gethsemani shocked me. Its length, height, narrowness, absence of pews, presence of choir stalls, and eerie lighting all added to my feeling of queerness.

My first full day at the abbey did not see me following the entire schedule. I did not get up at 2:00 A.M. for Matins. I was told that the monks chanted the Little Office of Our Lady from 2:07 A.M. (They were allowed *seven minutes* to

24

rise, wash, dress, and be down in their choir stalls for the beginning of that Office!) At 2:30 they began their morning meditation. At 3:00 they began to chant the Canonical Office of Matins and Lauds. Then came the Angelus. After that the priests offered their Masses singly. At 5:30 they were back in that massive monastic church for the hour of Prime. The canonical hour was always preceded by the hour of the Little Office of the Blessed Virgin. That meant two full Offices a day for these monks. At least one day a month they added a third Office for the dead. No wonder they called their home "a house of prayer." On the big feasts, when these monks would arise at 1:00 A.M., they put in practically eleven hours in the church chanting Office and offering Masses. There were two community Masses on certain days, one called the matutinal Mass, which was a low Mass; then, later in the morning, a sung high Mass which was often an abbatial solemn high Mass of a feast.

My first day I did assist at the Solemn Pontifical Mass, at which two monks pronounced their solemn vows. This was the first time that I heard anyone make a solemn promise to God of "stability," a promise made in public, and accepted by Christ's Church, to "live and die in the community of the Abbey of Gethsemani." I was used to the vows of poverty, chastity, and obedience, which all religious pronounce, but this day I heard two others added: a vow of "conversion of manners," and a vow of "stability."

The first was explained easily and quickly. It required that one live and die not only in religion and in the Order of Cistercians of the Strict Observance, but even in the community of the house in which he made his profession. Fr. Augustine chuckled as he told of the genesis of St. Benedict's idea of the vow of stability. It would appear that, when Benedict drew up his rule, there had been four kinds of monks in existence: hermits, gyrovagues, sarabites, and those whom Benedict dubbed "the strongest kind of monks," and for whom he legislated — the cenobites.

Back in his own century, Benedict saw what we call hippies. Unlike many we knew in the sixties, those in Benedict's day did just the opposite of what ours did. They had their heads shaved. Instead of jeans and dirty shirts, those of Benedict's day dressed as monks. This wise legislator said that if the sarabites were bad, and according to him they were very bad, the gyrovagues were even worse; for they "lied to God by their very tonsures, and what pleased them, they called 'holy,' and what displeased them was *verboten*." On top of that they "wandered from place to place with no superior over them."

I could account for such thinking and living. We are such self-centered and selfish beings, that we all readily rationalize what pleases us and are past masters at self-deceit. But I was still somewhat stymied by the whole idea of stability, this vowing to stay in one place with one group for a whole lifetime. How diametrically opposed it was to the ideas and ideals of the Jesuits. They practically vowed to be always on the move, ready at any moment to go wherever there was any hope of promoting the honor and glory of God by saving souls. In my sixteen years as a Jesuit, I had lived for varying lengths of time in every province, and had been under more than a dozen different superiors. If I chose to become a Cistercian, I would have to vow to stay right here in this one abbey, with this one community, and under this one abbot!

But it was not long before I realized that each and every religious is committed to his or her order or congregation for life, and while not taking an explicit vow of stability, the vow of obedience is tantamount to doing just that. So, very soon, stability ceased to bother me.

Yet there was still the other vow of conversion of manners. That did stump me. Listening closely to Father Augustine, I soon got the impression that it stumped him, too. He spoke of perfection. But every religious, without taking any specific vow, is obliged to strive for that. It is the Gospel mandate to all Christians: "Be ye perfect as your heavenly Father is perfect." So why this special vow? Father Augustine spoke of a change of life. Again, every religious makes a change of life the moment he or she enters the religious life. It would be years before I would find the one word that satisfied me, and which explains the vow fully. It occurs again and again in the Gospels and in the Acts. St. Paul uses it in his Epistles, too. It is the Greek word, *metanoia*.

I now believe that my conversion of manners began as I knelt in that gallery and looked down on that Cistercian Gothic monastic church. It had a quiet beauty that soon dissipated the uneasiness caused by the first impression of strangeness. It was long and narrow, but in the distance was a spacious sanctuary, steeped in a silence that stirred a reverential awe in any who looked down on it from this distant, quiet gallery. Here was the burning bush that Moses saw, for here was God. One could almost feel Him, hear Him, touch Him, and taste Him.

Directly in back and above the high altar stretched a massive picture window depicting the Madonna with her blue mantel stretched wide, sheltering Cistercian saints, all looking up with love-lit faces to Mary and her Child. Four other similarly large windows flanked this centerpiece. They carried the capsulized history of the Cistercian Order from its legislator, Benedict, to its leading light, Bernard.

Beneath these windows one could discern arches leading to alcoves holding altars for private Masses. From those arches hung delicately worked iron grilles, all of which had been shaped by the early monks themselves. What craftsmen they were! From those grilles dropped knotted cords, ending in tassels. It was a graceful, and a grace-filled semicircle — truly an awesome sight.

The transepts could not be seen in their fullness from this gallery, but their massiveness was readily suspected.

Lancet windows, delicately and artistically leaded, of multicolored stained glass, spaced along the side walls, held

27

readily recognized symbols of the Litany of Loretto. Directly behind me in the gallery, matching the massiveness of the Madonna window in the sanctuary, was a prayer-inspiring picture window of Our Lady's Assumption. Without those windows it would have been a dark and dismal church. With them it was a subdued and mellow place for prayer where one could all but touch God, and where one was certainly touched by Him.

That church is no more. It changed often during my forty years, but never as drastically as after Vatican II! We left up the original walls, but that is all we left. The beautiful windows are gone. The almost countless Gothic arches are only a memory. Many consider the remodeled church quite beautiful in its austerity and simplicity, but I know nostalgia almost every time I enter the "new" church.

The old church had other peculiar features. Right across the middle of the nave stretched a "bridge," artistically carved in mahogany. A curved stairway led to this bridge, and in its center was a bookstand. At that bookstand a monk would read the lessons during the Matins and at Vespers, and the abbot would read the Gospel every third nocturne of the vigils. This, of course, was all new to this Jesuit. It brought back the old saw that "Jesuits know not rubrics; they don't fast; and they can't sing." It is a libel, of course, but it arose from the fact that the Jesuits were the first order in the Church that was not obliged to choir, and were not monastic. Hence, they did not observe the monastic fast which ran from September 14th until Easter Sunday.

During the Office I noted the bridge separated the two elements which composed the community. The white-robed monks occupied the choir stalls above the bridge, while the brown-clad lay brothers filled those below.

It was the brown-robed, bearded brothers who attracted my attention magnetically those first few days. They were enveloped in silence, not only because they were in church, and, consequently, in the immediate presence of

Christ in the Blessed Sacrament, but because they were obviously absorbed in prayer. The serenity, peace, and quiet joy they radiated held me.

Among them were a dozen or more greybeards but, for the most part, they appeared to be young men. What were they doing with life? I knew their day, from 2:00 A.M. until 7:00 P.M., was devoted to hard manual labor, chiefly on the large farm which made this community self-sustaining. I caught glimpses of them setting out for their labors in the dark of early morning, and watched them returning as the sun sank toward the west. I noted that they always had a rosary in their hands. I labelled them "men of the beads and beards."

These bearded men had the beads in their hands even while the white-clad monks above them chanted the Office. Now, for some years I had been instructing the people in the pews about the proper way to assist at Mass; I begged them to participate actively and exhorted them to follow the missal. Yet, here I was looking at "professionals" saying their beads while the Divine Office was being chanted by the choir-monks, and even while the Holy Sacrifice was being offered! I was shocked and disillusioned.

Father Augustine again came to the rescue. He told me how the brothers had their own Office, which consisted of Paters, Aves, and Glorias. They were saying their own Office while the choir-monks were chanting the Divine Office above them. His explanation added to my admiration of and interest in the lay brotherhood.

I will never forget one morning watching the priests of the community file out for their single Masses. In absolute silence they marched out of the sacristy in single file, each preceded by a lone lay brother holding the missal in his hands before his breast. Around the apse they led that long line of priests, each with his chalice in the same spot before his breast. There was uniformity here! Unto the various altars they went, one by one.

This was a truly inspiring morning. The way the priests filed out, the low murmur of their voices as they offered Mass from the various altars, some twelve of them around the apse and in the transepts; the candlelight, and the reverence of those lay brother servers spoke to me of order, discipline, self-control, consideration for others, dignity, reverence, or to sum it all up in one word: holiness. I was awestruck, and I felt small, unworthy, and truly humble, to be in the midst of such men whose whole life was focused on God, and quite evidently on God alone.

I wonder now, reading one of my earliest letters from Gethsemani to my elder brother, Father Jack, if all this awe and admiration for and of these men, especially the lay brothers, caused me to be afraid that I could not measure up.

I looked at the life these men were leading and at the life I had just left. Nothing, and I mean absolutely nothing, appealed to me. The food was not exactly appetizing. The coffee was barley water! They used to roast the barley, add water and boil. Talk about it being "good to the last drop"; in those early days it was not good even with the first sip! There was no meat, no fish, no eggs. Don't forget I had just come from the Jesuits who are the only humans, as someone has said, who are like lions, for they like meat for breakfast. I learned from Father Augustine how these monks could make chapel in seven minutes every morning. They slept in their clothes, removing only their shoes. They slept on plank beds with straw mattresses, one coarse sheet, a pillow, and a blanket for each bed. Maybe that was good for the back, but how about the tired body and the almost exhausted person? Then there was the work — farming all day long. It was not that I disdained such menial labor, nor that I was afraid of work. Actually, I liked to work and even to engage in strenuous labor, for God had given me a strong physique and set it alive with energy. I soon told myself that it was God who was to be considered, and especially His vocation to the priesthood, His education, and His talents. There was the roughest rub. Could I deliberately bury my talents? I was not being arrogant. I was simply being honest. I had taught, preached, and lectured "successfully" for many years. So I had to recall the parable of the talents, and face reality, knowing well that I would be finally judged by Him who had told that parable. How dare I wrap His talents, or even His one talent in a napkin, and expect to win heaven?

Then I looked long at my priesthood. What were these Trappist priests doing as priests? I recalled how Christ said to His first priests: "Go forth and teach all nations, baptizing them in the Name of the Father, and of the Son, and of the Holy Spirit." These priests did not even baptize, let alone teach. So I kept on asking, what did they do? No baptisms, no preaching, no teaching, no marriages, no funerals, no confessions. None of the Corporal Works of Mercy. There was none of the counseling that is so prevalent today. Just what did they do with their priesthood? They offered Mass, but with no congregation behind them! And I? I could offer Mass outside the walls, usually with a huge congregation. I could preach, teach, baptize, marry, absolve, visit the sick, clothe the naked, feed the hungry, give drink to the thirsty — both the naturally hungry and thirsty, and more especially to those supernaturally starved and dehydrated. I could use my talents, which God had given me, even if I did not actually double them. Further, I could save my soul, and that was the ultimate object of life and living. Why should I stay inside these walls?

Then, there was my natural temperament. I was an extrovert who loved people. I was a social animal as well as a rational animal. These monks did not even speak or socialize with one another, let alone with other humans! I began to see the monastery as a hotbed for neuroticism. The monks were denying every God-given instinct. They were burying every God-given talent. They were living a life that was the antithesis of all God made man to be.

31

I had drawn up a watertight case against the Trappistic way of life — especially for me. I did admit they were glorifying God. But so were the Jesuits, the Dominicans, the Franciscans, the diocesan clergy, good Catholic parents, and good Catholic laity. I could use my talents, follow all my God-given tendencies, and employ every God-given bent of my temperament much more efficiently and effectively outside the walls than I ever could within them. In short, while I had every reason to leave the monastery I had none to stay within its confines.

What kept me from going away? Ignatius of Loyola. I pondered long and fruitfully on Ignatius' *Principium et Fundamentum* — the first Exercise of his Spiritual Exercises. I had made these Exercises every year of my adult life. I had given them to others. But it was only now that I was discovering the differences between knowledge of them and experience of them, the difference between getting the truth into the head and getting it into the heart.

Ignatius did not make life any easier. The beds were just as hard, the labor just as menial and tiring, the simple fare no more palatable. The coffee did not taste any better, nor was the soup any more succulent, and the vegetables still remained vegetables, but they all slid down more easily once I had plunged into the retreat. I must have plunged, for I had been hit by the opening Exercise with such force that I was knocked flat on my face before God, the Creator.

Creature is a word that has taken on such a variety of meanings that it can be used as a compliment of the highest order, or as a devastating condemnation. In Ignatius' "Principle and Foundation," it can have that double meaning, and it is the fundamental and principal word of this opening Exercise, the operative and dynamic word which sets the mind piercing to the truth of all truths, and the will beaming in on the genuinely good and the truly beautiful.

That was the purpose Ignatius had in mind when he laid down this foundation and stated his principle; the prin-

32

ciple is a beginning for the mind while the foundation is a beginning for the will — and a man, essentially and ultimately, is his own mind and will. From the Exercise, a thinking and prayerful man can discover the secret of life, and plumb to the depths the whole purpose of living.

It is stated with almost savage brevity: "Man was created . . ."; that is the beginning of all beginnings for a rational being. While we often say that an individual has the stuff to make a man, we actually do not know what we are saying, for the stuff of which any and every man is made is *nothingness*. That is what creaturehood means; it tells us that we are made out of nothing.

It can be devastating for a man, especially modern man, to be told he has come from nothing. He is right in considering himself lord of the universe, and with all his discoveries and inventions he has proved his claim. He has walked on the moon, scanned Mars, circled Venus, and scooped up rocks and dust from distant planets. Small wonder that he is proud. Yet it was one of our earliest astronauts, who from far out in space asked God an age-old question: "What is man that you should be mindful of him, or the son of man that you should care for him?" The soldier-saint from Loyola gives the only answer in those three words: Man was created.

The definition of creature says, "it is the production of something out of nothing by an act of God." There is the nobility of man: He is a product of the work of God Almighty, and is nothing less than a mirror of God Almighty, a veritable ikon of Infinity, a true image and likeness of Him who is Immensity, Omniscience, and Omnipresence.

Modern man seldom thinks of those attributes of God, for he very seldom thinks of God. Consequently, he does not know how to think rightly of man. Ignatius did, and he would have every exercitant begin his Spiritual Exercises by realizing he does not belong to himself, but to God, the only truly eternal. That is exactly what I heard during that re-

33

treat of election I made those early days at Gethsemani. Hearing that truth, I could close my ears to those lies I had been hearing about talents, tendencies, and temperament. That is why I did not depart.

I had decided to stay, pointing out to Father Jack the comparative easiness of this Trappist life when put alongside the life he had to lead as a Jesuit, as well as the life of my younger brother Father Eddie had to face as an Oblate of Mary Immaculate. This life — a life of silence, seclusion, and profoundest solitude; a life in which one ate no meat, eggs, or fish; a life in which one never saw a paper, magazine, or heard a radio (television had not been invented by then); a life in which a choir monk spent from seven to eleven hours in church daily, four to six hours at hard manual labor, and only six to seven hours in sleep was actually *easier*! Still, the end for Jesuit, Oblate, Trappist, or diocesan priest, was the same: the glory of God, the sanctification and salvation of souls — his own the first! The means were substantially the same: prayer and penance. Every priest had to be an *homo crucifixus mundo, et cui mundus crucifixus est* — a man crucified to the world, and to whom the world was crucified. The monks were engaged in an apostolate of prayer, while those outside the monastery had the apostolate of the Word. I told Jack that he would do the planting by his preaching and teaching, while I would do the watering of the seed by my prayer and penance.

My enthusiasm was generated by Ignatius, for he does not end his "Principle and Foundation" with the three words, "Man was created. . . ." He goes on to give God's purpose in creating man, ". . . to praise, reverence, and serve God, and by this means to save his soul." There you have the purpose of life, and the plan for living. Reason will tell you this truth, but it is revelation that hammers it home. Christ Himself put it clearly, concisely, and convincingly when He rebuked Peter for trying to dissuade Him from undergoing His Passion and taking on His Death and conclud-

34

ed with those impressive words: "If anyone wishes to come after Me, let him deny himself, take up his cross, and follow Me. For he who would save his life will lose it; but he who loses his life for My sake, will find it. For what does it profit a man if he gain the whole world, but suffer the loss of his own soul? Or what will a man give in exchange for his soul?" (Mt. 16:24-26) How those words clarify one's vision of life in this chaotic world.

Ignatius helps one put order into the seeming chaos that surrounds us as he goes on to state: "The other things on the face of the earth were created for man's sake, and in order to help him in the prosecution of the end for which he was created." He is saying that this wondrous world is God's work, and He made it all to aid man attain his one end. The cosmos is the blindingly beautiful handiwork of the Creator, and it was called into being as a means to help man find his way to God. Ignatius goes on: "Whence," he says, "it follows that man must make use of them insofar as they help him attain his end, and in the same way he ought to withdraw himself from them insofar as they hinder him from it." That is truth stated with practicality and prudence. That is the famous *tantum quantum* of the Exercises, and the life of every thinking Christian.

Ignatius is not finished yet. He concludes with his statement of what became known as his doctrine of "holy indifference": "It is therefore necessary that we should make ourselves indifferent to all created things, insofar as it is left to the liberty of our free will to do so and is not forbidden; in such sort that we do not for our part wish for health rather than sickness, for honor rather than dishonor, for a long life rather than a short life; and so in all other things, desiring and choosing only those which the better lead us to the end for which we were created." That "only" represents the other famous Ignatian word *unice*, which, with the *tantum quantum*, insures success as it guarantees sainthood — and that is the real purpose of any man's life.

I ended my letter to Father Jack with the words: "Yes, Jack, I have decided. I am off for the novitiate. I don't know any real fear. The food is terrible. The hours, awful. The silence, unbearable. The aloneness — heavenly! Nothing, absolutely nothing appeals naturally — but from the supernatural, yes, it is heavenly!!"

I had my reasons for all that enthusiasm, for it was most evident that these monks praised, reverenced, and served God every day, and all day long. How could any life more fully follow the purpose God had for making man? As for the reparation which had motivated me in choosing the life, what else was their penance, expressed by their silence and their austerities in food, clothing, sleep, and manual labor? As for glorifying God, I saw their lives as one long doxology. Indeed, I had my reasons! I saw that I could leave the Jesuits and live in the society of Jesus — and with ease, for He would be my constant companion in this "desert" which was steeped in silence, which was secluded from the madding world, and where one had to live as a solitary even though surrounded by others.

When Father Oddo one dark evening in early December called from the base of the stairs, "Father Flanagan! Father Abbot says you can come to chapter for this retreat with the community," I was delighted. I donned my cassock, threw my chinchilla overcoat across my shoulders, followed the waddling Father Oddo along the interior cloister and entered the chapter room for the first time, tingling with curiosity for a close-up of this community in which I had determined to stay. My first step inside the room made me blushingly self-conscious, for I was the only black-clad person in that large assembly of men whose heads were all close-cropped, and of those bearded brothers. I felt their eyes, and wondered how many were asking themselves, "Have we a black-sheep in our midst?" I did not satisfy my curiosity that evening, I was too self-conscious to even look around. But it was a new beginning for me.

2

Difficulties . . . Plenty
Doubts . . . None

†

While I was allowed in *with* the community, it would be weeks before I was *in* the community, and months, even years, before I would be officially *of* the community. I made that retreat with the community, but I still had to live in the "hotel."

The delay was due to the lack of those papers I should have had with me on my arrival, plus the fact that the Jesuit provincial had failed to answer a letter from Abbot Dunn. This failure embarrassed me to some extent, for I had always maintained that Jesuits were perfect gentlemen. I finally came to the conclusion that the provincial knew me a bit better than I knew myself, and that he was quite convinced that the silent cloister was not the most compatible environment for the young Jesuit priest he always addressed as Joe. In retrospect, I agree with him, but God's ways are not always our ways. It was a miracle of grace that I adjusted as well as I did, and actually revelled in the noncompatible environment.

The delay had its advantages. I met the retreat master, Fr. John Zeller, C.SS.R., and that was a delight. I used to visit with Fr. John every evening after the monks had gone to bed. We would go over the matter he had given in the retreat that day, and then branch out on many other matters.

I must have presented Fr. John with a "study," for some twelve or fifteen years later, Fr. John came back to Gethsemani, sought me out, and told me of the resolution he had made after our meetings in 1936. "I told God," he said, "that I would smoke my head off if that young Jesuit priest did not make it with the Trappists. And that very night I put aside my pipe and pouch, and I haven't touched them since." Now for Fr. John Zeller, that was a sacrifice! The jovial Redemptorist has long since gone to God and if ever the old saying about "heaven's gain being earth's loss" applied, it did in the case of John Zeller. He knew and lived the knowledge that the secret of Christianity is joy. He radiated cheerfulness, and had an infectious chuckle. A fellow Redemptorist told me, years later, that Fr. John was found dead in bed with his favorite book, the Bible, under his pillow. I would sum him up as a scholar who was truly humble, and a man who was the soul of charity and true simplicity. A greater tribute I cannot pay a real religious. He inspired me. I now recognize that he was a special grace from God. His retreat confirmed my own. I determined to stay.

It was not too long after Fr. John had left that the Christmas spirit must have taken hold on Dom Frederic, for he called me in one day to say that despite the lack of all the papers, I could join the novices as a postulant. As I laid aside the Jesuit cassock I felt a tinge of sadness, but as soon as I put on the all-white postulant's garb I was filled with a new joy and a tingling eagerness. My head was shaved to the skull bone. My razor was put aside. There would be no more need for a comb. I was denuded and then reclothed from the skin out with a habit, coarse as canvas for the underclothing, which was covered by white wool. The black sheep had come home!

Medieval as the garb was — for that matter, the entire structure of the life — I felt newly born and that I was entering the eschaton. There was much about this latest move that made me think of the angelic life and Paradise regained. In reality, I was treated as a postulant, and was given every assignment reserved for postulants. I carried the abbot's crozier in the regular weekly assignment. I was named to be miter-bearer in more than one abbatial Mass. I had to be servant-of-the-Church in my turn, and was treated no differently than was the youngest recruit who came in before finishing high school. Do you know what? I revelled in it!

It was a strange trip from the hotel to the novitiate. I had never walked long, dim cloisters before. I found the large cloister quite beautiful with its mosaic floor and Gothic-arched ceiling. The little cloister which led directly to the novitiate was an annex which had been built long after the pioneers had gone to their rewards. It was well named, for it was little compared to the beauty and massive width of the original cloister of the abbey proper. It was narrower and darker, and not very cheerful. In the novitiate, the floors, like those of the gate house, were made of the same wide, practically unplaned planks, with cracks between them. The walls and ceilings consisted of whitewashed plaster. There were no pictures, tapestries, or decorations to relieve the starkness of the walls, and no curtains or shades on the windows.

The scriptorium was furnished with backless stools and a very plain table, around which we sat for conferences and instructions by the master of novices. Around the entire expanse of walls, there ran a low bench with tiny individual boxes beneath in which we were allowed to keep pens, pencils, notepaper and notebooks. It was anything but spacious. A narrow corridor led from the front door of the novitiate to the scriptorium and divided the chapel, which could not have been more than thirty feet by fifteen, from three tiny cubicles which were the drying room, the singing room, and the master of novices' room. Next to the scriptorium was the shoe room, or the "grand parlor," where we hung our work apron and kept our work shoes.

Let me tell you about my first pair of work shoes. They were used unsparingly for five or six years — *at least* six hours every day except Sunday. They lasted all those years because the soles were very thick, and the heels were cut from discarded automobile tires. I well recall the master of novices leading me across the "yard" (Does that remind you of Sing-Sing or Walla Walla? Well, this is a penitentiary in the root meaning of that word! For this is a penitential order!) to the shoe shop, which was housed in one of the original buildings set up by the founders in the middle of the nineteenth century. It looked of that century! There was no real machinery to speak of. There sat the cobbler Brother Pius, who stood well over six feet and must have weighed over two hundred and thirty pounds. He had just passed his eightieth year of age, and was obviously dim of eyesight. Fr. Robert, the novice master, made a sign which meant work shoes. Pius shook his head in understanding agreement, and with no question about length or width, brought forth a pair which he must have fashioned rather recently, and handed them to the master. The master handed them to me, and led me back to the novitiate. I had no trouble getting into them, for I wore a size eight-and-a-half shoe, and these were closer to size twelve! "You'll get used to them," was the only comment from the master when I smilingly pointed out their roominess. Theirs not to reason why — anyway, I must have gotten used to them, for it was a good five years later that I turned them in — with no regrets, but with quite a few callouses!

The second floor, which was the top floor of the novitiate, held the dormitory. I was shown my cubicle, which was seven feet by five, walled in by planks that reached six feet above the floor, held three planks on which rested a tufted, straw mattress covered by one sheet made of sail cloth, one pillow stuffed with straw, and a blanket. There was no door to this cubicle, only a cloth curtain which could be pulled so as to give a modicum of privacy. There was a small crucifix on the wall of that cell, and it was more than a symbol. It told the entire story. A Trappist novice is as poor in worldly possessions as was Christ, and almost as naked as was He on the Cross, but all is well if he realizes he is one with Christ in the work the Father gave His Son to do.

But before he learns the depth of that reality, the novice has many other things to learn. I was not yet even a novice, only a postulant! What lessons were in store for me.

The very first afternoon I tucked up my woolen habit and tied it at the knees, took off my house-scapular, put on my work-scapular, threw over it a blue denim apron, then put on those durable work shoes. I fell in single file behind six choir novices, took out my rosary, and followed them to the woodshed down in the flour mill for my first afternoon of manual labor. I was all eyes, for this was my first close-up of my companions, and my first experience with monks at manual labor.

Only one of the novices, Frater Michael, was near my age. The other five were in or near their teens. The master passed out axes to all but one, and pointed to the fairly huge pile of cut wood that had to be split for kindling. Not a word was spoken. The only sound heard was the zing of the saw and the crack of the axes. Silence does sharpen the powers of observation, and I learned much about those novices by simply observing them.

I was at home with this assignment, but I soon noted that aside from Father Robert, the novice master, I was about the only one who was. There was young Patrick, all smiles and all willingness to work, but not very skilled at this kind of labor. He had just turned sixteen, stood close to six feet, and was all long legs and arms. He was a dangerous boy to be near as he wielded his axe, and because of his eagerness to split, and split, and split — and to laugh! "Plenty of speed, but no control," was my baseball summation of young Pat. Then there was Nivard, a shy, short youngster who obviously had never used an axe before. Barnabas, who was not much older than Pat, was delicately formed and not nearly as strong as Pat. Luke was a husky farm boy who was still growing, and was definitely clumsy. Anthony was built close to the ground, muscular, and had some rhythm to his swing. He had been a quarterback at a midwestern university before donning the Trappist habit. Frater Michael was of average height and build, seemed very intense and much more sober than the others. I soon learned that he was quite deaf.

Working so close to one another without speaking a word gave me a feeling of isolation even amidst companionship. We had been piling the split kindling for about an hour when the master clapped his hands. Everyone stopped his work, took out his rosary, and walked to a different spot to say his private prayer. The master went around offering each a cup of water which he had drawn from the cistern just outside the mill. After about five minutes the master clapped again, and all went back to their task. An hour later, with another clap by the master the novices laid aside their axes, fell into single file, and, with rosary in one hand and the other hand tucked under the scapular, headed back up the hill toward the novitiate.

My first period of manual labor was over, and I felt refreshed. I soon saw that this was our one form of recreation, and concluded that it did re-create!

Those early weeks in the novitiate flew. How could it have been otherwise, when every minute, from 2:00 A.M. until 7:00 P.M., had its own assignment? When seven hours (at the most) are assigned for sleep, seven to nine to choral chant in the church, and four to six to manual labor, you see how many are left for meals, study, reading, and the other needs of human nature. What would we have done if we had had to shave every day, get a haircut at least twice a month, and care for a wardrobe? A miserly monk might scrounge up seventy minutes which were not absorbed by regular assignments.

When we novices were not down at the mill splitting kindling for the smaller furnaces in the bakery, laundry, and kitchen, we would be down in the huge woodshed splitting logs for the larger furnace which was supposed to be central heating. The furnace had just been put in shortly before my arrival. Prior to this they had stoves in the abbatial church. The new furnace was supposed to heat that huge church, but it was only a game of "supposing." There were a few radiators around the apse, and they clanked loudly in the wee hours of the wintry mornings. Those clankings had a grand psychological effect on the chilled choir monks, whose breaths issued like fog or steam as they chanted their praises to God. So there was some practical meaning to all this wood chopping, for wood was our only source of energy those early years. Electricity came in with the furnace, but it was about as effective in the church as the central heating system! The lights were dim the few moments they were in use. Kerosine lamps and gas jets had just been removed from the scriptoria and chapter rooms as this "black sheep" came into the all-white fold. Finally, outdoor toilet facilities had just been abandoned at Gethsemani as I arrived. Believe it or not, these are the physical facts about Gethsemani in the mid 1930's.

When spring came, the entire community, which numbered seventy-two, spent all working hours out in the vegetable garden, or on the huge farm. Again, there was method in this madness, for the constitutions stipulated that the monks of our order should obtain their livelihood chiefly by manual labor, agriculture, and the raising of cattle. These monks were not only practical, they were pragmatists. When I read in the Rule that "the monastery ought, if possible, be so constructed that all things necessary, such as water, a mill, a garden, a bakery, and the various crafts may be contained within it," I saw that the pioneers of Gethsemani were men of the Strict Observance, that they had followed the Rule to the letter, and that I was living in a self-contained world within this world of ours. I realized that manual labor was something of a necessity for the community, for each monastery was supposed to be self-sufficient.

Yet I was not alone in seeing manual labor as recreation. Dom James Fox, the sixth abbot of Gethsemani, used to tell us that we were going out to play "Trappist golf" as he handed us our hoes to chop down iron weed, or to cultivate those long rows of cabbages, corn, or beets.

It was also at manual labor that I got my earliest belly-laughs. I was the only priest-novice until a middle-aged Irishman Fr. Joe arrived from Virginia in the late winter of my second year. Of course the afternoon work was down in the mill, splitting kindling. I know not when he had worked last, or if he had ever worked. But I gathered he was at Gethsemani on orders from some bishop. Suddenly, the absolute silence was shattered by a voice that was anything but bitter as it exclaimed, "Rather tough on the prodigal!" The shock instantaneously gave way to a real guffaw as I read all that was meant in that comment.

Fr. Joe did not last very long with us. But a few months later another somewhat older priest joined us. He was called "Sailor" Ryan by his contemporaries, since he had been with Dewey at Manila Bay at the turn of the century. Sailor was giving his all to the husking of corn one October afternoon when a well-meaning, but clumsy young novice, while carrying a mighty load of unstripped stalks, bumped into the industrious priest. An expletive slipped through Sailor's lips, which would have been funny enough for me, but the look of unbelief and utter consternation that came over the young novice's face as he dropped that load of stalks bent me over double.

I had to go deeper into the matter of manual labor than mere recreation or self-sustenance before I would be satisfied that I had found its *raison d'être*. It was not long before I found myself into the theology of manual labor. Yes, God had placed man in the paradise of pleasure to dress it and to keep it. God made the first man a gardener, something of a farmer even before the Fall; consequently, work is part of God's plan for us humans.

It was consoling to be convinced that I was following God's plan, that I was doing penance for my own and for mankind's sin, making reparation for our offending God. Years later, I came to realize that I could contemplate as I worked hand in hand with God as I helped Him bring forth a harvest. I planted, both He and I watered, but He alone brought forth the harvest. Co-creating with the lone Creator, truly being God's helpmate is the real meaning of Trappist manual labor.

But to show you how God works on a monk's soul and leads him by seemingly accidental happenings into the depth of reality, I'll quickly detail the developmental process of my education along contemplative lines.

Some fifteen or eighteen years ago I saw a Frater Benedict, who has since left us for what he considered "greener pastures," toiling all alone in the vegetable garden. I suppose I had just finished some manuscript, so I volunteered to help him. Under the broiling Kentucky sun during the simmering summer afternoons, I would hie myself out to the garden to weed, cultivate, spray, or harvest. I soon learned to drive a tractor and hitch it to a disc, cultivator, plow, or spraying machine. An overgrown weed patch was turned into a series of carefully tended beds of vegetables.

The following spring, Frater Benedict was given a new assignment, and those three acres of vegetable garden lay fallow. I did not like the looks of that, and to my query "What gives on the vegetable garden?" made to the cellarer, the laybrother in charge of all the temporalities of the monastery, I got the offhand answer, "It's all yours, if you want it."

I did not want it, but I love fresh radishes, lettuce, onions, tomatoes, cucumbers, and corn. Further, I had noticed how more and more canned goods were coming into our self-sustaining monastery. In my first decade of years at Gethsemani we purchased sugar and salt, and that was about it. We never saw any pepper in those days, not to mention other condiments. So the spring breezes were blowing around "Old Rasputin," as I called myself, as I hitched that tractor to plow, disc, harrow and planter. Thus, yours truly became head gardener at Gethsemani, and remained so until 1976.

Actually, I was the lone gardener, although in the early spring a few would volunteer their help at planting. As the balmy breezes of spring gave way to the burning heat of summer, and as the neat, long rows of newly risen plants saw weeds come in, I found myself more and more like the Ancient Mariner: "alone, all, all alone."

Again, I see that as part of God's plan. For when alone, to whom can one make signs or oversee? Not to no one, for God is always there looking, listening, and acting. Now, if contemplation can be legitimately described as "looking and loving" — and it can! — what was I going to do while out in that large vegetable garden "alone, all, all alone" with the Great Alone? I was soon endeavoring to simplify and unify all my drives toward penance, reparation, adoration, and contemplation by actualizing the lines of Dorothey Frances Blomfield Gurney. She once wrote:

The kiss of the sun for pardon
The song of the birds for mirth
One is nearer God's heart in a garden
Than anywhere else on earth.

How often, during those years as head gardener, as I watched the rows of radishes and lettuce begin to appear, did I sing to myself those lines Francis Thompson wrote about a field flower:

His fingers pushed them through the sod —
They come up redolent of God,
Garrulous of the eyes of God
To all the breezes near them;

46

Musical of the mouth of God
  To all had ears to hear them;
Mystical with the mirth of God,
  That glow-like did ensphere them.

That was years after my novitiate. To get back to the
difficulties of those early days — manual labor was not one
of them, but the sign language was. Now, every order and
congregation has its rules and regulations concerning silence. Since religious are human, those rules and regulations are not always perfectly observed. Now I was among
the silent monks, however, and they *were* silent! Never
once, in my first two decades here, did I hear a real breach
of silence. We did communicate, but it was only by signs.
That was my first task — to learn that language, and we had
to pass examinations to show our proficiency during repetition time.

We had been given a book of Usages, which contained
the vocabulary of the sign language. There were 496 different signs in that vocabulary. By combining them I suppose you could have some 520 to 530 "words" at your command. After World War II, when we had a veritable deluge
of applicants, the newcomers were most proficient at in-
venting new signs. By the time of Vatican II and its *aggiornamento*, those youngsters must have had a thousand words
in their vocabularies!

But my first difficulty cropped up at work time. I like
to work effectively, efficiently, and — God forgive my impatience — quickly. Imagine my frustrations those early
days, weeks and even months, before I had mastered the
language, when the senior in charge of the work would
make a very few unintelligible (to me) signs about the nature of the task I was to perform. It was easy enough when
we were simply chopping wood, but with the spring came
farming. When these signs were made up, the Trappists
were farmers. While they had horses, mules, plows, and

wagons, they did not have tractors or trucks. They had some primitive plows, discs, cultivators, and hay rakes, but no rotary tillers, baling machines, or combines. When I would be sent to the toolshed or the workshop for something that had been forgotten or unforeseen, imagine my puzzlement, when I saw only a sign to indicate what was wanted. I had to guess, and I did not always guess right.

We had only a two-hour period to complete a task, but little did I realize that these monks were working for eternity and not against time. Patience can be learned through successive exasperations! I got a real charge out of the remark Dom Frederic Dunn made to me one day when he said of the new arrivals, "They do not know which end of the hoe to use," but it was this mind of mine which did present some difficulties to me in those novitiate years.

We had repetitions almost every day. They would be held in the scriptorium, and we would all be seated around the table, with Father Robert McGann, the master of novices, at the head. One day it would be a repetition of catechism. The next day it would be one on the history of the order. The third day it would be on the Rule and constitutions. Then would come the Usages, the rubrics, or the customs. There would always be an examination on the sign language, occasionally a chapter of faults.

Father Robert had come to Gethsemani one year before I had been born. I soon saw, as I listened to him in those repetitions and instructions, that he was endowed with that very uncommon thing we name common sense. He was not a scholar, but a student — the difference being between erudition and well-grasped knowledge. His actions conformed to his teachings, his practice with his preachings, and his life showed that he really believed what he professed. He was simple, yet anything but a simpleton. I was soon to learn that simplicity is a cardinal virtue among the Trappists, and what is true for the poet — the height of felicity lies in simplicity — is even more true of the

48

priest. I found my master quite felicitous, but that did not prevent him from presenting me with some difficulties.

Yet, it was not only my youth, it was my background that brought me face-to-face with what I am now calling "difficulties." As a Jesuit novice I had been taught to dissect self, dismember asceticism, take the Rule apart, and study the constitutions joint by joint. In the juniorate we had put Cicero, Demosthenes, Horace, and Euripedes, along with Shakespeare, Webster, Longfellow, Shelley, and all the other masters, on the table and analyzed them until we knew what made them tick. In philosophy we got down to the causes of things, pierced appearances, and peered into substantialities, stripped off accidentals and viewed naked essentials. We always looked for the ultimate causes of things. In regency we, as teachers, were always analyzing, ever cataloging and laboring to form and fashion a well-rounded, liberally educated human being. Even in theology it was much the same, for we bravely, if somewhat vainly, endeavored to analyze the *actus purissimus* — God, and find parts in the *ens Simplicissimum*. That was the background which had shaped my mind and given me a habitual mental attitude to things and humans.

It was hardly an asset when one had to sit in with a group, ranging from uncompleted high school courses to a few who had been in universities, under a master who had to accommodate his teachings and lecturing to that conglomerate and who, himself, was practically self-taught. I will never forget the day we were treating the Holy Eucharist, and got embroiled in an argument over whether we received the Trinity when we received the Body and Blood of Christ. After much disputation, the bell rang for the end of the repetition. Who was saved by that bell? I am not so sure.

I sum up my master of novices now by saying he was a man's man, totally virile. He was simple in the best sense of that word — thoroughly sincere, and totally committed to

49

serving God as a Trappist monk. A greater eulogy I cannot think up.

In a letter to Father Jack, I wrote: "The sixteen years of intimate association with culture and refinement was a poor proximate preparation for a life of spreading 'culture' over four hundred acres of farm land, and for refining forests into firewood. . . . The close contact with educated men of delicate tastes, refined feelings, keen appreciations, polished manners, tender solicitude for others — in a word, with gentlemen — is sorely missed. . . . The world of books is as distant as the world of Mars. Boy, what wouldn't I give for half a day with a good book!" An "economical monk might salvage seventy minutes in the whole day for what we Jebs knew as 'free time.' But as for us novices, those seventy minutes are usually given to the study of this, that, or the other thing. In fact, Jack, novices have *no* free time."

I was from a family of ten children, five of whom had entered religion: three priests and two nuns. In those days we religious had next to nothing to say about where we were sent. At this time the religious side of my family was spread from Halifax, Nova Scotia to Indiana to Jamaica. We Trappists were allowed to write two letters four times a year: Christmas, Easter, August 15th, and November 1st. The first of those two letters had to go to one's parents. So I had to devise a means to keep in touch with my scattered family once a year.

Jack was concerned about my state of mind among the silent monks, and how I avoided mental stagnation in such a regime. Well, there was so much to learn about the Cistercians — their origin and aim; the history of their golden age, decline, and resurrection. There was the book of Usages. The night Office was a long one, but the lessons after each nocturne held excerpts from such masters of Latinity as Augustine and Bernard, such difficult styles as those of Ambrose and Chrysostom. I had been faithful in the discharge of my obligation to read the Office as a Jesuit,

50

but it was really a fulfillment of an obligation. Now it was my way of life. More and more it became personal prayer, heart-to-heart converse with God. But time was the cruel factor! I realized the cloister was supposed to be the home of contemplatives, consequently my prayer should be contemplative prayer. I craved time to study contemplation and the great contemplatives, but that bell was always ringing, summoning me to this duty and that.

I did experience some difficulties in my early years, but I never had the slightest doubt then, or since, that I was and am in the place God wants me. Those difficulties were solved by convincing myself that I would become what God wanted me to become by giving my all to the regime as lived here at Gethsemani. I would be regular!

I had no sooner come to that firm resolution than I was taught that while man proposes, God disposes. Our regularity became quite irregular as we novices, instead of the woodshed or the mill, were told to go to the front garth, which lay between the gate house and the main building of the monastery, to demolish it. A renovation program began then, and has been going on ever since. Never once in all my time here in Gethsemani has a year passed in which we were not building something new or renovating something old. Countless recreation periods, manual labor, were devoted to re-creating Gethsemani, and it has not stopped to this day. I have been everything from a cement mixer, hod carrier, bricklayer, carpenter, plasterer, cement block maker, mechanic, plumber, to ordinary day laborer. About the only task I have not had my hand into is electricity. Talk about a practical education or a trade school — where could one equal it?

We cleared that garth before the end of January, 1937 and, under the capable direction of Father Mauritius, who later became abbot of our daughter-house in Utah, laid out forms for the concrete walks.

Meanwhile, Father Eddie, my Oblate brother, made a

surprise visit to Gethsemani. Dom Frederic bent all rules and allowed me, a mere postulant still, to see Father Ed. A few days before he arrived it had begun to rain, and for eleven successive days it did nothing else but rain. It precipitated the great flood of 1937 for Louisville and other cities and towns along the Ohio River. The flood waters reached a height of fifty-eight feet in Louisville and inundated three-quarters of the city.

Dom Frederic told me privately that the creeks in Nelson County were over their banks, and the flood was nearing Gethsemani. He would not tell the community that, lest it distract them from their one work: the praise of God. He confided to me that he was ready to take in any refugees from the rampant waters, but as it turned out, it was not necessary. He did contribute to the aid of the victims with food, bed-clothing, and money. Where he got the money is beyond me, but I am sure he would have not only given the shirt off his back, but the very skin off his body to help others. He could be described as the soul of charity, and also as electric with energy.

In his first year in office Dom Frederic, in addition to changing the face of that front yard, had us out in the backyard building a corncrib, a new pig barn, a new chicken house, and a new garage. Meanwhile, workers employed by the Caldwell Construction Company, were raising a 125-foot steel structure as a base for a 50,000-gallon water tank. The tank would give running water to every faucet in the three-storied monastery, feed the hydrants that had been set in as fire protection for the many other buildings in Gethsemani, and could supply the irrigation system that was planned for the farm.

I did not learn the reasoning behind all this until summertime when we experienced a drought. Imagine the state of the storerooms for this community, which really lived off the ground, when a drought dried up an entire harvest! Dom Frederic had seen that happen more than once, so one of his first works when elected abbot was to plan for water.

We novices were part of that plan, for that spring and summer, when not out on the farm, we were up in the woods, chopping down trees, in preparation for the building of a dam. Once we had the tree down we clutched it with two iron tongs, like those used by icemen. Once we got the tongs set into the sides of the huge trunks, we waved to the laybrother atop the hill and he urged his mules to drag the trees to the top. Then we rolled them up to a wagon, which carried them to the sawmill.

Once, we had cleared out the woods, we threw a mighty concrete dam across the valley. It is twenty-three feet wide at the base, tapers up thirty-five feet, and stretches 307 feet across that valley. That took a lot of concrete! The rains from the surrounding knobs filled that reservoir-lake before the end of November. It measured thirty-two feet deep at the center of the reservoir. There was real elation among the laybrothers when the conduit, which stretched the mile from the lake to the monastery, was opened the day before Christmas Eve, and it was found that the water rose twenty-four feet, thanks to gravity and pressure, into the various workshops. It has since been named Dom Frederic's Lake, and while not actively supplying the monastery now, thanks to many other lakes we have since made, it stands as a true reservoir.

While we novices were hewing out that lake, neither the professed choir-religious nor the laybrethren were idle inside the monastery walls or in the monastery itself. My new home was changing! The church was changing, too, for new choir stalls were added, twelve in number because of the slow, steady influx of postulants. The community now numbered eighty-five. Four new altars were erected in the church, for the number of priests in the community was growing due both to ordinations within the community and applicants from outside. The most dramatic change was the replacement of the bridge, which had so fascinated and

53

puzzled me on my entrance, and in its place, the erection of graceful *ambos.*

It is amazing to me now to recall all this activity in this silent, solitary life. There must have been much noise and confusion, and not a little dirt and dust, while all these different projects were being completed, but all I can vividly remember is the quiet of the huge monastery and this very intense life of constant prayer and praise of God.

A brief glance at the annals for these early years of my monastic life makes me wonder how there could have been so many and such varied activities in this deeply tranquil and seemingly unvaried existence. We celebrated three golden jubilees, had state visits from the governor and his entourage, saw Jim Farley, the postmaster general, and even had the pope's apostolic delegate come to our humble, hidden home. Despite this veritable tidal wave of varied undertakings and transactions outside and inside the community, there never seemed to be a ripple on the surface of our day-to-day quiet existence. We saw many visitors for only a few moments, usually during the Mass. Some, like the various bishops, archbishops, cardinals, apostolic delegates, and governors, might say a few words to us assembled in the chapter room. The ever busy abbot and the guest master had to do all the entertaining and chatting with the various dignitaries. We monks kept silent.

The manner of burial for the monks was one of the things that held me back from joining sooner. It was in the middle of my novitiate years that I first experienced death and burial and thus had another difficulty disposed of. It was that of old Brother Mary, the lay brother who had fallen at my feet the day he opened the portals for me to enter Gethsemani. I looked down on his bearded face as we waked him in the open casket, a simple black box. It was a happy wake, for two monks were ever at his side praying the psalter from the moment he breathed his last until the last shovel of dirt was lain upon his grave. There was a special warmth even in the coldness of death around that casket. When I saw his corpse lifted from the black box and handed down to the infirmarian, who received the corpse and covered his face, and then watched the pallbearers shovel dirt over the habit-covered corpse, I felt a surge of joy for Brother Mary's state. I realized how sensible a manner of interment it was.

I blush now as I read the expression of my thoughts and feelings as I gave Father Jack my evaluation of my fellow monks and the life as I saw them leading it.

††

The Community has me still gasping. Absolutely regular! Not only not a 'cut-up' in the crowd, but not a half a dozen lively ones in the entire eighty-five. The rule is rigidly observed by all. Truth to tell, I sum the community up thusly: many genuinely pious; a few exaggeratedly so; and none tepid. The entire community is saintly, but it is not with the sanctity you and I look for and like — that virile, substantial, ever-active sanctity which is not given overly much to such externals as wearing the head on the side, keeping the eyes on the toes, and the hands in the sleeves, or the rattling of the beads; that real, red-blooded, manly holiness which is ever quiet and completely unobtrusive, and avoids anything that smacks of sanctimoniousness. Why it is, I know not, but most seem to be given to the opposite: perfect external modesty which borders on the immodest; seemingly a multiplicity of devotions and countless vocal prayers, which, to my idea and ideal of a contemplative and the simplicity of genuine sanctity, is utterly alien.

But I could be wrong. That they are genuinely pious is unquestionable; that, according to their lights, they are living saintly lives, is undoubted. The only thing I question is the intensity of their lights. After eighteen months as a novice I can account for all this to some extent. As I see it, there is nothing approximating a systematic training, never

55

a clear enunciation of the Trappistic ideal, a delineation of the contemplative model; no generating of an esprit de corps; no clarity as to specific end and aim; never a distinction between the substantials of sanctity and the accidentals; no proferring of a yard stick by which to measure appearances and actualities.

But I must stop lest I lead you astray. Let me sum it up by saying: They have a spiritual directory that is pregnant with solid and substantial doctrines. But to put that into the hands of a 15-, 16-, 18-, 20-, or 24-year-old youngster, and expect a timely birth, is defying all the laws of generation. The situation is brimming with difficulties. The candidates are received at any time during the year. Therefore, anything like classes belonging to the first-year novices and the second-year novices, is out of the question. That militates against anything like group instruction. The candidates range from fifteen-year-olds who know next to nothing about catechism, through transfers from some peculiar seminaries where warped ideas about sanctity must have been given, up to and including priests nearing their sixties who are quite conversant with real theology. Ergo, genius is demanded of the master as he labors to instruct and form so that he will not outrage the intelligent and yet meet the demands of the almost entirely ignorant. So you see, Jack, the circumstances are trying, if not actually tragic, and a mastermind will be needed to solve the situation.

As you see, fellah, it is the accidentals that irk. The substantials of the life are simply sublime! Look at Father Augustine, rector of a seminary, vicar-general of a diocese, prothonotary apostolic, and unquestionably, a bishop-to-be, coming here, and look at him today, at seventy-five, leading a life that calls for seven hours of Office, five hours of work, seven hours of sleep, little food, and no social intercourse — look at him and watch him living the Rule to the letter, living life with and for 'God alone' — and marvel. Look at thirty-three lay brothers working, working, working

— most usually at hard manual labor from 3:00 A.M. to 6:00 P.M., never speaking, subsisting on vegetables and bread — say it is inhuman, unhuman, and ahuman, and you'll be right. They have me speechless. They *are* saints! Yes, all in all, it is a miracle, a moral miracle, this community at Gethsemani.

Believe me, Jack, when I say I am happy, habitually so! The momentary fits of impatience with things as they are never reaches to the depths of my soul where I find perfect contentment with God's plan for me and His way of leading me home. Yes, I am completely content with this my latest vocation. Continuously so! The groanings of chained human nature, the occasional subtle, and at times not so subtle, eruptions of self, looking for some human gratification, the thoughts that 'this way of life is following John the Baptist and not following Jesus Christ,' or 'this way of life is utterly an exaggeration; the exotic dream of some half-starved monk, or 'these Trappists are living the letter of the Rule and not its spirit, and 'the letter killeth'; or even 'this is fanaticism and not Catholicism' are mists, sometimes quite thick and seemingly impenetrable mists, that *do* arise, but once I stand at the altar, bow over bread and wine, breathe those transubstantiating words He commanded us to, those mists are completely dissipated. So, too, when He gives me grace enough to sing a truly fervent hour of the Office. That is why, Jack, I can say in all honesty and real humility, Gethsemani and heaven are all but synonyms for me. That's why I stay.

That letter went out. That is why I say Dom Frederic never read it. Knowing him as I do, I would have gone out and not the letter.

3

Similarities
&
Dissimilarities

†

Dom Frederic so dominated, by force of his presence, personality and position, the first thirteen years of my forty behind these walls that if, under God, any one man shaped my cloistered character and my contemplative life, Dom Frederic was that man.

Before I get into that master sculptor's work, I must pick up some pieces I have dropped. I once bragged that I had learned all the ropes before the end of my first year as a novice. I only meant that I had passed all examinations on the Usages. That is a book which tells the monk just how to comport himself in all places, under all circumstances, and at every duty of the day and night. It tells you how to hold your hands, your head, your eyes, and how to make the various bows — there were three of these: an inclination of the head, a moderate bow with the head and shoulders, and the profound bow from the waist! That will give you some idea of the minuteness in these pages. It took some learning. There was no place, no person, no thing that was omitted from the prescriptions. No plebe at West Point or at Annapolis had to learn more about his feet, elbows, hands, chest, chin, shoulders, or abdomen in order to master all the details about his external comportment than did a Trappist novice. Some, no doubt, will consider all this quite exaggerated. Since Vatican II the Usages do not hold the same place of importance they held back in the days when I was working down at the mill or in the woodshed. Maybe that marks an advance. But I well recall the remark, almost in the tone of lament, made by our late abbot general as the spirit of Vatican II raised its head even in our cloisters. He said: "I would love to have a blank page inserted between every printed page in the Usages, and on that blank page write the spiritual reason behind each and every prescription in those same Usages." Yes, there was special method in this madness of our early Fathers. It was not only self-discipline, not merely to assure uniformity of observance, but deeper than all that, it was for that holy, truly humane, incalculably rich acquirement and requirement, so seldom seen today — reverence and respect, not only for all others and all things, but even for self.

They could be irksome. But they could also be very formative of character, not only for the individual, but for the community — and I soon saw that this community at Gethsemani had been formed. I remember at one solemn profession saying to those making their profession: "Only last week you heard from the lips of a golden jubilarian something of Gethsemani's history. It has been my duty to deal with little else these past ten years." (I was referring here to my book on Gethsemani for its centenary. It came out as *Burnt Out Incense.*) "I can tell you truthfully that she has always been great — not in numbers, nor in material possessions, but in the one thing that counts when monks are measured and Trappists are tried. She has always been great in *love for God* expressed in loyalty to the Rule of St. Benedict and the Usages of Citeaux. For over one hundred years this abbey has been famed for her regularity. Even in her awful eclipse she was loyal, for the first remark of the special visitors on the card for 1897 is an exclamation of wonder at Gethsemani's regularity. Under those stalwarts of God: Eutropius, Benedict, Edward, Edmond, and the saintly Abbot Dunne, Gethsemani's men were so regular that had the book of Usages been lost, it could have been rewritten from their lives."

It was not enough for the novice to learn the Usages, he had to live them. I was helped at this implementation of my knowledge by my brother novices and all the professed choir religious, in what we called the chapter of faults.

That is another august institution which some of the interpreters of Vatican II terminated in most monasteries. That chapter had its purpose, its practicality, and was highly productive, both of what is highest and best in human nature as well of what is the least admirable. Like all good things, it could be abused, and to some very minimal degree, it was — even here at Gethsemani. Like the Usages it could be irksome, but, like the Usages again, it was formative, both for the individual and the community.

I can't say that this institution kept me on my toes, for I was "proclaimed" often, and when one was proclaimed, he had to prostrate himself face downward in the sight of all the brethren. Was my face red — frequently! But the good brethren could not see it because of my prone position. I was proclaimed for making my profound bow "too profoundly," as well as proclaimed for not making my profound bow "profound enough." Abbot Dunne, as Dom Edmond Obrecht before him, would insist that we give our voice in choir, and I would be proclaimed for dominating in choir. It said in Scripture, and in every spiritual directory, that the Lord loves a cheerful giver, yet I would be proclaimed for being too cheerful. Believe me, there were times when I felt I could not win. Yet, I still maintain that it was a wise and wonderful institution, despite the seeming insignificance of some of the faults and the occasional pettiness in the proclaimer and the proclamation. It did give the individual monk self-awareness, self-composure, self-control, and self-command, and was well calculated to give him final mastery over self-will. It was conducive to humility and obedience. Are there any more important virtues for any religious or any Christian, especially since one can sum up the entire life of Jesus Christ as humility expressed in obedience?

As a novice I had to be present at two such chapters every week before the entire community of choir monks, and at least once a week before all the novices in our novitiate. I became quite proficient at prostrating myself, for while I always won a high mark on every written exam, it would appear that my fellow novices and the professed choir monks were less appreciative of my mastery over all these minute prescriptions. God love them for their acute perceptivity. They taught me the difference between learning a thing, and living it.

We can forget the chapter of faults for the time being, for it has ceased to be at present in the Abbey of Gethsemani. Its passing relieves me of many a physical prostration, but at the same time, it causes me a little uneasiness, for no substitute has been proferred for the unquestionable benefits it did produce for the individual and the community.

I was sufficiently educated in the religious life to know that the Usages and that chapter of faults were but means to an end. There is an intimate linking between Usages, the Rule, the constitution, the vows, the virtues and the end: Perfection, which can be described as putting on Christ, or conformity to Christ, or transformation into Christ — the real *raison d'être* of religious life. So, after reading the Usages, and long before I had learned them, let alone lived them, I turned to the Rule.

That reading was unavoidably colored by my Jesuit background. Now it is true that Ignatius of Loyola did not found a military order, but he did found what he called the Company of Jesus. The word company tells a story, for the Spanish soldier who had been wounded at Pampeluna could only have been thinking soldierly thoughts when he called his order a company. His constitution and Rule call for soldierly action, and the characteristic virtue of his men is that of a true soldier: obedience. The ranks of his followers have been filled with men who have been known for centuries as "the Pope's Flying Squadrons," and whose lives have ever exhibited those crowning virtues of military men: readiness for combat, unswerving loyalty to their leader, and utter selflessness as seen in their unquestioning obedience. His Spiritual Exercises unavoidably set one hearing bugle calls, the din of battles, and send one plunging into war. Undeniably, there is tangible evidence of much that is military about the order Ignatius did found.

With all that in my blood, I was thrilled when I read such words as *militaturus*, *militanda*, and *militans* before I had completed my reading of the first chapter of the Rule of St. Benedict. I felt right at home! For in his first sentence Benedict tells to whom he is addressing his Rule and for what purpose as he says: "Listen . . . to the precepts . . . willingly receive and faithfully fulfill the admonition . . . that by the labor of obedience you may return to Him from whom you have departed by the sloth of disobedience." I thought I was listening to Ignatius. "To you, therefore, my words are addressed, whoever you are, that renouncing your own will, take up the strong and bright armor of obedience to fight under the Lord Christ, our true King." I found Ignatius, in his entirety, expressed in his Exercises, as I read the prologue and the first sentence of the first chapter in Benedict's Rule. He was asking us to renounce our own wills, take up the arms of obedience, and fight under the standard of Christ, our true King. I felt right at home, but I had a lot to learn, and, I did much later.

As I analyzed the Rule, I felt even more at home. The characteristic virtues of the Jesuit are humility and obedience. Ignatius, in all sincerity, called his society, or company, "this *least* . . .," just as Benedict had ended his Rule by naming it this "*least* of rules written for beginners." In Benedict's, as in Ignatius', nothing is stressed as much as humility and obedience. So I plunged into the new life, thinking I had hardly changed my manner of living to any real extent. Then came my first Lent as a Trappist!

As I entered my first Lent here at Gethsemani I was awakened to the fact that there were some legitimate grounds for accusing the Jesuits of not fasting, singing, or knowing their rubrics. I very soon realized that the Jesuits did not fast as did these monks!

It is said that comparisons are odius. Maybe they are, but parallels bring out perfections and imperfections. I was paralleling more than comparing. I found that while the Jesuits stressed interior penance more than the exterior, yet in the matter of corporal punishment, the Jesuits actually outdid the Trappists. While the monks used only once a week what the Jesuits called "the flag" (a corruption for "flagellum"), a tiny whip made of knotted cords, the Jesuit novice used it twice a week, and further added to corporal punishment by binding his thigh or his abdomen with a chain which had sharp, piercing points of metal that bit into the skin. The Trappists had no chains. Yet, the Jesuits had never been known as a penitential order, while the Trappists very name is synonymous with penance.

As for prayer, the Jesuit novice had more formal mental prayer than did the Trappist. While the former had one hour of meditation every morning, and a half-hour every evening, the Trappist had but thirty minutes each day. Again, in the matter of examen of conscience, the non-penitential Jesuits outdid the very penitential monks, for while the latter made only a five-minute examen at noon and at night, the Jesuit employed a full fifteen minutes every noon and night. In the matter of communal, vocal prayer there was no comparison. The Jesuits were not without these, before retiring the entire community assembled in chapel for litanies, and many added shorter vocal prayers. So there were many similarities and some dissimilarities between the two, but in this matter of fasting . . . well, the Jesuits do fast, and they do observe all the days of abstinence, but if we compare them to the Trappists, I must say that if we use the word fast regarding the Jesuits, we will have to use some other word for the monks. The closest would be *starve*. That is the way I felt that first Lent at Gethsemani.

Throughout the year the monks never have breakfast. On all Sundays, Holydays of Obligation, and from Easter until the Feast of the Exaltation of the Holy Cross in mid-September, the monks do have what is called a *mixt*. Don't ask me where they got that word. It is utterly non-representative of the food allowed the monks in the early morning hour on those days, for there was nothing mixed about it. It was simply a cup of barley water and two slices of dry bread, weighing never more than four ounces. That was verboten all during Lent.

We had to wait until high noon before we ever broke our fast. Even that was an indulgence to us weaker men. In the early days of the order, right up to the reformation of the order in the late nineteenth century, the monk waited until sundown, or about 4:30 P.M. before he allowed food to cross his lips. At this dinner we did have our two cooked portions, as the Rule prescribed, and I do not exaggerate when I say it was the same old story of beans and potatoes one day, and potatoes and beans the next. There was a variety to the beans: green beans, wax beans, Boston baked beans, string beans, and stringless beans, but there was no variety, save in the method of preparation, to the potatoes. I do not recall ever seeing a sweet potato in those early days. Even at dinner we went without soup on the first three Fridays. On the last three Fridays we subsisted on bread and water all day — well, almost all day, for in the evening there was a "collation," a spoon of apple sauce, four ounces of bread, and a cup of barley water.

Let me tell you now how I came to look forward to Sunday mornings and Sunday evenings during Lent. Like

Christ, after fasting (for only a week) I was hungry. They served a small spoonful of molasses every Sunday morning with the four ounces of bread and one cup of barley water. Believe me, it was delicious! At Sunday evening collation they served a potato, usually boiled in the jacket, with a raw onion, and some watercress. That, too, was scrumptious!

Now, remember that Lent always comes, in this clime, during the early spring. For agriculturists that means plowing, harrowing, discing, and planting, and Trappists are agriculturists. We had extra work many a morning, and most afternoons during the holy season of Lent — all that on well nigh empty stomachs. But the very air of springtime is a tonic. Further, I had read the section of the Rule which stated: "Although the life of a monk ought at all times to have about it a Lenten observance, yet since few have strength enough for this, we exhort all, at least during the days of Lent, to keep themselves in all purity of life, and to wash away during that holy season the negligences of other times. We shall worthily accomplish the same if we refrain from all sin and give ourselves to prayer with tears, to holy reading, to compunction of heart, and to abstinence. In these days, then, let us add something to the usual measure of our service: as private prayers, abstinence from food and drink, so that everyone of his own free will may offer something to God with joy of the Holy Spirit, something beyond the measure appointed to him, withholding from his body somewhat of his food and drink and sleep, refraining from talk and mirth, and awaiting holy Easter with the joy of spiritual longing. Let each one make known to his abbot what he offers, and let it be done with his blessing and permission. What is done without leave of the spiritual father shall be imputed to presumption and vainglory, meriting no reward. Everything, therefore, is to be done with the approval of the abbot."

I did not have to worry about less food and drink. Nor did I have any concern about extra reading, nor extra work.

For all these were already prescribed. So what could I of my own free will offer to God with joy of the Holy Spirit? What was there to offer beyond the measure appointed to me? Don't forget I was a novice and my primary motive for coming here was reparation. I was in a box as I looked for something to offer, which I had to make known to my abbot.

On one of the earliest days after Ash Wednesday in 1937 I knocked on Abbot Dunne's door. We novices had to visit him once a week, and this was my day. I entered once I had heard the stamp of his foot on the floor. That is the way he said "Come in." Silence was sacred to Abbot Dunne, and to all under him, but let me put to rout that wildly mistaken idea that some monks lost their voice because of their perpetual silence. How could we, when we were obligated to sing to God from seven to nine hours every day, confess every week, and talk to our abbot, or spiritual father, at least once a week? We always had easy access to talk things over with the master of novices. I early concluded that we silent monks used our vocal chords much more than the ordinary run of mortals! No, never did any Trappist monk lose his voice because of nonuse. Well, after my *Benedicite* and his *Dominus* we discussed my progress, or lack of it, during the past week. Then I blurted out, "Reverend Father, I would like your permission to use a hair shirt all during Lent." He smiled, toyed with his ever-present letter opener, and said, "We'll see." Two days later, as I bowed before him after compline and he sprinkled holy water on my head, he slipped me a small package which held a homemade hair shirt. It was made out of a rough burlap bag, a potato sack, I suspect. I used it every day that Lent, but never a day since. I was a novice, and I was gung ho.

Yet, that will give you some idea of the kind of man Dom Frederic Mary Dunne was. He told me privately that he was born of a soldier and raised by a soldier. His father was Captain Hugh Dunne of the 78th Ohio Volunteers, an infantry outfit which saw plenty of action during the Civil

66

War. Aside from his carriage, however, there was little of the commanding officer about Dom Frederic Mary Dunne. His commands were mostly requests, and far from any military bark about them, they were usually presented gently and with humble warmth. He was a tartar with himself, but almost tenderly motherly with his subjects. Yet, I must retract that statement about only his bearing being soldierly. There was something else, the stern, solid spirit of no compromise. Where the Rule was concerned he was like Gibraltar.

Dom Frederic puzzled me. He was the most active monk I had ever met. As far as that goes, he still stands in my long experience as the most active monk I have met to date. Yet he was abbot of what was supposed to be a contemplative community, and I was naive enough in those early days to think there was an opposition between action and contemplation. I had come from an active order in which contemplation was mentioned only in the final exercise of Ignatius' Spiritual Exercises. Actually, he mentions contemplation in the other weeks of the Exercises, but for him contemplation was a simple form of mental prayer in which the will is more active than the intellect. It consists in listening to the words of certain persons with the object of stirring up and deepening our love for Christ. I had been contemplating in this fashion all my religious life. But now that I was in a contemplative order, I set myself into a study of the recognized contemplatives in the Church, especially of Teresa of Avila and John of the Cross.

After reading about Teresa's "mansions" and John of the Cross' "nights," I was expecting to hear Dom Frederic discourse on these subjects, but what I did hear morning after morning (we had to go to the chapter room every morning after prime) was the abbot expatiating on the Rule. While we "silent" monks may be the most talked *of* body of men, because of our strange way of life, we are also among the most talked *at* body of men. We sat and listened to our abbot every morning of the year, then sat and listened to almost every priest or prelate, from a monsignor to bishop, archbishop, cardinal, and apostolic delegate who ever visited the monastery. Occasionally some celebrated layman or secular dignitary, such as the governor of the state, would have us as a captive audience, too.

I don't recall Abbot Dunne ever using any of the consecrated contemplative terms during those morning sessions. He did insist that we get rid of self, that we deny ourselves, that we could give nothing to God but what we took from self. It struck me as a very negative approach. Oh, he stressed doing the will of God, but in those early days, I took this to mean never doing your own will.

Now the spirit of the abbot is the spirit of his community. How could it be otherwise in a Trappist community when the abbot enunciated his doctrine every morning of the year? I soon awoke to the fact that Dom Frederic was teaching and preaching the doctrine of abandonment. I was not out of the novitiate before I came to realize that this doctrine was *the* doctrine of the order at that time. Dom Lehodey, a French abbot, had written a bulky book on the subject, titled *Abandonment,* which was something of a bible for the Trappists, especially the novices. It is a magnificent doctrine, but I was too young, too ignorant, and, I confess now, too arrogant to recognize this doctrine as fundamental for a contemplative — just as I was too dumb to realize that all Dom Frederic's negativeness was, in its way, nothing other than John of the Cross' *nada.* I did come to recognize Ignatius of Loyola as a true mystic, and Dom Frederic as a wondrously real contemplative, but that was only years after losing my ignorance and arrogance.

Late in my first year as a novice I went to see Dom Frederic, and he asked me with his ever-present smile but with deep earnestness, "Just how do you find our Trappist life, Father?"

"Very similar to the Jesuit life," I replied without hesitation.

"So?" said Dom Frederic.

"Yes, Reverend Father. The Jesuits motto is A.M.D.G. — *Ad Majorem Dei Gloriam.* We Trappists have U.I.O.G.D. — *Ut in omnibus glorificetur Deus.* Same difference, no? We both seek the glory of God."

"Uh-Huh."

"Then look at our characteristic virtues. Humility and obedience mark the Jesuit. Humility and obedience mark the Trappist."

"Yes?"

"Then the Jesuits hear 'The Call of the King' and answer it, fighting under His 'Standard.' The Trappists are told by St. Benedict to 'take up the shining armor of obedience to fight under our true King, Christ.' That is the 'call' I heard in the very prologue."

"Good," said Dom Frederic. "But, tell me, don't you find any dissimilarities?"

I was not expecting that, but I did seize on it to express my distress about the lack of intellectuality I claimed to have found in the house. I saw Dom Frederic's smile vanish and a look of concern deepen in his blue eyes. I thought it was interest in my subject that brought this change about. Little did I realize I had practically insulted my abbot by saying there was little intellectuality around here, yet he was talking to us and teaching us every morning of the year! But the truly humble abbot ignored the stupidity in my statement by asking why I thought thusly. I told him my impression of the theological conferences we had every month, of the sermons I listened to every feast of sermon, of the scantiness in the courses of philosophy and theology I found were being given in what we dared call our seminary.

In my boyish enthusiasm I did not realize I was talking to a man who had made all his studies within these walls; consequently, I was telling him he had not been educated properly for the priesthood.

But can you guess the outcome of my stupidity? He

69

very gently asked me to draw up what I considered a proper curriculum for monks. I followed the *Ratio Studiorum* of the Jesuits to a great extent. It won praise from more than my abbot. The abbot general liked it and told me, personally, that he would submit it to the general chapter. It won what Juvenal said virtue won in the days of pagan Rome: *laudatur et alget*. It was praised but left out in the cold.

The same matter of intellectuality came up in a later discussion with Abbot Dunne. I had been hard at my analysis of the Trappist specific vocation, which is to contemplation. I told Dom Frederic that I had learned from Thomas Aquinas that the greatest mistake we mortals make is to confuse means with ends. I went on to tell how our asceticism was only a means and not an end; that it was meant to prepare us for our real end, which was contemplation. Again I received his approbation, as I thought, by his still pleasant and even smiling, "Yes?" Then came my clincher. "Before one can come to know and love God the way a contemplative should, one must have an intellect."

That won a broader smile and the very pleasantly spoken, "We are not here to make our men Jesuits."

Instead of catching the profundity of his remark, I flippantly replied, "You couldn't."

He did not throw me out of his room, let alone throw me out of this contemplative order. All he said was, "You keep on praying, Father, and all will yet be well." Note he did not say, "keep on studying," or "keep on analyzing," but keep on *praying*. Oh, for the wisdom in this genuinely sound and profoundly wise spiritual guide!

I must have prayed, or maybe it was only that God, in His great mercy, took pity, for He enabled me to write at Dom Frederic's death: "Undoubtedly Abbot Dunne was a contemplative. That statement is going to be challenged by those who have been brought up only on modern commentaries of St. John of the Cross and know something of the ceaseless activity of Dom Mary Frederic Dunne. How could anyone so Martha-like, so continuously busy about so many things, be also like Mary? He began his abbacy with sixty-eight souls. When death took him so suddenly, he had one hundred and fifty-five monks in his Abbey of Gethsemani. What a continual outpouring of self such a charge entailed. How could he have been a comtemplative?

"Add to this his monopoly of all the offices necessitating contact with the outside world. Watch him hurry down to Georgia to look over sites for his first foundation. Then see him arrange every detail of the preparations and supervise the packing of everything from patches for clothing to the golden vessels for the altar, and even the altars themselves. Follow him as he makes three trips to Utah and purchases the William C. Parke Ranch. Plunge with him into the thousand details of preparing all the necessities for this foundation; then realize that, almost immediately, he had to go through the same distracting experience for his third foundation on the Luce Plantation at Mepkin, South Carolina, and was deep in negotiations for his fourth foundation in upper New York when he died; then you may admit that his love for Christ was goading him on, but you may also ask how he could ever be a contemplative.

"Were you to sit beside him as he slit his mail and sped through it finding therein everything from intricate moral cases demanding almost immediate solution to contracts for buildings in Georgia and Utah, for books to be published in New York, Chicago, and Milwaukee; and applications for admission from all over the world; were you to stay and listen to the continual stream of interruptions from the phone and the door, and hear him offer consolation to everyone and advice to most, you would wonder even more why I say that he was a contemplative.

"But, if you had read something of Teresa of Avila or reflected a bit on the life of St. Paul, you would not be so surprised. Better still, if you had seen, as did the English woman, Caryll Houselander, that 'Christ is man's con-

71

templative' and drawn all the logical consequences inherent in that truth, which she so rightly labels as 'almost blinding in its tragic glory,' you would understand. God looked at man and loved him and became like him, taking on Himself the shape and color of man's sins; that shape being the shape of the Cross, and that color, the stripes on His Body which brought forth that Blood. Thus does that English woman tell the whole story of what is contemplation, and what are its consequences.

"When one gazes so steadily and with such love at another that he becomes like that other, you have a true contemplative. That is what happened to Mary Frederic Dunne. All unwittingly Miss Houselander has depicted Dom Frederic to the life as she expertly paints a true contemplative as 'standing not before a painted Cross, but before blankness, himself cruciform; his arms extended, his hands empty, his naked feet still, his heart broken open for his Lord's sorrows. . . .' Intuition had led this young lady to the truth that the real contemplative 'becomes like the Crucified on Whom he looks always with the dark eyes of Faith; for man cannot help becoming like one on whom he gazes steadily forever.'

"What intrigues me more than Miss Houselander's intuition is the pen-picture she drew so perfectly of Dom Frederic as she went on with her description of the true contemplative: 'He is stripped of everything, he is empty-handed; because arms stretched out wide enough to embrace the Crucified reach out to a width that embraces the world, and hug nothing to self because hands which open to receive the nails must let go their hold on everything else.'

"How perfectly that 'embrace of the world' and that 'hugging nothing to self' portray Gethsemani's abbot. He had seen that it is only the selfless man that God can use, and he had resolved to be useful to God. His very occupations, which so many falsely imagine would have precluded all possibility of his becoming a contemplative, were the very things that saved him from all delusions about genuine sanctity, and actually brought him to the perfection of the contemplative life; for that perfection is found in intense faith generating a love that is *ardor*.

"It was the Cistercian, William of St. Thierry, who said: 'Your vocation is to be united with God . . . to possess Him in the union of perfect love.' Dom Frederic fulfilled that vocation, for very early in his life, he realized with St. Teresa that sanctity lies not in the prayer of quiet, nor even in the quiet of prayer, so much as in fraternal charity; not in mystical experiences, but in union with the will of God. But he knew that if he were to be a saint, he would have to be a contemplative saint, and I believe it was God the Holy Spirit who, in jealousy, gifted him exceptionally, and led him to the truth St. Augustine has expressed so perfectly and pithily when he says a contemplative is one who 'lives in the Word' — *Vivere in Verbo* are the Saint's exact words.

"That resolve to 'live in the Word' turned Saul, the tentmaker from Tarsus, into that torch of truth we call 'The Apostle of the Gentiles'; it changed Augustine, the self-confessed self-indulgent rhetorician from Tagaste, into that self-denying saintly Bishop of Hippo, and Holy Mother Church's Doctor of Grace; it made the ever-active American Frederic M. Dunne into a true Trappist and a full-blown Cistercian contemplative. For it is Etienne Gilson who has rightly described the latter for us when he says: 'The Cistercian contemplative is a lover who is so deeply in love that he forgets himself entirely as he devotes all his energies to the Beloved.' Frederic Dunne was always on the go, but never without his Invisible Companion; always preoccupied, but never oblivious to his ever-present Beloved; always busy about many necessary things, but never without constant leisure for the 'one thing necessary.' He had literally countless works in life, but only one life-work: the continual contemplation of the God who continually contemplates man.

"Hence, his life became cruciform; his living became Christ; his every heartbeat nothing but a further 'filling up of those things that are wanting to the Passion of Christ.' And he well knew the joy that prompted the Curé of Ars to make the startling statement that 'Even if there were no Heaven or hereafter, it were Heaven enough to serve God here on earth.'

"Merciless is the only word which describes Dom Frederic's attitude toward his own body in his later years; but merriment is as good a word as any to describe the atmosphere in which he moved and the dominant tone of his soul."

It took me years to come to that proper evaluation of my first abbot just as it took me almost as many years to come to a clear concept of just what contemplation is. The point I was making was Dom Frederic's handling of me in those very early years of mine as a Trappist. In my youthful impatience, impetuosity, and impulsiveness, I wanted to become a contemplative immediately! I was looking for directives. I was expecting my experienced abbot to take me by the hand through Teresa's mansions as well as guide me in John of the Cross' dark nights. What did I get? As I told you my abbot told me he was not going to make Jesuits out of the men under him, and urged me to keep on praying.

What I garnered from all my study of the celebrated mystics was a little knowledge and some understanding. What was behind Dom Frederic's seeming non-guidance was that rare gift of the Holy Spirit: wisdom. My knowledge and understanding of the subject came from books. His came from life and living. I could discourse on all kinds of prayer. I learned from heavy tomes that there was vocal prayer and mental prayer; that mental prayer could be divided into meditation and contemplation; and that contemplation had two forms: acquired and infused. I learned much about affective prayer, the prayer of quiet, the prayer of simple regard. And, of course, I had read much about transforming union and the mystic marriage. I doubt that

Dom Frederic could have held his own if I had entered into what I might arrogantly term a deep discussion on the various states of the soul in the various forms of prayer. But he prayed! He was so united with God that he knew much about God's ways with individuals like me. That is also the fruit of wisdom or what we learnedly call discernment. He was wise to simply urge me to go on praying, for he well knew what would happen if I followed that directive.

Just look what happened in the matter of finding out what this Trappistic fasting in Lent was all about. I got that hair shirt. I worked like a Trojan those sweaty spring days. I kidded myself into believing I was really going places as I felt that burlap scratch my rib cage as I hoisted buckets of cement up to the scaffolding where professed laybrothers and a few professed choir monks were laying brick for our new garage. We used just a wheel and a rope as our cement-elevator, and plenty of my arm and back muscles. This was really observing Lent I kept telling myself, as I grew thinner, harder, and I thought, truly ascetic. It was not until Holy Week that I finally saw clearly what it was all about.

††

This is truly the great week in the liturgical year, especially for monks who lead the liturgical life so absolutely as we do. Truly, it was something tremendous to me that first year as a Trappist, and has become even more tremendous with each succeeding year of the forty I have spent behind these walls. The Gospels became alive. I see now that the Holy Spirit had pity on this young Trappist novice who was ending his first Lent as a monk. But, truth to tell, all I was really conscious of that Holy Week was *Jesus.*

The liturgy is a wondrous teacher of true contemplation, especially when *lived* as here at Gethsemani. I see that now, but was so wrapped up in its discharge this first year I was unaware of its pedagogy.

Palm Sunday opened the week with loud hosannas

which centuries back shook the city of Jerusalem, and which in this year of 1937 really shook the walls of our cloister and our gothic church. We had our blessing of the palms, then our procession around our gothic-roofed and mosaic-floored cloister, and into our abbatial church for that Mass in which the Passion was sung by three priests. My dear Father Augustine, at 75, took the part of the Christ and when he came to that cry of *Eloi, Eloi, lama sabachthani* — My God, my God, why have you forsaken me — I heard the voice of Father Augustine, but the cry of Jesus Christ. I was living with Christ minute by minute, and that is how, after hearing the loud hosannas and watching the gentle Jesus enter the city "riding on the foal of an ass" as the people waved their palm branches and laid their very garments before the little beast, I saw the same gentle Jesus become flaming indignation as He scourges the money-changers out of the temple, and in holy wrath tells them not to make the house of His Father a "den of thieves." That same evening I saw Him weeping over the city that would not accept Him, and was startled to hear Him predict its destruction. It was a kaleidoscopic day. I saw the Christ of God in majestic dignity, in fiery anger, and in deep sorrow. He moved me to true compassion as He stirred identical sentiments in my soul.

On Monday I came with Christ over from Bethany, one of His favorite retreats: the home of Martha, Mary, and Lazarus. On the way to Jerusalem I saw Him do a strange and frightening thing: He saw a fig tree, went up to it, and found it all foliage and no fruit. He cursed it, and the tree withered and died. It was not yet time for fruit! I wondered why He had done such a thing, but I had no time to solve the matter, for as He entered the Temple, the chief priests and the elders of the people gathered around Him. With subtle questions they tried to trap Him, and this gentle Jesus answered them with a bewildering prediction: "Publicans and harlots are entering the Kingdom of Heaven before you. . . ." Tax collectors, who were hated by the people because of their cheating ways, and women of the street, whom so many disdained, would enter heaven before the chief priest of His chosen people! I realized that this warm, loving, and very lovable Lord could be chilling.

That evening, back in Bethany, there was a banquet. Many more than those who had been invited gathered in and around the home of Martha and Mary. I knew that many had come not only to see Jesus, but also to see Lazarus whom Jesus had raised from the dead not too long before. It was a curious crowd and they saw and heard something unexpected. I saw and heard it, too. I saw Mary come up behind Jesus, break open an alabaster box, and pour its contents over the head of the Lord. The whole house was filled with its fragrance. The ensuing silence was broken with the query I had heard levelled at us Trappists: "Why this waste?" Before any reply was forthcoming, to what was more a condemnation than an interrogation, I heard the face-saving addendum: "This could have been sold for three hundred denarii, and given to the poor." Was perfume that valuable? But then came the gentle, calm voice of Jesus: "Let her be. She has anointed my Body for the burial." He knew that they were about to kill Him. He knew the man who spoke against Mary and for the poor was about to betray Him. He knew that many of the onlookers at that very banquet who only yesterday had cried "Hosanna to the Son of David" would be crying "Crucify Him! Crucify Him!" a few days hence. Yet He was calm, in quiet full possession of Himself, appreciative of and compassionate for Mary, and even gentle with Judas. What character my Christ had! And I was here to put on Christ!

Tuesday I was back in the temple with Him. I watched the scribes and Pharisees gather around Him, not to learn from Him, but to badger Him with their subtleties. I heard from the lips of the gentle Jesus eight woes, any one of which was enough to make the bravest man blanch. "Woe

77

to you scribes and Pharisees, you hypocrites! You who shut up the kingdom of heaven in men's faces . . . Woe to you, scribes and Pharisees, you hypocrites! You who travel over land and sea to make a single proselyte, and when you have him, you make him twice as fit for hell as you are! Woe to you, blind guides! . . . Fools and blind! . . ." On and on He went relentlessly. "Woe to you scribes and Pharisees, you hypocrites! You are like whitewashed tombs that look handsome on the outside, but inside are full of dead men's bones and every kind of corruption. . . ." What anger! What defiance in His words: "You are the sons of those who murdered the prophets. Very well, then, finish off the work that your fathers began." He was saying, "Kill me!" They did not answer. Never had they seen or heard Him like this; at least, never so clearly. He was incarnate wrath as He thundered: "Serpents, brood of vipers, how can you escape being condemned to hell?"

It had been a frightening day for me, staying as close as I possibly could in the company of this Jesus who could be so tender and so terrifying. As we left the city some of His disciples called His attention to the beauty of the temple as it lay in the warm glow of the setting sun. It was a magnificent sight. But, instead of glowing with appreciation, Jesus rather sadly said: "You see all these? . . . I tell you solemnly, not a single stone here will be left upon another: everything will be destroyed." Then He wept: "Jerusalem, Jerusalem, you that kill the prophets and stone those who are sent to you! How often have I longed to gather your children, as a hen gathers her chicks under her wings . . . and you refused." He paused and looked down longingly and lovingly on the city and the temple, then, after brushing the tears from His face, He seemed to sigh as He said: "So be it! Your house will be left to you desolate, for, I promise, you shall not see me any more until you say: Blessings on Him who comes in the name of the Lord!"

It had been a chilling day. I had seen Him afire with

78

indignation and ablaze with defiance. I had watched Him weep. I had heard Him prophesy the destruction of that masterpiece that was the temple of God in God's holy city. I went to bed weary and all lost in wonder over the manhood of this Son of God who had become like us in all things. He, indeed, was a passionate Man whose eyes could flash fire and whose lips could hurl thunderbolts. Those woes rang in my ears and those loving tears wrenched my heart.

Wednesday was quieter and yet sinister. He was alone with His Father. Judas was alone with the high priests. I was alone with my thoughts.

Then came Holy Thursday, the Upper Room, the Seder, the Last Supper, the institution of the Eucharist, the ordination of His first priests, and the Offertory of His Mass!

I had been through it all before. But what a different week it was here at Gethsemani. As a Jesuit I had prepared for Holy Week. We had the Tenebrae. I sang in every choir that had been formed from 1920 until 1933 when I was ordained. We had used polyphony, Palestrina being prominent. Here we used plain chant. There we had rehearsal after rehearsal for weeks on weeks. Here we *lived* the liturgy day after day. There I was absorbed in the production of marvelous harmonies. Here I was absorbed by the main character in the Passion. There we were recounting. Here I was reenacting. There I was conscious of the love Jesus had shown. Here I was with the loving Lord. There I had recalled what had happened centuries before. Here it was happening around me and in me. Time was telescoped in such a way that the 14th day of the month Nisan was today.

Holy Thursday night I was with Christ in Gethsemani. I saw this young Priest agonize as He contemplated the consecration He was to make in His Mass of the morrow. I heard Him cry to His Father to "let it pass." Again and again He prayed that same prayer: "Let it pass." He was shrinking back from celebrating His First Mass. Then, with the drops of blood, came His final triumph over fear and

79

self: "Not my will, but Thine be done." He rose a conqueror to face His captors-to-be.

I did not realize it fully then, but I did see, at least vaguely, that the liturgy lived, as it was being lived in this monastery, brought one closer to God than was Moses by that burning bush. He had the Shekinah in his desert trek: the pillar of fire and the covering cloud. We had the Christ.

I went with Him to Annas and Caiaphas. I went down into the dungeon as the high priests and the Sanhedrin awaited the dawn so that they could drag Him to Pilate. I watched the Roman governor try to free Him and to wiggle out of the fix the bloodthirsty Jews had placed him. I went before Herod and saw Him clothed as a fool. I went to Calvary with Him that first Good Friday behind these walls, and in the late afternoon was wandering about our cloisters sobbing in my heart: "Jesus, my Love, is crucified!"

Saturday was the emptiest day of my Trappist existence as I went into a church whose altars had been denuded and whose tabernacle door stood ajar and I realized how exact Leon Bloy had been when he had written: "Jesus is always being crucified, always bleeding, always expiring, always mocked by the populace and cursed by God Himself in accordance with the precise wording of the Ancient Law: 'He that hangeth on the tree is cursed by God.'" I thought also how exact Pascal had been when he wrote: "Jesus Christ will be in agony until the end of the world." Even before the Mass of Easter began, I saw the purpose of Lent as the Trappists live it with their fastings and penances. We were "filling up what is wanting to the Passion of Christ . . . for His Body, which is the Church." It made sense. It made us co-redeemers with, in, and through Christ Jesus.

That Easter was the most glorious Easter I had ever lived, for I was living the liturgy. I was at the tomb early with the women. I stayed behind with the Magdalene. I heard Him call her by name. I walked to Emmaus, and I "recognized Him in the Breaking of the Bread!"

When I next visited Dom Frederic I smilingly told him I was really in the society of Jesus. He smiled and then asked me again if I found any dissimilarities, and I was able to blurt out, "Plenty!"

"Yes?"

"Yes, indeed. As a Jesuit I was a soldier. Hence, I looked on all superiors in much the same way a soldier looks upon the captain of his company, upon all officers. Our general was our commander-in-chief."

"And now?"

"Well," I smiled, "I call you Abbot — Father, don't I? That makes me your child. That makes all my confreres — priest, non-priest, laybrothers — members of the family. I could call the Jesuit quarters barracks in some truth, but this monastery is our family abode, our home. That makes a mighty difference. It is very like my old life, Reverend Father, and yet very unlike."

He gently but enthusiastically remarked, "God is good."

Indeed He is, and He had been very good to me!

I am reminded of Michelangelo as I recall what Dom Frederic did to me. When that Italian genius had finished a lifelike statue of Jesus, he stood back studying his completed work. Then he prayed: "Lord, I have just formed Thee with these feeble hands. Lest I should appear a greater artist than Thee, form Thou me! Form me — a servant of vile passion — according to Thine own Image and Likeness that I may be both pure and free. The first man Thou didst fashion from clay — I, alas, am of harder stuff. Thou wilt have to use both hammer and chisel, Lord — but do! Strike, Oh Great Sculptor, God. For I am Thy stone."

Whether the great Florentine, who knew such agony and ecstasy, ever actually said that prayer, I have no way of knowing, But for showing what God actually did to me, under the expert hands of Dom Mary Frederic Dunne, it serves perfectly. He quietly allowed me to see all the similarities between the Jesuits and the Trappists. He allowed me to, jokingly, but quite seriously, tell him that I was now really living in the society of Jesus, but he would never allow me to forget how much more I had to learn about the dissimilarities. Yet, he never verbally pointed them out. That was part of his wise sculpturing, too. As I admitted to him, "I'd rather argue than eat." Of course, I told myself I was simply seeking the objective truth! Aren't we all masters at kidding ourselves along!

This same morning in early Eastertide I asked Dom Frederic for the key to the shower. At Gethsemani in those days there was but one shower for a community now numbering over eighty. Even the name "shower" is a misnomer, for it was only a pipe to which a shower-head had been fastened. My first visit to Dom Frederic as a novice saw me asking for the key to the shower. After my second visit Dom Frederic exclaimed, "Why, Father, you took a shower just last week!"

"Yes, Reverend Father, I did. But as a Jesuit I used to shower every day, sometimes twice a day." He gave me the key, but quietly added: "You'll get used to this life." I smiled externally, but internally I was deciding: "I'll show you!" I did by asking for, and getting that key every week of my first year. The winter was more than mild that first year. But as I entered my second year cold came down our way from off the Canadian Rockies. In mid-January I made my usual visit, and my usual request. When the pipe thawed out it sent a jet of ice water down upon this novice. The next visit I did not ask for the key. The wise abbot did not seem to notice the omission. Nor did he ever once say: "I told you so." Things have changed since then.

I was not out of the novitiate before my good abbot gave me an assignment which, contrary, I am sure, to his intention then, became something of a second vocation, and something of my life's work.

4

Discoveries

†

It might seem that I was in almost constant turmoil during my novitiate days, but the fact of the matter is that I was enjoying a peace of mind, of heart, and of soul such as I had never known before. There was a profundity to this peace deeper far than I had ever experienced as a Jesuit.

I was conscious of the intellectual difficulties I had about this life, just as I was intellectually conscious of the discoveries I had made concerning the similarities and dissimilarities. At the same time I was deeply conscious of experiencing the most wonderful, thrilling, and joy-filled tranquility in my living. There are three separate faculties in the human soul: the intellect, the memory, and the will. (You can see how that triplicity in unity shows how we are in the image and likeness of our Triune God.) While I was wrestling in my intellect, I was at perfect peace in my will. I had made up my mind, when in actuality, I had made up my will that I was going to stay at Gethsemani. But that will-action did not stop my intellect from wrestling with the many problems this life presents.

Like Jacob, who after wrestling with the angel, walked with a limp, I, too, hobbled along after much wrestling, but my heart was always high, and my spirits soaring. While I was fighting ideas, I was enjoying peace of mind. That is

83

why I could tell Dom Frederic I was in difficulty, and tell Father Jack it was all smooth sailing, and be telling the truth about the one same individual.

Here is something that may enable you to understand what I was calling my "difficulty" to Dom Frederic. I was in a community that was gradually changing from an almost wholly European composition to one that was more and more American. Americans like to see results, but what results could Dom Frederic show these young men from New York, Chicago, Detroit, Boston, and other large cities in the U.S.A.? There was the huge farm, and that ever present wood pile. We had begun to change the face of our land by hewing out the lake I have already mentioned and transforming the looks of our inner courtyard. But those projects would hardly justify the Trappistic life to eager young Americans who had left home to become religious! The motto of *Ora et Labora* was being implemented literally. We could see the results of our labors. But what tangible results could we see of all our praying? I believe that is one of the reasons Dom Frederic resorted so frequently to Sacred Scripture to tell the story of Moses and Joshua.

It is a stirring story. Moses was in trouble — deep trouble. He told God that the people would soon be stoning him if water were not found — and soon. That was no idle fear. The Jews had just left the desert of Sin, and after traveling by stages, had arrived at Rephidim. There was no water in that territory for themselves or their cattle. They turned on Moses and angrily asked: "Why did you ever make us leave Egypt? Was it just to have us die here of thirst with our children and our livestock?" Moses turned from the people and turned to God who told him to take his staff, go over to the rock in Horeb, strike that rock, and water would flow. He did so, and the people were quieted. But then Amalek came to wage war against these wandering Jews. It looked like no contest, for the Israelites had but recently left Egypt where they had been slaves, not warriors, while Amalek had a real army behind him. Yet Moses calmly told Joshua to "pick out certain men, and engage Amalek in battle." Brave man that he was, Joshua did as he was told. Moses went with Aaron and Hur to the top of a hill which overlooked the scene of the battle. Then Scripture tells us: "As long as Moses kept his hands raised up, Israel had the better of the fight, but when he let his hands rest, Amalek had the better of the fight. Moses' hands, however, grew tired; so they put a rock in place for him to sit on. Meanwhile, Aaron and Hur supported his hands, one on one side and one on the other, so that his hands remained steady until sunset. And Joshua mowed down Amalek and his people with the edge of the sword."

There was a story from the New Testament which was another of the abbot's favorites: that of Martha and Mary. Martha, good woman and grand hostess that she was, sat Jesus down and then flew into her kitchen to prepare a meal worthy of her delightful guest. Mary sat down at the feet of the Lord. After working herself up into some sort of a sweat, Martha seemingly lost patience. There was her good sister, Mary, quietly sitting at the feet of the Master. There is nothing more delightful than an entertaining member of the family to engage the guest's attention. But, evidently, Martha thought her sister was being just a bit too gracious, and not a bit helpful! Finally she could not contain herself any longer. She blurted out: "Lord, do you not care that my sister is leaving me to do the serving all by myself? Please tell her to help me." The Lord didn't accede to that request. Instead, He seems to chide Martha by saying: "Martha, Martha, you worry and fret about so many things, and yet few are needed, indeed only one. It is Mary who has chosen the better part; it is not to be taken from her."

In those talks after prime, we heard only the finale: "Mary has chosen the better part." I saw Dom Frederic's purpose in stressing this saying of Jesus. I also knew that he had many fathers of the Church on his side, for many see in

85

Martha and Mary prototypes of the active and the contemplative lives. Toward the end of my novitiate, however, these stories began to get under my skin a bit. I began wrestling with these stories, and Dom Frederic heard the results of that wrestling one day when he made some reference to the efficacy of prayer and to Moses on the mountaintop while Joshua was battling down on the plain.

"Father," I asked as quietly as possible, "did you ever wonder what would have happened to the Israelites if Joshua had not been down there swinging his sword?"

He looked at me and a quizzical frown gathered above his bushy eyebrows. "What do you mean, Father?"

"I mean that, while the Good Book does tell us what happened when Moses held his hands up, Joshua never let his hands down."

"But look what happened to your friend, Joshua, when Moses let his hands drop," said my abbot. He was not smiling as kindly as usual.

"Yes, but look at what happened to Amalek when Joshua went to work again."

"But Father," said the abbot, "this is the Word of God."

I did not answer, as we do today, "Thanks be to God!" While I knew he was trying to bring out the power of prayer when he used this illustration, I always thought that there was another side to the story: that of Joshua. I also pointed out the defect I found in his other illustration by saying that if Martha had not busied herself about many things, the good Lord would not have had much of a supper that evening at Bethany.

Dom Frederic smiled with that, and added, "Right, Father. Martha was a saint, too. I am sure she loved the Lord. Yet it still remains a fact that Jesus did say that Mary had chosen the better part. I hope you will, too."

I see now that Dom Frederic saw into my soul even though I do not believe he saw into my arguments. He dismissed those as he directed me. He told me to pray on and then reached into one of those many cubbyholes atop his desk and brought forth a pamphlet which gave an unexpected turn to my Trappist life. "Father, I wish you would read this and give me your criticism of it."

What he gave me was a "Souvenir of Your Retreat." It was a synopsis of the retreat given to laymen by one of the community. I read it. The first thing that struck me was the title: "*Before the Silver Cord Is Snapped.*" That was taken from the book of Ecclesiastes — the Preacher, as we called him in far-gone days. Today many refer to him as Qoheleth, a Hebrew name which, perhaps, means "He who convokes an assembly." Ecclesiastes would always attract any man who was assigned to give retreats, for Qoheleth is concerned about the purpose and value of human life. In both his prologue and epilogue, Qoheleth states very directly the whole purpose of any and every retreat. In the first he says: "I applied my mind to search and investigate in wisdom all things that are done under the sun." Of course, we do not ask retreatants to investigate all things that are done under the sun, but we do have them set out to "search and investigate in wisdom" what they have been doing under the sun, to see if they have to conclude with Qoheleth that "all is vanity and a chase after wind." At the end of every retreat we say what Qoheleth says in his epilogue: "The last word, when all is heard: Fear God and keep His Commandments; for this is man's all."

You can see why I was enthusiastic about reading the retreat souvenir. Those words of the title are taken from verse six of Qoheleth's last chapter: "Before the silver cord is snapped and the golden bowl is broken, . . ." That's magnificent imagination and expression. The golden bowl suspended by a silver cord is a symbol of life. The snapping of the cord, with the consequent shattering of the bowl, is a symbol of death. In a retreat we stare, and stare until we see, what life is all about, and how certain death is.

In a letter to Fr. Jack, I wrote, "A tiny booklet of about sixty-thousand words (price 5¢) was put out down here as a 'Souvenir of a Retreat.' Its purpose was to serve as an echo of what they had heard while here from Friday night until Monday morning. Swell idea; for it is only too true that a few vague impressions of this and that represents the sum total of what they take away after nine to twelve talks. Well, sir, I read the booklet and then told the abbot that it was a grand idea — to give such a souvenir — and that in this booklet some excellent topics had been touched, but as a whole, the work was flat, dry, and rather dusty. Whereupon my good abbot comes out with: 'You do better for next year. But write it this year.' "

It was a command and a challenge. Actually, I believe I went into the abbot's office in my weekly turn, tossed the booklet on his desk, and smilingly said: "Oh, Reverend Father, that is awful. I could do better than that in my sleep." I meant to be pleasant even as I meant to be honest. I did not realize that Dom Frederic so loved his community that he deeply felt any slightest criticism of anyone in the community, and here, before him, on his knees, was this young novice saying that one of his oldest priests had produced something that was awful.

I thought about what I was going to write while I was out in the fields those last days of August, under that Kentucky sun which often had the thermometer nearing 100°. But before the month was out, I was snatching every available moment to sit at the one typewriter in the novitiate, to set down in typescript some of those ideas.

Before the harvest of corn was in, my manuscript of *A Trappist Asks: Are You?* was dropped into the abbot's box. It practically wrote itself. I had been giving retreats just before I came to Gethsemani. I was convinced then, and am even more convinced today, that the Spiritual Exercises of St. Ignatius form the best possible set of unified, progressive, personally profitable Exercises for anyone at any time.

If he were not directly inspired, then he most assuredly was highly enlightened to set down a series of meditations and contemplations that are well calculated to engage the whole man — intellect, memory, emotions, imagination, even his passions — to lead him on to a will-action that can be called an election or resolution for the honor and glory of God and the sanctification and salvation of the individual. Ignatius was not only a master of the spiritual life, and analyst of the human soul, but psychologist *par excellence*. For good reason, then, I followed Ignatius' Exercises in much the same fashion that I had done when giving retreats and preaching missions.

After chapter the next morning the Reverend Father Abbot beckoned to me. I followed him to his office, wondering just what it was that I had done amiss again! Once inside his room, he walked directly to his desk, picked up my manuscript and thumping it with his free hand, said, "This is good."

I smiled and modestly said, "Of course. I wrote it."

He did catch the playful twinkle in my eye, and responded, "Oh, you! I am going to have it printed. I am going to order ten thousand copies."

"Whoa! Reverend Father," I called out. His blue eyes snapped in inquiry. "How many copies of *The Silver Cord* did you have printed?

"Five hundred. Why?"

"How many have you got left?"

"About two hundred."

"And you're going to print ten thousand of my thing?"

"Yes, Father, and I am going to sell them. We gave the other retreat souvenir away. But this one, we will sell."

I dropped my flippancy and became serious as I told him I felt sure the name Trappist would sell almost anything. I insisted that we were people who aroused curiosity, and were practically unknown in America. Dom Frederic winced when I said that. I suggested that it pays to advertise, and plunged into my theme, enlarging on the attractiveness of our name, and the value of the printed word to make ourselves known to Americans.

"Yes, Father," he said quietly. "That is why I am planning a series of booklets similar to this, and books about our life. This will do for men," he said, holding up my manuscript. "I now want you to write one for women."

That's how it all started for me. That was back in my novitiate days, and it has not stopped since. After *Life Is a Divine Romance*, my effort for women, Dom Frederic suggested, "Now, Father, I wish you would write something for priests." Once that had been completed, it was, "Now, Father, I would like you to write something for the good nuns." On and on it went in this manner for years. If it was not "something for married people," or "the home," or "for those in the service," it would be "something on the Mass," or "the Holy Spirit," or "the Sacraments."

The abbot had me turning out a booklet every two months, and assigned to me "for composition — two hours on Monday; two hours on Wednesday; two hours on Friday." God, I was convinced, had given me a vocation to be a cloistered contemplative. Dom Frederic, it appeared, was giving me an avocation — that of a writer of booklets. Was this writing taking me away from my real vocation? Every now and then, during meditation, or examen, or at manual labor on the farm or on the woodpile, or in the "stilly silences of the night" before falling asleep, I would question whether all this mental activity was not militating against my becoming the true contemplative the cloister is supposed to form.

It was a temptation. The master of deceit, father of lies, and author of confusion was at work to destroy my peace of soul and distract me from both my true vocation and my abbatially-conferred avocation. He failed because he was up against a divinely inspired, and spiritually wise abbot. Dom Frederic put out all the fires of fear by saying, "Obedience is better than sacrifice."

And I discovered, with the increasing demands, that even behind these walls we do fall into that most prevalent of all illnesses: "Poor me." But the real discoveries lay in another direction. I discovered that there were censors of the order, censors for the diocese, censors for archdioceses, all officially appointed, and then that there were some unofficial, self-appointed censors. Though none of these were in Rome, some people do not have to be in Rome to do as the Romans do! We often say: "In Rome the wheels turn slowly." An adaptation of that old, true saying might be: "The mills of God grind slowly, but they grind exceedingly fine." Well, whether it was Louisville, Cincinnati, New York, Milwaukee, Indianapolis or St. Louis, I found out that the censors took their time.

I believe that Dom Frederic was as disappointed as I with all the delays, but being ever so much wiser and trusting in God's providence, he just smiled and said: "Maybe in tomorrow's mail, Father. Be patient." He had a soul-deep fear of pride in any shape or form in any of his sons, and I, with all my impatience, must have been a source of peptic ulcers for him in this matter.

He did furnish me with some encouragement one day by saying he could not keep the gate house supplied with sufficient copies of *Are You?* I was highly pleased that my prediction about the sales value of the name Trappist was proving correct. At the same time, when my abbot told me how Cardinal Spellman had ordered copies of *The God-Man's Double* for every priest in the New York Archdiocese, how the nuns had ordered so many copies of the booklet *Doubling for The Mother of God*, and that he had had to order a double reprinting, I was both amazed, embarrassed, and scared. Were my efforts that good? Had I been theologically exact? What was God's purpose in all this?

Then one day when I was kneeling at my abbot's feet he said: "Father, I have a story I wish you would write up.

Now, I do not like to criticize anyone, nor say anything that might hurt anyone. But this man had a temper. And he was always 'getting even.' " Then he went on to tell me about John Greene Hanning. I left the abbot's office with about six words on the back of a used envelope. (In those days our only note-paper consisted of the backs of used envelopes.)

I went from that office tingling with excitement, feeling that I could write this story with zest. The abbot had meant another booklet, but I never stopped until I had typed over two hundred pages. Although I was atingle with the triumph of having written the story, I was embarrassed over the bulk of pages.

"This is too big for a booklet, Reverend Father. Why don't you try it in book form."

"I don't know anything about getting books published," he said.

"Neither do I," said I, "but we could try to find out."

"Whom would you suggest as a publisher?"

"I think Bruce is a truly Catholic publisher. Why not try him?"

"Where is he?"

I chuckled. Was the abbot under the impression that I knew something about publishers? "I don't know for sure, Reverend Father. But I could find out easily enough by looking at some book he has published."

That's how it all started. That was thirty-seven years ago. It has not stopped yet. As with the booklets, so now with the books, I was due to make discoveries. Only this time it was not amongst the hierarchy or the priesthood; it was in the publishing field.

After I had given the abbot the address of the Bruce Company, I heard no more about the matter until one day, some six months later, he called me to his office and gave me a bundle of galley proofs. I was to read them, correct what I wanted corrected, then give them back to him as soon as possible.

I got those galleys back to my abbot sooner than he expected, and in a condition no one could have expected. I hadn't gotten beyond the second paragraph before my short fuse began to sizzle. It was not my writing! It wasn't long before I took my pencil and drew a long "X" from top to bottom of each of those galleys, scribbling on the side: "Delete, and restore the original!" That is the condition in which I gave them back to my abbot. He did not say a word as he glanced through the sheets, but I did notice a compression of his lips. Finally, as he folded them, he said, "Very well, Father, I shall ship these back to Bruce."

I heard no more about the matter until some two weeks later when Dom Frederic sent for me. It was about *The Man Who Got Even With God.* He smiled a bit slowly as he said: "I fear you are the man who got even with Bruce." Then he grew quite serious as he told me about the contract he had signed, how the Bruce people had insisted that, instead of "A Trappist," which had already become something of a pen name for me, they be allowed to print "Rev. M. Raymond, O.C.S.O." Knowing Dom Frederic, I am positive the Bruce people had to use every possible argument before they ever won my abbot over to that idea. As for myself, I did not give "a good Continental," as my dad would say. Then, he very quietly told me that in the contract was a clause which allowed the editor to make any changes he deemed beneficial. Again, I protested saying that the writing of the man whose name is given as the author should be in a book bearing his name, and that the editor would not have to take the brickbats or bouquets that might come to the one whose name was on the outside cover. I should have saved my breath, for as Qoheleth had said, I was "chasing the wind." I finally said: "You are the abbot. I will do whatever you say."

I did not have much time to fume over the discoveries I had made about publishing, for Dom Frederic had set me to writing about the earliest Cistercians, hundreds of years before they were ever known popularly as Trappists. That assignment resulted in *Three Religious Rebels* and *The Family That Overtook Christ.*

Bruce rejected *The Family That Overtook Christ.* When Dom Frederic ever so gently gave me what he called the "sad news," I laughed and said: "So what, Reverend Father? Bruce is not the only Catholic publisher in the United States. Send the manuscript on to P. J. Kenedy and Sons in New York." He did. Many years later I learned that Kenedy immediately wired Bruce asking, "How come you reject the second manuscript of a man whose first book has become a runaway best-seller?" I never got that information from my wary abbot. In the four times a year I was allowed mail I would find a letter from Father Jack, telling that *"The Man . . .* is still at the top of the Catholic best-seller list." I did not even know there was such a list. It was Father Jack who learned from Kenedy that Bruce had replied by wire: "Raymond is dynamite!" That is how Kenedy came to publish my next three efforts, the three volumes of "The Saga of Citeaux."

What a discovery I made when Father Jack saw fit to write: "As I read *The Man Who Got Even with God,* I considered it more an autobiography of Joe Flanagan than a biography of John Greene Hanning. Change the names and the accidental differences of antecedents, concomitants and aftermath, one who knows you, follows you. The vital principle in this book is the character, the ideals, the high hopes and best wishes of Joe-Raymond. Hanning's difficulty was vindictiveness. Yours is pride." Did that make me jump! I sat back and tried to analyze myself. I recalled a day, years and years back, when my darling mother had puzzled me by saying: "You are conceited, Joe." I suppose I had just experienced some boyish triumph in athletics or public speaking and was showing that I enjoyed it, but I had always detested any and every conceited person. Her statement stung. I knew I was confident, but conceited? That was the

94

last thing I ever wanted to be. I respected my mother's judgment and knew she would never say such a thing unless there was some ground for it. I smarted under that statement for days, but being but a boy, it was soon forgotten. Now, here was Father Jack, whose judgment I respected even more highly, saying I was proud.

He was basing that judgment on what I had written. Jack went on to say: "As Hanning had the potentialities of a saint, as he had to actualize them through long and trying self-conquest under, through, and with Christ, so Joe-Raymond has to do the same. The *to-esse* and the *to-fieri* is really the only distinction between the biography and the autobiography. Read your own book, brother, and see Joe-Raymond en route to sanctity. In your book you have his heart-pearls and his getting even with God. That's the only way for Joe-Raymond. I'm betting that Hanning and you are going to have it out on the balconies of heaven for eternity, and that Christ is going to smile, as He does now, at your many . . . what-shall-we-call-them."

Was it not Bobby Burns, the Scotch poet, who prayed: "Would that God the grace would give us/To see ourselves as others see us"? To think of all the years I had spent trying to discern my predominant fault, wavering ever between sensuality and pride. As Jesuit novices, we were told that one or the other dominated in us.

I have a magnificently short fuse! Being human, I am an inheritor of the seven capital sins, the first of these being pride. I had rightly concluded that every sin is basically an act of pride. It was with Lucifer. It was with Adam and Eve. It is with every one of the offsprings of those first parents. But when we say that an individual is a proud being, we mean that attitude of mind the Greeks called *hubris*, and the Latins set down as *superbia*, and we Americans recognize as overweening, ungrounded, unfounded, self-esteem, or as one of my earliest teachers used to put it: "an abnormally exaggerated, unprecocious case of over-developed ego." Father Jack's statement, "Yours is pride," told me it was back to the drawing board in this most important of all important matters: knowledge of self.

Well, Ignatius had given me Three Degrees of Humility. He wanted the soul to be perfectly detached and afire with generosity. He wanted a man to be so completely attached to the will of God that he would be absolutely detached from his self-will. Such an attitude of mind, heart, and whole being was not only wise, it was simply just. It told the whole truth about our human condition. We are creatures, and since everything we are or have has been given to us by the Creator, it is only right and just that we thank the giver for whatever He has given us, and show that gratitude by using our greatest gift, our free will, to do His will. So Ignatius' first degree of humility comes down to this: "I so humble myself in all things concerning the law of God, that I would not enter into deliberation about breaking a commandment, whether divine or human, which binds under mortal sin." Once I know the will of God, as expressed in His Commandments, I won't trifle with any temptation, give it no consideration whatsoever, for I so love God (and rightly love myself) that I would never commit a mortal sin.

His second degree manifests the same practicality. He says: "I find myself in such a state as not to desire to have riches rather than poverty . . . and never to enter any deliberation about committing a venial sin. . . ." As you can see, that is a much higher degree than the first. And yet, is it not obviously a matter of sound principle? The first degree gives us the fundamental principle of any sound spiritual life and living. The second degree makes us, when we have this attitude habitually, men of high principle. Any good religious would at least aspire to this. But Ignatius was never satisfied even with high principle. He had no time for mediocrity. So he gives us his third degree — and it is that in any sense you like to use the term — in which he says:

96

"The third is the most perfect humility: when, the first and second being included, and supposing equal praise and glory to the Divine Majesty, the *better* to imitate Christ the Lord, and to become *actually* more like Him, I desire and choose rather poverty with Christ poor than riches." As you can see, Ignatius' stress here is not so much on detachment from creatures, which is clearly necessary for the first two degrees, but on attachment to Christ the Lord. In conclusion, Ignatius' degrees of humility are in reality three degrees of love. I had meditated on these three degrees all my adult life, but was I practicing them?

Long years ago I had seen that Ignatius was no dreamer in presenting us with this third degree. No, indeed. Actually, he had given us nothing new. It was all there in the Sermon on the Mount, in the eighth Beatitude: "Blessed are you when you are reviled, or persecuted, or made a target for nothing but malicious lies — for My sake. Be joyful — leap for joy; a rich reward awaits you in Heaven." That was Christ talking, and He was not addressing religious! Thomas Aquinas has called this the "summary of all the Beatitudes." St. Paul had "determined to know nothing among you save Jesus Christ, and Him crucified." No, Ignatius was not a dreamer. This degree was not only for those mighty saints of God. It was for any and every religious.

As I turned to St. Benedict, who was now my "Father," what did I find? Not three degrees of humility, but *twelve*! That set me reeling at first, for I had spent sixteen years of my life focusing on three degrees. I had always loved "Ockham's razor" which in philosophy, shaved closely. William of Ockham said, *entia non sunt multiplicanda sine necessitate*. Ignatius' degrees gave me trouble enough. What was I going to do about Benedict's twelve?

Yet this seventh chapter of the Rule, which is entirely on humility, has been called the heart of the Rule, the finished expression of monastic spirituality, and has won from

97

many the title of *Doctor humilitatis* for Benedict. I was living under this "doctor" now, and was having my life regulated by his Rule.

I found nothing really new in them, yet every one of them gave me pause. I hung on every rung, for Benedict would have us erect a ladder such as that which Jacob beheld in a dream, and the rungs in that ladder numbered twelve. By mounting them one by one we "presently arrive at that love of God which is perfect and which casts out fear; that love, whereby everything which in the beginning the monk observed not without fear, he shall now begin to do by custom, without any labor, and, as it were, quite naturally — not now through fear of hell, but for the love of Christ."

How I remember those degrees as they hung framed in the little cloister which led to the novitiate. They held a capsulization of Benedict's paragraphs. I passed them at least a dozen times a day. The first degree reminded you of God's omnipresence; that He was looking on you at all times; that you were going to be judged by Him. The second reminded you that you were never to do your own will. The third told you to be obedient for the love of God. The fourth exhorted you to embrace hard and difficult things with patience. The fifth reminded you to make known to your abbot all your evil thoughts. The sixth told you to be content with all that was mean and poor. The seventh commanded you to believe yourself inferior to all. The eighth said you were not to be singular, but to follow the common rule and the example of the seniors. The ninth cautioned you to speak only when questioned. The tenth insisted that you should not be easily moved to laughter. The eleventh said that you should use few words when you do speak, and then use them in a reasonable manner. The final degree stressed that you should be humble not only interiorly in your heart, but exteriorly in all your comportment.

I saw the sound psychology and proven pedagogy in

98

hanging those capsulizations on the walls leading to the novitiate and to the professed scriptorium. They served as a constant reminder of what the life was all about, and by implication, what human nature was in itself after the fall. To me, they looked like the ABC's of the spiritual life. Although I was not yet a solemnly professed in the Cistercian life, I was not a beginner in the spiritual life. As I recall my earliest reactions to Benedict's twelve degrees, I wonder if they did not indicate pride in myself. I saw that Benedict had been thorough, for he covered the whole man: body and soul; interior and exterior; mind, will, imagination, emotions, and passions. But I saw nothing really new in them, save in their number. I had known them from my earliest days as a Jesuit novice.

The scriptural image of Jacob's ladder was used in such a way that the paradox of life was obvious; not only of the Christian life, but of the life of the Chosen People, the paradox of all people. I saw it as the paradox of all creation of intelligent beings, the angels as well as those who were made little less than the angels — all humans. We go down by trying to ascend; we climb by going down. That is evidenced by the entire history of intelligent beings. Lucifer would ascend to the throne of God, and was plunged into the depths of hell. Adam and Eve would aspire to knowledge of good and evil, and lost that paradisal knowledge they had when they walked with God in the cool of the evening. Mary of Nazareth called herself the handmaid of the Lord, and was crowned queen of heaven and earth. Jesus Christ became a worm and no man, and thus redeemed all men. So the paradox was as old as Creation and as new as the morning's dawn.

I went on thinking of how I could climb by going down, and ascend by descending. Soon I saw that Benedict had not only given me the ABC's, he had given me the entire alphabet. What at first I had considered elemental, I now saw as total. I also came to the realization that humility was like quick-silver. The moment you thought you had it in hand, it slipped from your fingers. The tighter you sought to grasp it, the more readily it ran out between the cracks. It seemed so simple; yet, the longer you looked at it, the more mysterious it became. Soon this study had me saying about humility what Thomas à Kempis, I think, said about compunction: "I'd rather feel it — that is, possess it, than know its definition."

Finally, I turned to prayer and said the words a wise old missioner once said to God: "Lord, I am not humble by nature. To be honest, I am not too sure just what humility really is. Right now it seems to me that it is seeing myself in my true relationship to you; a recognition of my creaturehood, my total dependence on you, the realization that all I have and am is a gift from your creating hands and heart. So, in this sense, make me humble. When I am myself, grant that I may be grateful to you. Help me to become the 'me' you had in mind when you created me. To do that you will have to empty me of all the 'me' I have put there, and would like to keep. So, Lord, I ask a lot, and I may not now be prepared to pay the price it will demand. But I know that you are all-wise, as well as all-loving and all-powerful. Therefore, what I am afraid to do, you can do for me, and in me. So, please, Lord, in your own way, in your own time, make me, under the guidance of your Spirit and for the glory of your Father, make me a humble man."

I still went my way using the Ignatian principle of "working at humility — as though it all depended on me; but, at the same time, praying as if it all depended on God." I am still at it.

5

I Find a "New" Christ

†

In the late thirties of this exciting and somewhat mad century, I did find a "new" Christ. Now, I agree wholeheartedly with St. Paul when he insists that "Jesus Christ is the same, yesterday, today and forever." So, you have every right to ask: What am I talking about? Well, to understand my statement about finding a "new" Christ you must remember that I made my theological studies in the earliest years of the nineteen thirties. Hence, what was new to me in the late 1930s will not be in the least new to any reader who was born after that time.

God gave me an exceptional set of professors throughout my philosophical and theological studies. I made those studies long before Pius XI ever thundered at Hitler and his Nazism with that marvelous encyclical *Mit Brennender Sorge*, which the then Monsignor Spellman, later Cardinal Archbishop of New York, is said to have smuggled out of Rome under orders from Pius XI to broadcast to the world, years before the same sturdy mountain-climber of a pope told Stalin what he thought of him and his Communism in *Divini Redemptoris*. So, if you know your dates, and your Church history, you realize I had studied all about the Church more than a decade before Pius XII put out his stupendous *Mystici Corporis*, the encyclical that first set me flippantly saying, "The pope agrees with me." For, towards the end of my novitiate here at Gethsemani, I came across a little book by Daniel A. Lord, S.J., titled *Our Part in the Mystical Body*. That book was a revelation to me, and is the source for the title of this chapter.

In our study of the Church, under the very able Arthur Sheehan, S.J., we found no thesis on the Church as the Mystical Body of Christ. The term was a novelty to me back in the late 1930s. But I had long admired Dan Lord. I first met him through his pamphlets and his work amongst the Sodalists of Mary. Dan could capture your attention, fire your imagination, rouse your enthusiasm, and set you tingling with the truths he presented so clearly and convincingly. Imagine with what avidity I picked up his book on our part in the Mystical Body! I thought then that it was simply my admiration for Dan, plus my starvation for some stimulating reading, that had me so thrilled with his pages. I see now that it was God's way of preparing me for my vow of stability in the Abbey of Gethsemani, and for the main theme of all my writings. It was a real revelation!

To appreciate and really understand my statement, you must know that St. Benedict tells his masters of novices to watch their subjects closely to "see if they truly *seek God*." That is the first and final sign of a true vocation, according to Benedict. I wonder how many thousand times I have heard that phrase: "seek God." Now, the purpose of any search is to find. I was asking myself: Where and how am I, a human, to find God, who is divine? The creature is supposed to seek and find the Creator. Do they expect me to touch the Intangible, view the Invisible, know the Unknowable? I was quite lost in this, to me, new approach of seeking the One I had already found. Don't let anyone tell you that all religious orders are the same, or that all schools of spirituality are alike. Essentially, yes, but specifically — oh, what a difference! Then came Christ, through Dan Lord, and He appeared new!

At this time we novices were building the wall. It still stands — and I call it a monument to my impatience. In 1939 we numbered twenty-one in the choir novitiate — quite an increase in less than two years. Each day, in that beautiful Indian summer, the twenty-one of us would seek God as we mixed sand, gravel, and cement, and made cement blocks. We raced each day to break the previous day's record. We needed thousands of those blocks, for the wall was to be twenty-three feet wide at its base, and was to taper up some twenty-one feet before we crowned it, and was to stretch over fifty feet from east to west.

No one who used the phrase "seek God" was ever very definite or explicit about what he meant. We had to dig out, or up, the meaning for ourselves. If someone had only said: Now all we mean is that you are to find God's will for you from day to day, hour to hour, moment to moment, the search would have been over. For we novices were always and everywhere under obedience. I was experienced enough to realize that I could look upon any directive from abbot, or master of novices, or confessor, as God's will for me. I knew that the Rule had been approved by Christ's vicar on earth, and I realized that Christ meant what He said when He told us, "Who hears you, hears me," as He talked about His vicars. But how about the other twenty youngsters who did not have my background in theology or the spiritual life? If I was having difficulty with the phrase — and I was — how about those other novices?

Were they, like myself, while pounding cement into blocks, saying, "My Jesus mercy," as I very frequently said in those days? Or were they imitating me in other moments when I'd look at one of my awkward confreres and think to myself, "Boy, are you clumsy," or even, when someone opened the form too soon and thus spoiled the block I had just pounded, were they saying to themselves, "Damn!" How does one seek God when laying tier after tier of cement blocks?

We novices were under the supervision of Brother Hugh, who was over seventy at the time, although no one would ever have guessed that from the quiet, efficient, gentle, kind, and understanding way he went about supervising the young novices. We were novices as well at laying blocks — I, too, who was made foreman. I suppose it was because of my age. At any rate, Brother Hugh depended on me to some extent. Well, it began to rain during the night after a day of hard digging for the foundation. That meant we novices next morning would have to remove mud from the depths we had dug the day before. That went on for four consecutive days and nights. On the fifth, after getting the mud out, I tested the ground and made the sign to Brother Hugh to throw it in. Since we had no ready-mix in those days, but only ready backs, ready arms, and ready hands, it stands as a monument to that saintly Brother Hugh and his patience. Some of those novices had never seen a trowel before. Many had no idea what a plumb line was for. As for the level, some looked on it as a plaything. Some four or five months after we had crowned it, however, I noticed a crack running up that wall. Six months later I noticed that the crack had run almost to the crown, and had widened six inches near the base. It dawned on me that one corner had sunk, and the long, tall wall showed its weight by that widening crack. Brother Hugh looked at it one day and simply smiled. The next day he had me and others plugging cement into the crack. It can be seen to this day; yet, I dare professionals to fault that wall today in any other respects.

The wall was erected to hold back the dirt we extracted from under the monastery proper so that the lay brothers could have a modern lavatory. Actually, we added a full storey to the monastery, without adding an inch to its height. Now that is some feat for a community of farmers. We had plenty of *labora* in those days, and there was plenty of *ora* during all that *labora*. But where was the God we were seeking?

104

Before I entered Gethsemani, I had spent sixteen years in religious life. During that time I had made two novitiates, one from 1920 to 1922, another from 1934 to 1935. So I had a very clear concept of the goal of all religious living: perfection. I knew one way to seek perfection: follow Christ. I had already made two month-long retreats, an annual retreat of eight days' duration each of those sixteen years, and annually two tridua in preparation for renewal of vows. Daily meditation for at least one hour was a Jesuit prescription. Spiritual reading from various masters in the spiritual life was almost as regular as three meals each day. There was Mass and Communion every day. So I was no mere novice in the religious or the spiritual life when I came face-to-face with the command that I seek God.

Still, I was somewhat mystified. It seemed a new and different approach to me, and appeared to call for an entirely different orientation of my spiritual life. The one thing novice-like about me in those early days was my burning sincerity to learn the Cistercian way, and a boyish enthusiasm to follow every directive perfectly.

My sanguine temperament would be satisfied with nothing less than the best: the best I could give, and, yes, the best I could get. It is possible that I wanted to *see* God, not just to *seek* Him. I knew enough about the spiritual life, and even about the mystical life, to realize that all the human can do is dispose himself, remove the obstacles, and humbly pray for the grace and the gift which lie entirely in the hands of God. But my temperament had me not only striving, but actually straining to grasp, to get firm hold on this concept and command about seeking God.

About the only help I got was from a confessor who said something about it meaning union with God. I already knew about union of wills being what love is all about. I also knew that the Our Father and Christ's words "Not My will but Thine be done" told us what life is all about. But that seemed too facile a solution to what I thought was a gigantic problem. So I went to the acknowledged mystics, Teresa of Avila and John of the Cross, to learn what I could about the mystical marriage, the transforming union, the consummated union, and deification. While Teresa and John stirred both my admiration and envy, even they did not greatly help.

It was then that God took pity on His floundering novice and placed Dan Lord's book on *Our Part in the Mystical Body* in my hands, and changed my life.

Dan's influence on me was reflected in my first sermon as a Trappist to Trappists. It was given on Palm Sunday of 1939, five full years before Pius XII wrote his monumental encyclical, *Mystici Corporis*. I was ablaze, and admittedly, not so brief.

My text was taken from Matthew 21:3: *Dominus Opus habet* — " 'God hath Need' . . . of you!"

†††

"The world is saved by those who do nothing." That was the opening sentence in an article titled "Idleness," an article about you and me — the lazy monks, the drones in the human beehive, the idlers of humanity — the men who do nothing, yet save the world!

Startling statement, isn't it? Yet one that is in perfect harmony with the rest of our religion, for Christianity is nothing but a tissue of seeming contradictions, a maze of palpable paradoxes, founded by the God-Man, history's greatest enigma. Here we are at the beginning of a week in which we commemorate the greatest horror of all history, yet we call it Holy Week. The darkest and direst Friday ever known to man, we call Good. The murder of the God-Man wrought our redemption!

The Lord, He the Omnipotent, Omniscient, and Infinite God, has need — real need of tiny you and tinier me! Yes, it is all confusing and mightily contradictory when we look at it with merely human eyes, peering at it through the thick twilight of unaided human intelligence. Then it is only too true that we are lazy drones, men who do nothing. What can we show to a world that demands tangible results? What can we show to a wise world that weighs human worth on the only scales it has — those of material accomplishment? For almost a full century a community of monks has been in this abbey of ours. What substantial good has it done the county, let alone the country? What material benefit has it brought the State of Kentucky, never mind the United States? Oh, it is very true that we are the worthless ones in the human family, as the world values worth. Yet, it is equally true that we who do nothing save the world! For we are Christ's doubles, and Christ redeemed mankind.

Christ's Doubles! That's what we are here for — to double for the God-Man. Oh, what a destiny! What a dignity! What a deification is ours — to double for Jesus Christ. That is the need God has of us this day.

Now you know what a double is, and what a double does. He is a perfect reproduction of the original. There are times when the original cannot act, and things the original cannot do. The double must act and do, in such a way that the people looking on will think that it is the original acting, and the original doing. The double must be more than an understudy or a stand-in. He must be a perfect reproduction of the original. He must have the same form and figure, the same height and the same build, and, as far as it is humanly possible, the same human features. He must so exactly reproduce the original that you cannot detect the difference. That's what a double is, and that's what a double does — and you and I are doubles for Jesus Christ.

That is the true concept of our vocation. All else is either error or eroticism! We are not here to be other Bernards, other Benedicts, or other Little Flowers. We are here to be other Christs! The voice of unerring wisdom said:

107

"Come, follow me!" The voice of infallible truth said: "I am the way!" On both occasions that voice was the *verbum divinum* — the voice of Jesus Christ! That is why we who do nothing save the world, for we double for Him who was the first and great redeemer, and we are His replicas, His little redeemers.

We are to double for Him this day and this week. We are to do for Him exactly what He did 1900 years ago. We are to reproduce Jesus Christ, who rode into Jerusalem triumphant, and staggered out of it accursed. He who was welcomed on Sunday with loud hosannas was hooted at on Friday with "Crucify him! Crucify him!" He who today heard: "Blessed is he who comes in the name of the Lord," five days later listened to: "Away with him! Away with him! . . . We have no king but Caesar!" On Sunday He rode in over rich robes, on Friday he staggered out, reddening withered palm branches with blood that had been scourged from His inmost veins. That is the Christ we are to reproduce — the Paradox! The only way we can do it is paradoxical. We save the world by doing nothing!

To be a little redeemer, to be Christ's double — oh, it is thrilling, but is it true? Is this fact or fancy that I am spinning? Fancy it is, and fancy it will ever remain unless we get down on our knees daily and pray.

God has need of us today! What He did, physically, 1900 years ago, He wants to do today — just as really, just as truly, but *mystically!* What He did in His physical body that first Sunday of the Palms, He would do again today in His Mystical Body. Hence, He has need of you and of me, for we are the Mystical Body of Christ. We are not merely imitators of Christ, not merely lovers of the God-Man; we are much more. We are His *members!* That is why I say we must double for Jesus Christ, for we are living cells in the living Body which is the Body of Jesus Christ. That is what the doctrine of the Mystical Body means. That is the truth it tells us about ourselves. That is what Paul meant when he said: "I live, now not I, but Christ lives in me." That is what I mean when I say, Christ has need of us. My head has need of my hand, if I am to bless; my head has need of my heart, if I am to love; my head has need of my tongue, if I am to speak, and Christ has need of you and me, if He is to live — and He is the Eternal Galilean!

He wants to make a triumphant entry into Jerusalem today, but physically, He is in heaven. Actually, Jerusalem is every city we call modern. But He can do it, and He will do it, if you and I but render Him our *reasonable* service. That is the kind of service commended of us by the Holy Spirit through the great St. Paul — a service not merely of the audible word and more external act, but a service of head and heart, a service of mind, memory, and will, a soul's service! Action! Always action, for activity is life! Let it be *human* action, and not merely the acts of a man — *actus humanus*, as some ancients have said — and not merely *actus hominis*. The distinction is very real!

Christ wants to relive Palm Sunday. Now tell me, why Palm Sunday? Why did Jesus, who was ever and always shunning the praises and plaudits of men, set the stage for a loud-sounding triumph? Why did the meek and humble Christ demand public glorification? Certainly not for Himself! He who knew all things, who looked through all time and across all space, who knew the hearts of men, was not going to seek the hosannas of a people who would soon cry: "Crucify him! Crucify him!" No, the triumphal entry was not for Himself. Nor was it for His friends. That would have been deception, and Christ cannot deceive. That would have been a contradiction, and Christ cannot contradict Himself. For months He had been predicting His Passion and Death, not His triumph. Only a week before, He took the Twelve aside and said: "Listen, we are going up to Jerusalem, and all things shall be accomplished which were spoken by the prophets concerning the Son of Man. For He shall be betrayed to the chief priests and to the scribes and ancients. And they shall condemn Him to death, and shall deliver Him to the Gentiles, and they shall mock Him, and spit upon Him, and scourge Him. And after they have scourged Him, they shall put Him to death." To His friends He had always insisted: "My Kingdom is not of this world." No, the waving palms and loud hosannas were not for His friends. Then for whom? For His foes! For Annas and Caiaphas. For scribe and Pharisee. For all who hated Him and were plotting His death.

Jesus arranged His triumphal entry that He might fulfill an outstanding prophecy about the promised Messiah. For almost three years now the hating high priests, the hypocritical Pharisees, and the sneering scribes had been asking for a sign. For three years he had answered them with words from the prophets. On Palm Sunday, He gives them not promises nor predictions, but fulfillment. These hating leaders knew the prophets! They knew that Isaiah had spoken in his song of victory about the entry of the savior into Jerusalem. But, if Isaiah lacked clarity, they could never mistake or misinterpret Zechariah; for he explicitly stated: "O daughter Jerusalem! See, how your king shall come to you; a just savior is he, meek, and riding on an ass, on a colt, the foal of an ass."

Jesus wanted Jerusalem, He wanted the hating Annas, the hypocritical Caiaphas, the critical Pharisees, the sneering scribes and Sadducees, and all Jerusalem to accept Him for what He was — not the prophet from Nazareth nor the wonder-worker from Galilee, but the Christ, the Son of the Living God, the Savior, their promised Messiah. Yes, the triumphal entry was staged for His foes. He fulfilled a prophecy, that they might *see*!

Today He would repeat His act through you and me. For Stalin is a modern Caiaphas, and Hitler is a modern Annas. Spain and Mexico are Jerusalems over whom He weeps, for He loves them. He fulfilled a prophecy that His enemies might see, that those who hated Him might recognize Him for who He was — the Son of the Living God. Today, this Sunday of the palms in 1939, you and I fulfill a prophecy that atheist and Communist, anti-clerical and ir-religionist, that Nazi and Bolshevik might see, see that He — the Eternal Son of the ever-living God — lives, and that He loves Red and revolutionist, just as He loved the high priest and Pharisee, and loves them with the same unselfish love even unto blood. His prophecy was that of Zechariah. Ours is that of Himself, for He did say: "Behold, I am with you all days."

See how perfect is the parallel. To fulfill His prophecy He needed but two things — an ass and a colt. Today, to fulfill His prophecy, we need two things: our *opus Dei* and our *opus diei*; our prayer and our penance — our sacrifice of word and our sacrifice of act, our sacrament of labor and our sacrament of reading. With these we can be Christ's doubles. We can show Godly love for those who hate God. We can fulfill a prophecy and redeem a world. But to do that we must use them properly. Each must be more an *actus humanus* than an *actus hominis*. Each must be an act having in it mind and will. Each must be an act of a religious, and not of a robot. A robot is a mechanical man, while a religious is a man of God!

Are you wondering how I can be so absurd? How can you redeem a world by milking cows, cleaning pens, or carting dung? How can you be doubles for Jesus Christ with a pitchfork, an axe, or a pair of mules? Will caring for cattle convert Communists? Or clearing forests sanctify Nazis? Pretty absurd, isn't it, when we leave the romance of rhetoric and come down to the drab details of everyday life? Yes, it is absurd, but not quite as absurd as that other stable — the stable of Bethlehem. Not as absurd as the Incarnation. Nowhere near as absurd as that Jesus Christ should become the village carpenter.

My brothers in brown, see how perfectly you double for Christ. Look at Him there in Nazareth. See hands divine become hardened and calloused from handling plane, saw, and hammer; arms divine, that were omnipotent, become weary from work; and brow divine grow damp from sweat. Jesus, the God-Man, deified labor. He divinized work. He sanctified sweat. That is why I call manual labor a sacrament, for it is an outward sign, instituted by Christ, to give grace! Remember, He was redeeming the world just as much at Nazareth as He was on Calvary, for it was not His Passion that won salvation, it was His action! Not His Agony and Death, but His obedience! Not His suffering, but His submission. Not the cruel way of the Cross, but the crushing of His own will. It was not His immolation that saved us, it was His oblation! Let everyone grasp the truth: physical torture, brutal bloodletting, thorns, spittle, spikes, spear, not even the Cross itself, *ex natura sua*, were essential for our salvation. Obedience was! The Cross and Calvary happen to be the consummation. But obedience, the oblation of self, the doing of God's will — that is what wrought our salvation! Jesus was doing that will at Nazareth as He worked on wood, just as truly as He was doing it on Calvary when He was laid on wood. So, my brothers, you are other-Christs. You are redeemers of the world, so long as you work under obedience. So long as you do everything because it is the will of God, just so long are you doubling perfectly for the God-Man. It is not *what* you do. It is *why* you do it. God has great need of you with your simplicity, your honesty, your humility, your very real sanctity. Don't ever disappoint God, my brothers in brown. Make this Holy Week *holy*!

We in white — how simple it is for us to make this week sacred! We have the two things needed: our sacrifice of praise and our sacrifice of the Mass. God has given me lips and tongue and teeth and arched roof to my mouth, so that the labials, the gutturals, the liquids, and the vowels can be heard distinctly. In my Divine Office my enunciation will be perfect, for my God has need of me. My pronunciation will be exact, for my God has need of me. My heart will be in my song, for my God has need of me. My Office is a sacred thing, and to it I consecrate my whole being: my mind, my memory, my will, my intellect, my imagination. All that I am, and all that I have, I give to my God, for He has given them first to me.

Fathers and brothers, no extras to save mankind! No private devotions, but the whole man in the public prayer of the Church. Obedience saves the world; not private prayers and penances! So, this day and this week, I will obey Christ, who says to me through His Church: 'Sing your Office *digne, attente, ac devote. Viriliter age!*

Allow me a word about our Mass. Yes, it is *our* Mass; and when I say our, I mean everyone in this room, from Reverend Father to latest postulant. It is our Mass, for we are all priests! A bishop's hands may not have been laid upon your heads, but baptism's waters flowed over them, and baptism is the *ordination* of the laity. It gives each recipient a share in the priesthood of Christ. St. Peter says: "You are a royal priesthood, ordained to offer up spiritual sacrifice; you are a kingly priesthood." Pope Pius XI, addressing all the faithful, says, "Pray the Mass."

That is why most of us will never again *go* to Mass, or *hear* Mass, or *attend* Mass. Never! That would be passivity, and passivity never sanctified a soul, let alone saved a world! We must *say* the Mass; for it is *our* Mass! How personal is the Mass! You and I are on the paten with the host. You and I are in the chalice with the wine. You and I are offered up with the Christ, for we are His members! That's what the *orate fratres* tells us. That's what the *in spiritu humilitatis* after the Offertory tells us. The only proper prayers are the Mass prayers. The only proper book is the missal. When I can't be the priest at the altar, I will be a priest in the choir, and I will sing my Mass as solemnly, as reverently, as attentively, as if I were the priest at the altar. I must put my soul into my song. I must put my heart, mind, and will — I must put the whole of me into this most sacred act possible to man in time, or Eternity!

Had I been on Calvary's top, I would not have drowsed! I would not have been indifferent! Drowse while they are hammering my Jesus to the tree? Indifferent while Jews howl and Romans sneer and mock? Drowse or be indifferent while my God dies, and my Mother's heart breaks? Never! Well, the Mass is Calvary!

That's how to save the world, my fathers and brothers. The *opus Dei* and the *opus diei* are all we need. But we must vivify, vigorize, virilize them.

If I cut my finger, and it becomes infected, what happens? My whole body is affected and immediately the leucocytes, the tiny, vigorous, life-giving corpuscles in my bloodstream, race from all parts of my body to the infected part, and there do battle to the death with the phagocytes causing the infection. My body is a unity, hence the healthy parts rush aid to the members that are diseased, so that the whole may have well-being. Christ's Mystical Body is just as much a unit. The Church is not an organization; it is an organism. It is a living Body, the Mystical Body of Christ. But some parts are diseased and dying; some are already dead. But we are the healthy part. We are some of those robust, vigorous corpuscles. Hence, we must give strength to the weak, health to the diseased, and life to the dying, and even to the dead. There are tens of millions of actual, and hundreds of millions of potential members of Christ's Body out there beyond our cloister walls.

Fathers and brothers, a contemplative is not a Buddha with eyes closed, hands folded, intently looking inward, thinking only of self. Never! A real contemplative is another Christ, with arms flung wide, eyes open, side open, heart open, thinking only and always of others. They are actual or potential members of our Body, and Christ is our Head! Yes — Christ the paradox, Jesus the meek, Jesus the master; Jesus the king, Jesus the criminal; Jesus the judge, Jesus the

114

condemned; Jesus the priest, Jesus the victim; Jesus who saved others, but would not save Himself — is our Head!

And we, we will be paradoxical: lazy monks, yet ever active lovers of mankind; idlers of humanity, yet humanity's energizers; drones, yet dynamos; do-nothings, yet saviors of the world; faulty, frail, finite nothings, yet doubles for the Infinite God! What a sublime paradox: We, the personifications of weakness, this Palm Sunday and during this Holy Week satisfy the needs of God! Omnipotence has need of us; let us not disappoint God!

I can see why some looked at me askance during that Holy Week. I had been too fiery for a quiet, contemplative community. I had presented a new Christ to them — one who had a need, and even a need of us! Doubtlessly, the doctrine of the Mystical Body was as new to them as it had been to me. Doubtlessly, also, I had much to learn about this new Christ; especially did I have to learn how old He was, and how ancient the truths were I presented. Some four hundred years before me Teresa of Avila wrote: "Jesus has no body on Earth but yours, no hands but yours. Yours are the eyes through which His love is to look out on the World. Yours are the feet on which he is to go about doing good." So we are back to square one, or better still, back to Qoheleth's declaration: "Nothing is new under the sun."

It was brand new to me, and it fired me with a determination to learn all I could about this "new" Christ. That determination led me to, using Cardinal Newman's term, a "development of doctrine."

115

6

Development of Doctrine . . .

The Pope Agrees with Me

†

The new Christ appeared to me as one who had need of His members. I had taken my analogy, or illustration, from Hollywood, but many of my own brothers had never seen a movie, while many of those who had, had no clear idea of what a double was nor what he had to do. Yet I hoped I had proven my point even for those from foreign lands.

I fell in love with this new Christ, but I well knew how exact the ancients were when they insisted that you can't love what you do not know. I wanted to fall more deeply in love with this new Christ, so I resolved to gain greater knowledge of Him. God Himself was aware of both my enthusiasm and my need of more intimate knowledge of this doctrine. As so often, He cared for both through another. This time it was my darling sister, whom I was now calling my partner in the service of Love. I could do that, for she had changed her name from Mary Agnes Flanagan to Sister Mary Clare of the Sisters of Charity of Halifax.

These good sisters had taught each of us Flanagans in St. Peter's Parochial School in Dorchester, Massachusetts. So it was quite natural that my two older sisters, Catherine and Mary, should sail out of Boston Harbor, head for Halifax, Nova Scotia, to give themselves to God as "Black Caps of Mother Seton," as they were then known. Catherine, as

Sister Leo Stanislaus, took off for heaven the year before my ordination. But Mary Agnes came back to Boston as Sister Mary Clare and Superioress of St. Margaret's Convent in Dorchester the very day Hitler blitzkrieged his way into Poland. Jubilant as she was to be back in the U.S.A. after many years in Nova Scotia, and delighted to be stationed in the parish next-door to home, she was also concerned about my enthusiasm over my new Christ. One of her first unofficial acts on her return to the States was to purchase and send to me a book titled *The Whole Christ*, with the subtitle: The Historical Development of the Doctrine of the Mystical Body in Scripture and Tradition.

What a revelation came to me from the introduction, which had been penned by Fr. Joseph Husslein, S.J. I thanked God, who had really sent this book, for humbling me to the dust. Fr. Husslein had written: "We (with this new doctrine) are indeed the heirs of all the ages, and we can turn to this book (Emile Mersch's *Whole Christ)* which has for its particular purpose to make us comprehend what each successive period has contributed to mankind's fuller and richer knowledge of this sublime subject. Ours, as the latest comers, is the accumulated treasure of the centuries."

I won't weary you with my detailed study of this classic, but I must share some highlights, so that you can see what God did to my soul.

Emile Mersch wrote: "We propose to study what St. Paul calls "the mystery of Christ in us. . . .' This mystery is before all else a prodigy of *unity*. . . . In the first place, it unites us with Christ." You already know that I had come here to "live in the society of Jesus." Here was my new mentor telling me that my purpose had already been accomplished. "For us, from a supernatural standpoint, to exist means *to be in Christ*."

If that truth thrilled the Trappist in me, what do you think his next lines did to the theologian in me? "To understand this unity, we must understand the nature of the In-

117

carnation, which has brought it to our earth, the nature of Divine Life, whence this unity flows, the nature of Justification, of which it is one aspect, the nature of Original Sin, of which it is the reparation, the nature of the Eucharist, of which it is the supernatural effect; in a word, we must understand the whole of Christian Doctrine."

He was saying that were I to understand this new doctrine, I would have to understand all theology. How had it come to pass that I, who had had four very full years in the study of theology, could not recall having so much as heard of this doctrine?

There was some relief for me in his next paragraph wherein he admitted "it would be absurd to lay claim to perfect knowledge of the mystery here on earth. Only in the rays of the Eternal Light, 'on that day' spoken of by Jesus in the Gospel of St. John, shall we know how Christ is in the Father, and we in Him, and He in us. Meanwhile, we must rest content with the half-light of this world, a light that may be increased by study and reflection, a light that is most fruitful and most desirable, but always imperfect."

I found that passage an echo of the words I had used one day when talking about contemplation with Tom Merton. I held that there is such a thing as active contemplation, which is quite distinct from that marvelous gift from God we call passive contemplation, and which to me is really the mystical life. Tom sided with those who held there was only one kind of true contemplation: passive. I had concluded our friendly, but by no means unheated discussion, with: "Tom, what you are talking about is a very special gift from God, one that we cannot obtain by our greatest efforts even when aided by grace. To me, what you are calling true contemplation is really close kin to what I know as the beatific vision, and I am perfectly content to wait for heaven to be granted that. You have some very fine theologians on your side.

"I admit the passages you have quoted from the recognized mystics, like Teresa of Avila and John of the Cross, have been cited by others as proof of your contention. But I have a few fairly able theologians who hold as I do, and they have interpreted those same passages a bit differently. To tell you the truth, Tom, I believe I would fall dead if I had an experience of the Triune God within me as described by certain mystics. I am perfectly content to wait for heaven for anything like that."

Mersch was saying something very similar as he said we must rest content with the half-light, but what spurred me on was his contention that this "light may be increased by study and reflection." He set me doing both as he began with Genesis, then immediately insisted that we had to go to the New Testament to understand the Old. All my professors of Sacred Scripture had insisted that "the New is concealed in the Old. The Old is revealed in the New." Mersch put that truth to immediate application by straightway citing the opening lines of St. Paul's Epistle to the Ephesians to shed clearer light on Genesis: "Blessed be the God and Father of Our Lord, Jesus Christ, who has blessed us with every spiritual blessing on high in Christ. Yea, in Him He singled us out before the foundation of the world, that we might be holy and blameless in His sight. In love He predestined us to be adopted as His sons through Jesus Christ, according to the good pleasure of His will."

I saw that Mersch was taking me back before the creation of the world, back into the very mind and will of God, to enable me to understand this doctrine. He stunned me when he said: "What the first verse of Genesis is for a religious understanding of the universe: 'In the beginning God created heaven and earth,' and what the Prologue of St. John's Gospel is for the understanding of the Word: 'In the beginning was the Word' — the opening lines of Paul's Epistle to the Ephesians are for the Doctrine of our elevation to the supernatural order and our incorporation into Christ. They tell us that God, who in the beginning made

119

all things, loved us, at the beginning of all His graces, in the Word, who was 'in the beginning.' "

God had me in His mind and heart before He said: "Let there be light!" He loved me before He had said: "Let us make man in our own image."

What an intoxicating experience it was for me to read Mersch's first chapter, in which he was showing how the Mystical Body was prefigured in the Old Testament!

Echoes from the New Testament came to me with each succeeding reference. As Mersch told of the first Adam, I heard Paul telling of the second. When Emile told how God looked upon the Jews as His vineyard, I heard Christ, in His sacerdotal prayer, saying: "I am the vine, you are the branches." When this scholar told of how God spoke of His Chosen People as His sheep, I heard Christ telling His parable of the Good Shepherd. When he had me listening to God talking to His people in the Old Testament and calling them His bride, not only the favorite song of contemplatives and mystics, the Canticle of Canticles, came to mind, but also John's vision of the New Jerusalem as it came down out of heaven adorned as a bride. One peak was reached when Mersch had me hear God call His people His son. Addressing Pharoah, God said: "Let my son go." How could I fail to hear God, again and again, saying of Christ: "This is My Beloved Son"? Indeed the New does reveal what is concealed in the Old. No wonder Paul so often speaks of us as having our *esse in Christo* — our very being in Christ Jesus!

I confess that despite my intimate acquaintance with some truly wise ancients, both Latin and Greek, who had often warned me to be moderate, I had gone so far overboard about this doctrine, that I was brash enough to plead with my brothers, Fr. Jack and Fr. Eddie, who had been preaching parish missions and giving retreats for years, to recast all their matter and use this doctrine exclusively.

Wise old Fr. Jack replied by quietly warning me about excessiveness. He saw the possibility of one falling into what he called panChristism. I did not agree with him, but I was pulled up short when I found Mersch, in his earliest pages, warning about certain false notions some had about this doctrine. His first was exactly what Fr. Jack had warned me against. Mersch wrote: "One would ill understand this unity (with and in Christ), or to be more exact, he would not understand it at all, were he to imagine that the faithful are really and absolutely Christ Himself. This would be a kind of pantheism, or rather 'panChristism,' quite as contradictory as it is naive, and fraught with the most absurd consequences." I read on with greater concentration and learned that some were relying more on their imaginations and sentiments than on reason and faith, and thought they could picture to themselves this reality. "It goes without saying," concluded Mersch, "that whosoever allows himself to be misled by his imagination is exposing himself to all kinds of absurdities." Since I do have a vivid imagination, I became much more cautious.

Emile's last warning was about false mysticism. He admitted it would be quite useless to describe all the forms which the illusion takes, but he did mention illuminism, quietism, and the very false notion that this truth, about our being made a member of Christ by baptism, did away with all call for asceticism, self-denial, or mortification. I felt sure I had not fallen into any of these errors, but I was grateful for his warning, and resolved to be on my guard.

I well knew that public revelation had closed with the death of John the Beloved. What is called ongoing revelation is, when it is right, nothing but what John Henry Newman called the development of doctrine, which consists of a fuller understanding and expression of what has been revealed. In other words, revelation does not grow, but man grows in his clearer understanding of what has been revealed.

I have always admired Newman, not only for his mastery of the English language, but also for his astounding integrity. He, like Paul, is my ideal of a real man, a true mind.

He was a theologian who thought things through, who listened to God, who loved his Christ. It was he who first awakened me to the mighty difference between a notional assent and a real assent. The first is a nod of the head in agreement with a truth that has been presented. The second is an assimilation of that truth into one's very blood and bone. With the first, you can tell that truth to others. With the second, you live that truth in the presence of all others.

As Mersch took me through the Old and New Testaments, he had me in awe as I saw the true development of this doctrine. But he also set me back in consternation at my obtuseness in having missed this doctrine all my life and in having missed adoration of God's ongoing revelation of it from Genesis to the Apocalypse. No wonder St. Jerome had said: "Ignorance of Scripture" (referring to both the Old and the New Testaments), "is ignorance of Christ." The seventy-two books tell of no one else, and it is revealed therein that He and we are *one!*

Emile's painstaking explanation of the further development of this doctrine by Fathers of the Church, both those of the East and the West, filled me with joy. Before I had completed his study of the Oriental Fathers he had me singing:

> "When men shall say to you: Lo, Christ is here;
> When men shall say to you: Lo, Christ is there;
> Believe them! And know that thou art seer
> When all thy crying clear
> Is but: Lo here! Lo there! Ah me,
> Lo everywhere!"

Mersch's champion of champions among the Occidental writers was Augustine of Hippo. The Latin mind has a more practical turn than that of the East. Hence, in the Occident, greater stress is placed on moral problems and Christian conduct, which should result from our incorporation in Christ. And no one has stressed this more emphatically than Augustine. I had always admired this man from

122

Tagaste, but as I read on in Mersch, my admiration turned into what can only be called love. Emile rightly called him "the greatest of the Church's Doctors. He was a genius of rare versatility and brilliance; a true African and a true Roman, yet the first of the moderns." Since psychology has taken so advanced a place in our day, I always enjoy referring psychologists and psychiatrists to Augustine. He anticipated all their insights, and did so back in the fourth and early fifth centuries! Augustine was a man as well as a mind — man of such sterling character that he was as ready to lead men as he was to spend himself for them. There were never any half-measures for Augustine. When he sinned, he sinned, as he tells us in his *Confessions*, wholeheartedly. When he turned to God, he turned completely. His real love, and it was a passionate love, was for Truth. This is evident from his constant use of *within*. We must seek within; we must turn our eyes within; everything is within. Thinking is not so much an association of concepts as a searching within one's self for Truth. His whole soul, his whole self, reaches out for that Truth. It is Augustine's confession: "O Truth, Truth, how intensely did the marrow of my soul even then sigh after Thee!" That soul was satisfied, as every one who has read the *Confessions* knows.

But it was the development of the doctrine of the Mystical Body that I was looking for now, and not the inner soul of Augustine. In looking for the one, I found both. Just imagine what it meant to this young monk who was seeking God and longing for union with Him to read: "Let us rejoice and give thanks. Not only are we become Christians, but we are become Christ. My brothers, do you understand the grace of God that is given us? Wonder, rejoice, for we are made Christ! If He is the Head, and we the members, then together He and we are the whole man. . . . This would be foolish pride on our part, were it not a gift of His bounty. But this is what He promised by the mouth of the Apostle: 'You are the Body of Christ, and severally His members.' " Augustine taught that Christ was even more truly within us than He was truly the Christ when He walked the roads of Judea, for faith is more perfect than evidence, and grace more perfect than nature. "It is a greater thing," he says, "to believe in Christ than to see Him always bodily present; for when we believe, He is present to the eyes of the spirit. Let no one regret His ascension into Heaven as if He had abandoned us. If we believe, He is with us. His presence within thee is more real than if He were to stand beside thee, before thy very eyes. If thou believest, He is within. If thou wert to receive Christ as a Guest in thy room, He would be with thee. Behold thou dost receive Him within thy heart — is He not with thee?"

I was finding, on each page on which Augustine was cited, ever greater reason to fall ever more deeply in love with Christ, especially in the Eucharist. This, to my way of thinking, is the real focus of the contemplative life, and the source and center of contemplation. What amazed me was that Augustine was explaining the mystery of the altar: Christ's Sacrifice and Sacrament to neophytes, and not to profound theologians. He was explaining it by teaching the Doctrine of the Mystical Body. "If you would understand what the Body of Christ is, listen to what the Apostle says to the faithful: 'You are the Body of Christ, and severally His members.' Since then you are the Body of Christ and His members, it is your mystery that is placed on the Lord's Table; it is your mystery that you receive. To words that tell you what you are, you answer 'Amen,' and in answering you subscribe to the statement. For you hear the words: 'The Body of Christ,' and you answer 'Amen.' Be, therefore, members of Christ, that your 'Amen' may be true.

"But why is this mystery accomplished in bread? Let us offer no reason of our own invention, but listen to the Apostle speak of this Sacrament: 'We many are one bread, one body. Understand this and rejoice. Unity, truth, piety, charity. 'One Bread.' What is this one bread? It is one body formed of many. Remember that bread is not made of one grain, but of many. During the exorcisms you were ground like wheat; at Baptism water was poured over you, as flour is mingled with water, and the Holy Spirit entered you like the fire which bakes the bread. Be what you see, and receive what you are.

"This is what the Apostle teaches concerning the bread. Though he does not say what we are to understand of the chalice, his meaning is readily seen. . . . Recall, my brothers, how wine is made. Many grapes hang from the vine, but the juice of all the grapes is fused into unity. Thus did the Lord Christ manifest us in Himself. He willed that we should belong to Him, and He has consecrated on His altar the mystery of our peace and unity."

For a cloistered monk, whose whole day is centered on the Mass and Holy Communion, whose life's aim is union with God, whose one work is to become who he is, that passage was more than manna from Heaven. It was, more precisely, the Living Bread who came down from heaven.

All my straining ceased when I came across Augustine's passage about holiness. "Can I say," he asks, "that I am holy?" He proceeds to answer his own question, and mine, too. "If I mean a holiness that I have not received, I should be proud and a liar. But if I mean a holiness that I have received — as it is written: 'Be ye holy, because I the Lord, your God, am holy,' then let the Body of Christ say these words. And let this one man, who cries from the ends of the earth, say with his Head and united with his Head: 'I am holy. . . .' That is not foolish pride, but an expression of gratitude. If you were to say that you are holy of yourselves, that would be pride; but if as one of Christ's faithful, and as a member of Christ, you say that you are not holy, you are ungrateful. Since all the faithful who are baptized have put on Christ, as the Apostle says: 'All of you who were baptized into Christ, have put on Christ,' and since they have become members of His Body, they offer insult to their Head if they say they are not holy; for then His members would not be holy. See where thou art, and from thy Head accept thy dignity."

Augustine's teachings marked a high point in the development of this doctrine. After him, in the early Middle Ages, and on into the age of the Scholastics, there was something of a decline. I shouldn't have been surprised, for all life is undulant. Now you are on the crest. Then you go down into the trough. But, when down there, don't get excited, for you will soon start rising toward the crest again. I believe I learned that fact more from Ignatius and his Spiritual Exercises than I did from any of the so-called masters in psychology or psychiatry. That is Loyola's teaching, practically speaking, about consolation and desolation.

Mellifluous Doctor though he was, my father, St. Bernard had little to say about the Mystical Body. I did gather comfort from the fact that two of his disciples, William of St. Thierry, and Isaac of Stella, did speak of the truth, and speak beautifully.

It disappointed and disturbed me that the great Scholastics had not marked an advance in the development of this doctrine, but perhaps it was part of God's Providence. God had assigned the schoolmen the task of summing up the revealed Truth, of expressing the dogmas of the Faith with the greatest clarity, logical order, and coherence. Since they were so devoted to precision, and since this doctrine will always retain a certain mystery, I came to understand their reticence to deal with it in detail. They did deal with it, however. Aquinas treated it in his Soteriology. The Scotists say little about it. The Jesuits, that is the theologians, were brief about it, but their exegetes had much to say. The doctrine suffered something of an eclipse, but the schoolmen prepared the ground for its further development.

It was the popes of my lifetime who spoke out on it. Leo XIII, who died the year I was born, wrote of it explicitly in his *Satis Cognitum*, as he dwelt on the Church. Pius X, who made it possible for me to receive my First Holy Communion at the age of seven, treated of it in his *Il Firmo Proposito*, which dealt with *Catholic action*. Pius XI, my beloved mountain-climber, called it this most beautiful doctrine, and asserted it was peculiarly well suited for our modern age. For it is a remedy for Naturalism, for Liberal Individualism, for Nationalism, and that unbridled economic Liberalism that has and is driving so many nations into the hands of dictators. But especially is it a remedy for that summation of all heresies, Modernism.

But God waited for Pius XII, whom I consider one of the great theologians, to give us the masterpiece, *Mystici Corporis*. It was given at Rome, at St. Peter's, June 29, the Feast of the Holy Apostles Peter and Paul, 1943, the fifth of his pontificate.

The world at that time was literally falling apart. Hitler had blitzkrieged his way east and west, nation after nation had been dominated, and the Axis powers seemed capable of winning the world-wide war. As usual in wartime the animal in man had been unleashed, and morals were at their lowest ebb. The immediate future for mankind in general, and for the Church in particular, was bleak indeed. Yet, here was Christ's vicar talking to the world at large, and the Catholic world in particular, about a doctrine many of the most learned had feared to face. With his usual brilliance and boldness, Pius wrote: ". . . some through empty fear look upon so profound a Doctrine as something dangerous, and so they fight shy of it as of the beautiful but forbidden fruit of Paradise. It is not so. Mysteries, revealed by God, cannot be harmful to men; nor should they remain as treasures hidden in a field useless. They have been given from on high precisely to help the spiritual progress of those who study them in a spirit of piety."

Pius was using many of the Fathers and Doctors Mersch had presented to me as he showed the development of this doctrine down the ages. Further, Pius, like Mersch,

127

cut through the confusion and the uncertainties which had set in over the centuries as the various interpretations and analogues had been introduced in an effort to explain and expound the richness and splendor contained, yet concealed, in this sublime truth. But Mersch, for all his magnificent work, was only a theologian and something of an historian, whereas Pius XII was Christ's vicar and visible head of the Church Jesus had established and was here writing with his full pontifical authority.

In a masterly introduction Pius gave his reasons for publishing this encyclical. They were three. First, the terrible (and I add, terrifying) state of society made it imperative that all spiritually minded men should be possessed of the light which is contained in the doctrine. Secondly, the Holy Father was grateful for the united love, which all his children, even though their countries were at war with one another, had manifested to their common Father in Christ. He rightly claimed that the truth of the Mystical Body was the secret of this wonderful unity. Finally, there was his own pastoral duty to the souls entrusted to his care, for the renewed interest in the liturgy, the growth of Catholic Action, more fervent devotion to the Sacred Heart, and the spread of more frequent Holy Communion had prepared men's hearts for a better understanding of this sublime mystery. At the same time, there had arisen certain wrong tendencies deriving from some misunderstandings of the doctrine which it was his duty to condemn and proscribe.

Emile Mersch was right in his claim that this doctrine includes all the others, for the pope is saying practically the same thing as he talks of the Church, visible and invisible, the Sacraments, the Sacrifice, the various states of life witnessed to by the different members in the Church as the Body, touches on Creation, the Fall, the Incarnation, Redemption, Merit, Grace — all in his opening paragraphs. Pius set down who were members of Christ's Body, saying: "Only those are really to be included as members of the

Church who have been baptized and profess the true Faith and who have not unhappily withdrawn from Body-unity or for grave faults have been excluded by legitimate authority." Lest there be any doubt about his meaning, the pope reiterates the same fact at the close of this same paragraph saying: "It follows that those who are divided in Faith or government cannot be living in one Body such as this, and cannot be living the life of its one Divine Spirit."

After treating of the Body as a body, Pius went on to show why it was Christ's Body. He was the Founder of the Body through His life, Death, Resurrection, and sending His Spirit into that Body. Then, expounding on the theme of my first sermon, "God has need," he says: "Because Christ the Head holds such an eminent position, one must not think that He does not *require the Body's help*. What Paul said of the human organism is to be applied likewise to this Mystical Body: 'The head cannot say to the feet: I have no need of you.' It is manifestly clear that the Faithful need the help of the Divine Redeemer, for He has said: 'Without Me, you can do nothing,' and in the teaching of the Apostle, every advance of the Body towards its perfection derives from Christ the Head. Yet, this too, must be held, marvelous though it appears: *Christ requires His members.*" (Italics added)

Pius gave me a clearer view of my life's work as a Trappist, and justification for my claim that we were to be little redeemers. Pius said: ". . . in carrying out the work of Redemption He wishes to be helped by the members of His Body. This is not because He is indigent and weak, but rather because He has so willed it for the greater glory of His unspotted Spouse. Dying on the Cross, He left to His Church the immense treasury of the Redemption; towards this she contributed nothing. But when those graces come to be distributed, not only does He share this task of sanctification with His Church, but He wants it in a way to be due to her action. Deep mystery this, subject of inexhaust-

129

ible mediation: that the salvation of many depends on the prayers and the voluntary penances which the members of the Mystical Body offer for this intention."

Did that passage lift the heart of a man whose life is prayer and penance! Life behind these walls can be very hard on a red-blooded American. Americans are a nation not only of competitors, but a very practical, pragmatic, and productive people. There is the rub for Americans in a cloistered contemplative life. Due to our culture and character, we like to see results for our work, but what can we see after weeks, months, and even years here at Gethsemani? Nothing. Oh, we have taken in a few harvests, and we have built a few buildings, lakes, and walls, but a pagan or an atheist could produce those things. What can we look upon as Catholics, sons of God, religious, or priests? Again I say: Nothing.

But here was the pope of Rome, the vicar of Christ on earth, the visible head of the Body known as the Catholic Church telling me that the salvation of many depends on the prayers and voluntary penances I offered as a member of Christ's Mystical Body for this intention. Indeed that strengthened me in the discharge of my vow of stability.

Pius XI had encouraged me prior to this. In 1924, Pius had written a letter known by its first word *Umbratilem*. In that letter he boldly said that those in the cloistered orders save more souls than do those in the active ministry. I seriously questioned the grounds on which he made such a statement. Then in 1925, he addressed us Trappists directly. (*Umbratilem* had been addressed to the Carthusians.) This letter is known as *Monachorum Vitae*, and again Pius XI made practically the same statement. I took this a bit more personally, since it was written to the Cistercians of the Strict Observance. Both of these letters were letters of congratulations. Knowing something of Vatican diplomacy, I told myself His Holiness would say much the same were He addressing the Jesuits, the Dominicans, or the Little

Sisters of the Poor. It was sound psychology on the pope's part to build up the ego. Then again, it was charity. The Father of us all was giving us a pat on the back, encouraging us to keep agoin', for he well knew it was tough going behind cloistering walls. But then on February 18, 1926, this same mountain-climber of a pope, wrote an encyclical letter: *Rerum Ecclesiae*, a letter to promote foreign missions. In it he exhorted every bishop in foreign lands to obtain cloistered communities for their various dioceses if they wanted the active missionaries to have real success. This, since it was an encyclical, commanded more of my attention than the others; still, when analyzed, it did no more than stress the importance of prayer.

Opening the second part of his *Mystici Corporis* Pius says: "Here, Venerable Brethren, We wish to speak in a particular way of our union with Christ in the Body of the Church. St. Augustine has justly remarked that this union is something sublime, mysterious, and divine; but for that very reason it often happens that many misunderstand it and explain it incorrectly." I wondered if I had misunderstood it and explained it incorrectly? "It is at once evident that this union is very close. In Sacred Scripture it is likened to the pure union of man and wife, and is compared with the vital union of branch and vine, and with the cohesion found in our body." So far, so good, but His Holiness is not through. "Even more, it is represented as being so close that the Apostle says: 'He (Christ) is Head of the Body of the Church,' and the unbroken tradition of the Fathers from the earliest times teaches that the Divine Redeemer and the society which is His Body form but one mystical person, that is to say, to quote Augustine: 'the whole Christ.'" I had grasped all that, but now comes the clincher: "Our Saviour Himself," writes Pius, "in His high-priestly prayer, has gone so far as to liken this union with that marvelous oneness by which the Son is in the Father and the Father in the Son."

I could only fall down in adoration and thanksgiving when I read that passage. My work was done. No more searching. No more straining for union. God had accomplished it all, and had done so from the moment the waters of baptism had been poured on my brow! Now Augustine's exclamations were more clearly understood — not because he was a passionate African, but rather because he was a humble and grateful Christian who had heard, much more clearly than I, Christ Himself telling this truth as He prayed before His Last Supper.

I had been swimming in a sea of theology for some time, due to Mersch and Pius XII. I had been looking deeply into those fonts of Revelation: Scripture and tradition for weeks and months. Sound reasoning was always present. It was a delightful swim, but it also was exhausting, even as it was exciting and exhilarating.

My brothers, both priests and non-priests, looked different to me after that swim. I was not granted what was once granted, for a time, to Caryll Houselander. For some months, after she had learned this truth, she saw the face of Christ in every human face. The faces of my Trappist confreres, bearded and unbearded, did not look like that to me. But I did see all in Christ Jesus.

My day, in choir and out of it, changed. In choir I knew myself to be *labia Christi* — the very lips of Christ, as I praised Father, Son, and Holy Spirit in the official prayer of the Mystical Body, the Divine Office. When I went to the altar the union was even more real, and much more profound, for then I was acting in the very person of Christ! My priesthood, appreciated before as something special, now became truly awesome.

The liturgical life, lived so completely in the liturgical year by us monks, took on newer vitality and commanded greater vigor, as I strove to become who I was: *Jesus Christ.* Let me tell you about that in my next chapter.

7

Reliving
the Greatest Story Ever Told

✝

My first reaction when I encountered the phrase *opus Dei* was not favorable. I took it to mean what we priests had always called the Office, meaning the recitation of the breviary, saying the canonical hours. It does mean all that, so why multiply terms? Why not call it by its correct name: the Office? Why do they call it the work of God? It's not that, but our work, our duty and our obligation — a serious one, binding, under pain of mortal sin. I had a point. But I was not pointing in the right direction!

As I studied Benedict's rule, I saw what stress he laid on this work of God. He devoted thirteen of seventy-three chapters in his Rule to the *opus Dei*. Obviously, he thought it to be an essential element in the life of a monk. In fact, it is the second requirement he lays down as proof of a genuine vocation to the cloister. The novice master was to see if the aspirant was truly seeking God. After that, Benedict tells the master to see if the one seeking entrance among the brethren were *sollicitus ad opus Dei* — zealous for the work of God. Then, one of the greatest punishments Benedict prescribed for delinquents was excommunication from the *opus Dei*. It dawned on me gradually why this wise legislator for monks wrote: "*Nothing* is to be preferred (put before) the work of God." He was a God-oriented man, a truly

God-conscious individual, so I was soon translating his *opus Dei*, not as the *work* of God, but as the *worship* of God.

That did not call for any great mental acuity, far less any mental ingenuity, for it was obvious from the reading of the Rule that while the Divine Office was not the *sole* work for the monk, it was his primary and principal work. Further, reading between the lines, one soon saw that Benedict considered this worship of God as the focus of the monk's life, and the formative element of his monastic character. He did not come behind these walls for himself, but for God. He was not cloistering himself to seek *his own* perfection, or "fulfillment." He had come to *glorify God*. Actually, it is not a matter of getting so much as of giving.

I had said my Office faithfully for years before I came to Gethsemani, but I admit that, at times at least, it was done as an obligation that bound under pain of sin. I got it in during my busy day. Now I was not simply saying my Office, I was praying it. What a difference! I hope I honored God in the old days, but I confess it wasn't very much of a real prayer, far less the pure prayer that Benedict exhorted us all to offer. I had more time for it now — from six or more hours every ordinary day and up to more than nine hours on special days. Contrast that with the hour I used to devote to it, not infrequently just before midnight. I think the greatest difference came from the fact that in the old days I had always said my Office alone. Now it was always with the community. It is in choir with the brethren that one can understand clearly the meaning of the word "comunio" — we are many and yet we are one — and this unit is assembled for the one work of glorifying God! Once I had mastered the many mechanics — posture, place in psalter and antiphonary, the various bows, the different officers, the eight separate modes in the Gregorian Chant — the *opus Dei* became the most inspiring, satisfying, and the most exciting work of the day.

The point I want to make is the fullness of the phrase:

opus Dei. As I got into my study of the *opus Dei*, I felt dissatisfied with the usual translation work of God, and translated it into *worship* of God. I went so far as to take two words emblazoned over the entrance door of our church as the freer, yet more exact translation. Those words read: *Venite Adoremus*. That was my capsulization of my whole life here at Gethsemani. I was here to *adore God*.

Remember that I was brought up on the fundamental exercise of St. Ignatius which had taught me that I had been created to glorify God. I was so taken with this idea in my early days here, and still am to a great extent, that I told the community in both sermons and conferences that we were here for no other purpose than to become animated doxologies. When you realize that we end every psalm and practically every hymn in the Office with those words, you can see how the *opus Dei* was something very heavenly, if not heaven itself, to me.

This heavenly worship of God was not always bliss to me when I was still a very young monk. While I did try to do as Benedict bade me, and be conscious of the angels, in whose presence we were singing, I was anything but unconscious of the humans in whose midst I was discharging the *opus Dei*.

One Sunday of Recollection when I was assigned to give the conference on "The Divine Office as a means to Union with God, and how to make it such," I insisted we don't make the Office a means to union with God. It already is that. "What is union with God," I asked, "if not the fusion of the mind and will of man with the mind and will of Omnipotence? Since prayer is naught but the lifting of the mind and heart to God, and since the Divine Office is prayer, to say that the Divine Office is a means to union with God seems like saying the same thing to me." So I repeated that I was at a loss on how to carry out my assignment.

I had early seen the greatest danger for anyone in this life: routine! I also had, praised be to God, the one solution:

135

thought. I told my confreres that while dwelling on that distinction between man and a machine, I saw that I could carry out the assignment and give a talk about the Divine Office being a means to union with God, and show them how to make it such. The latter could be summed up in one word: think.

††

How about it, fathers and brothers, doesn't that make sense? We are men; therefore, we have minds. If we use them, we can be consciously united with God. All we have to do is *think*. Did it ever strike you that man is the only creature in God's visible creation who can *think*, and therefore, pray? Did it ever strike you that, since Thomas' definition of glory is correct, namely, *Clara cognitio cum laude*, man is the only creature in God's visible creation who can give God glory? Man alone can have that *clara cognitio*, which means 'thinking clearly,' upon which the *laudes*, or 'praise' is founded! Betelgeuse, the brightest star in Orion, has been on the wing since God first said *fiat*, and never once has it deviated from God's appointed course. The Andes, Himalayas, and Rockies have thrust their brave peaks into the clouds for aeons, just as God ordained that they should. The Atlantic, Pacific, and the other five seas have ebbed and flowed just as God appointed that they should since the Spirit first brooded over the waters at creation. What a flawless obedience to God these creatures have shown! But what is it, though it has been going on for ages, what is it compared to a single sigh of a thoughtful man, whose sigh is a thought-provoked sigh of love? These wondrous creatures cannot praise formally, cannot pray, cannot think. But you and I can be the conductor of the symphony of the spheres, the Coropheus of the cosmos, we can give voice to the voiceless sun, moon and stars; song to rocks, rain, wind and waters; tongues of praise to bird and beast, if we but *think*! Unless we do think I greatly fear that

136

our Divine Office will be neither Office, nor divine. So don't you agree the best way to make our Office a means of union with God is to think — think before we go to Office, think while in Office, and think again after we leave Office?

Think what you are as a man. Oh, I know that the best spiritual writers and some of the greatest saints have always insisted on our littleness, and with reason. Even the old ancients had this horse sense. It was Alcibiades, I believe, who had his pupil study a map of the world, then asked him to point out Greece on that map. The lad traced the outline of his country. Then the wise teacher had him compare it with the rest of the known world. The boy saw how small his country was. Then Alcibiades asked him to point out Athens. The disciple had a little difficulty finding the pinpoint which represented that home of highest culture and loftiest thought. The teacher smiled. 'Can you now show me the street on which this building stands in which you and I are holding this conference?' The lad grinned sheepishly. It could not be done. If not that boulevard, lined with such massive buildings, how much less the room in which the two stood. The lesson of one man's relative smallness had been well taught. It's so simple to parallel that illustration and make you feel smaller than a sub-electron.

What are we Catholics compared to the total population of the United States? One-sixth. What are we religious compared to that Catholic population? Near beer: one-half of one percent. What are we cloistered contemplatives compared to that population of religious? I was never very good at calculus or trigonometry, but I would hazard a guess that we are not six one-hundredth part. And what are we Cistercians of the Strict Observance, or better still, we men of Gethsemani, compared to the number of cloistered contemplatives? Approaching the vanishing point, aren't we? But that is only one side of the medal, and not the embossed side. Look at yourselves with the eyes of God, and tell me what you are. No, let Him tell you. Fathers and brothers, you are *unique*! In all God's wide creation there is not now, there never was before, and there never will be in the hereafter, another just like you!

When Almighty God, the Omnipotent Maker of men, had fashioned you just as you are, with your particular temperament and temper, your talents and tendencies, your character and composition, He took that mould and shattered it, for He wanted no replica of you! For He had a work for you to do which only you could do provided that you were endowed with those qualities and qualifications that mark you off from every other human. That work can be done by no other. If not done by you, it will remain undone 'til skies be fugitives' — and long after. Stupendous thought, isn't it? Yes, and thrillingly true. Dogmatically sound, and philosophically accurate. As a man, you are tremendous! Look now at what you are as a monk.

When you and I stand in choir, what are we? We are *Christ*! Fulton Sheen has a passage which proves this point ineluctably. He says Christ would be limited and imperfect without the Church. "For, without His Mystical Body," he asks, "where would He find tongue with which to speak forgiveness to other penitent thieves, or hands to lay on other little children? Without His Mystical Body where would He find feet to receive the ointment of other Magdalenes, or breast to receive the embraces of other Johns? How else could He, as Incarnate God, console other widows than that of Naim, visit other friends than those of Bethany, attend other nuptials than those at Cana? Without His Mystical members how could He call other Apostles than those of the Lake, convert other women than the one by Jacob's Well, or other men than the Centurion on Calvary? If we do not see Christ living in His Mystical Body, then we would not have believed Him Divine had we seen Him in His Physical Body at Galilee. If we miss God, it will not be because He is too far away, but because He is too near!"

In his encyclical on reparation Pope Pius XI exclaimed:

"What a spectacle for Heaven and earth is the Church at prayer! For centuries without interruption, from midnight to midnight, is repeated the divine psalmody" — and the Church is Christ! St. Augustine, in his commentary on Psalm 85, is even more pointed. "When we address God in prayer," he says, "we do not separate the Son from the Father; and when the Body of the Son, the Church, prays, it does not separate itself from its Head. No. Our Lord Jesus Christ prays in us, for us, and is prayed to by us. He prays in us as our Head; prays for us as our Priest; is prayed to by us as our God. Let us, then, recognize our utterances in Him and His utterances in us. Let no one say, when he hears this Psalm, 'It is not Christ who speaks,' nor again, 'It is not I who speaks.' Nay, if he recognizes himself in the Body of Christ, let him say both: 'Christ speaks and I speak.'"

Indeed this is no dream, but soundest dogma. Never were the words of Pius XII, found in his immortal encyclical, *Mystici Corporis*, more true, or more applicable to us than when we stand in choir: Christ *needs* His members.

Since you are Christ in Choir, don't you see the *value* of your actions? *Actiones et passiones sunt suppositorum:* Actions belong to the person, not alone to the members. Look, brothers, we say *you* milked the cows this morning. We don't say your fingers did! It is the father we proclaim for allowing a door to slam, not his hand for not having guided it, for actions belong to the person, not alone to the members. So is it with the Mystical Christ. You and I, as members, are infinitesimal. But when we act in Him, with Him, and through Him, and He acts in us, then our acts are truly *Theandric* — acts that are Divine and human all at once. They take on the value of the Person whose members performed the acts, and the Person of Christ, you know, is Infinite, Divine, the Second Person of the Trinity!

Think of that before Office. Think of what you are as a man: unique, with a unique work you have to do for God. Think of what you are as a monk: Christ! Then you'll be united with God as you chant your Office. Christ-consciousness means success in your every effort, and what a dynamic drive it gives you to every Office. This is what I mean. Have you ever noticed how when one member of your body is ill, the other members, which are thoroughly healthy, suffer in sympathy? The explanation is not difficult: the body is a unit. So, too, is Christ's Mystical Body. Hence, my whole being aches, my heart breaks for that diseased section of Christ's Body known as Russia. And how my very soul sobs whenever I hear that one of Christ's essential members, one of His priests, has gone off the track. But I also know that in the physical body, the living parts give life to the dying members. In the Mystical Body of Christ, the same law holds! Then how I will chant my Office for Russia, and for priests, because I have developed Christ-consciousness and I know they are *my* members! This necessarily unites me with God not only during the Office, but all the day long, and all the night through.

If we want to make our Divine Office really divine and truly Office, we will think *after* each hour. By that I mean we will examine ourselves immediately at the conclusion of Matins, Lauds, Tierce, Sext, None, Vespers, and Compline. We will ask ourselves: Did I chant that with Christ, as Christ, in Christ? That will be enough, for that will obviate the one thing that can keep us from being united to God in my Office: *laziness*.

If I am lazy physically, mentally, or morally, I won't be united with God. Physical laziness will induce drowsiness, and ultimately, will produce sleep. I can't think when I'm sleeping; nor can I sleep when I'm really thinking! If I am mentally lazy, I will not make the necessary intellectual effort to follow the sense of the words, and I will gradually lapse into some form of robotism. If I am morally lazy, I will not stir myself enough to realize who I am: Christ; nor realize what I am doing: helping Him praise the Father, and to save the world, by being the *pleroma* of His Passion! I won't stir myself enough to love those diseased and dying members in so real a manner as to win for them the grace which will bring them back to life and to robust health.

Oh, how we have to watch out for laziness. It can produce in us that which so sickens Almighty God that it turns His stomach, and has Him spewing such lukewarm members out of His mouth! It is well to remember that lukewarmness is worse than coldness, just as indifference is worse than hate. Let me adapt some lines to make the point:

> When Jesus came to Golgotha, they nailed Him
> to a Tree;
> They drove great spikes through hands and
> feet, and made a Calvary.
> They crowned Him with a crown of thorns; red
> were His wounds, and deep.
> For those were crude and cruel days, and
> human flesh was cheap.
>
> But when Jesus came to Louisville, they simply
> passed Him by.
> They never hurt a hair of Him; they only let
> Him — die!
> For men had grown more tender, and would
> not cause Him pain.
> They only just walked down the street — and
> left Him in the rain!
>
> Still He cried: "Forgive them; for they know
> not what they do."
> While clouds poured down that wintry rain that
> drenched Him thru and thru.
> They all went home, and left the streets without
> a soul to see;
> While Jesus crouched against a wall, and cried
> — for *Calvary!*

141

Of course He cried, for hate is better than indifference, and coldness than lukewarmness. May the Mother of God, the Mother of men, the Mother of monks, keep us from laziness!

Be generous! For God's sake — and for our own. God made us for happiness, and He made us for happiness in time as well as for all eternity. Happiness, whether in time or eternity, depends on generosity. Mother Ponnet, a very holy Visitandine, used to strive to make each succeeding prayer holier than the one before. That's the kind of generosity I am talking about. Let us do that with our every Office and its every hour. To one of His saints Our Lord pointedly said: "Make room, and I will come like a torrent." I am sure He is saying that to each and every one in this room. Give Him your heart, give Him your head. Think!

Leon Bloy was right when he said: "There is only one sorrow: not to be a saint." We can avoid that sorrow by developing Christ-consciousness before, in, and after every Office. Antoine Martel, a deep thinker and a splendid Catholic, said: "Our Age is not satisfied with good Religious, but waits impatiently for saints." Should we not ask ourselves: What kind of a religious am I? A bad one? God forbid. A good one? That is not enough. A saint? Well, it is no great gamble to say I am far from it. If I am satisfied with that, however, I am betraying my Rule, disappointing my superiors and confreres, the lawful expectations of God, and I earn the very legitimate impatience of the secular world.

Eva Lavalliere, the French actress, who was converted from a thoroughly shameful life, wrote: "My past I will entrust to You, my God, with confidence; as for the future, I shall march on to sanctity!" Are we to be outdone by this girl? Take naught as your measuring rod but that plain, plebian devotion to duty. That marks the man, the monk, the real mystic, and the true saint.

††

It was inevitable not to be alerted to and aroused by the insistence on the importance of the Divine Office here at Gethsemani. While the Rule speaks plainly enough that Benedict meant what he said about preferring nothing to the *opus Dei*," the regime and the regimen I found here spoke even more plainly. Immediately after the night Office we novices were supposed to devote the time between Matins and Prime to the study of the Psalms. Three days a week we had to attend chant class immediately after dinner. Beside these three classes, we had to attend a weekly repetition of chant, immediately after chapter, at which the entire community of choir monks was present. In the chapter of faults, which was held at least twice every week the most heard proclamation dealt with faults committed while in choir, for the opportunity to make mistakes while discharging the Office seemed limitless. How often did I hear our good abbot insist: "Give your voice. God gave it to you, Give it back to Him." That was Dom Frederic. When Dom James was elected, one of his first moves was to hire a Frenchman, a doctor of music who graduated from the *Schola Cantorum de Paris*, to come across the waters, remain with us for six months, and teach us the proper execution of Gregorian Chant.

How Doctor Francois Lefevre worked! There would be a class immediately after Prime every morning but Sunday. At 10:00 A.M. there would be a special class for the various scholas — that group of from four to eight who had fairly good voices, and who would sing the Gradual and the Offertory in each Mass. Promptly after dinner, another class was held for novices and simply professed; then, just before Compline, a class for the entire community. Sandwiched in between were special classes for the proper rendition of our celebrated Salve Regina, with which we closed every day of our existence. Yes, Frenchy, as I came to call the good doctor, worked! So did we!

But the point I am making is that no one, and I mean

143

no one, could miss the place of importance of the Divine Office, or the *opus Dei* here at Gethsemani. But it was never looked upon as the *sole* work of the monks. I must have given that impression in my conference to the then young Frater Louis, Tom Merton. Shortly after that recollection Sunday, Father Robert made an appointment with me, and much to my surprise, I found a young novice with Father. It was Tom Merton. I knew nothing about Tom at the time. The first time he had been pointed out to me was while he was pushing a damp mop over the linoleum in the infirmary. The then new novice had contracted a cold. But even in the infirmary, so long as one is not in the death throes, a Trappist works. Well, Tom was working with a Father Dennis, a short, lively Irish-American from Jersey City, who was then Mass secretary for the monastery. He had to visit the abbot every day to get the list of Masses to be offered, and always managed to pick up the latest news from the abbot (squeeze it out of him might be the better expression; for Dennis had a way with him — inquisitorial). Dennis pointed to Frater Louis, and made the sign to me: "He's a poet." I looked at the slightly-built, sandy-haired, serious-faced new novice, lifted my shoulders, my eyebrows, and my hands in the sign-language meaning: "So what?" For at that time, after my almost twenty years in religious life, I had met and lived with more than one poet. I had, invariably, found them different, if not actually dreamy, so I was not greatly impressed by Father Dennis' revelation.

As I stood in the presence of Father Robert and his rather new novice, however, my interest quickened. It was so exceptional for the novice master to seek a session with one of his ex-novices, and more than exceptional to bring along a new novice for such a session. To me, it was unheard of. So I looked Tom over more closely, as I awaited Father Robert's revelation of the purpose of the meeting. I saw an alert young man with eyes alive with intelligence,

144

and felt a sense of pleasure and joy. Father Robert quickly came to the point and said something to the effect that Frater Louis wanted to know if I was preaching and teaching the doctrine that monks exist solely for chanting the Office. My eyes narrowed as my forehead came down in a frown of puzzlement, if not disbelief.

"No, no, no, Frater," I said. "We must distinguish between a *prime* purpose and a *sole* purpose." I held out my not very small hands so that he could see the callouses and said something to the effect that when he had tossed as much hay, laid as many bricks or blocks, handled hoe and axe as often as these hands had, and developed similar callouses he would agree that chanting was not the *sole* work of choir monks here at Gethsemani. It was a brief session, but a very revealing one to me. I suspect that our lack of social contact sharpens our powers of observation and makes our perceptions very keen. At any rate, when Father Robert dismissed the novice and then asked me what I thought of him, I replied: "An exceptionally intelligent young man." Then the master told me how he had asked Tom what he thought of my conference and had also learned that Tom was exceptionally intelligent and had already looked deeply into our life, so deeply that I had disturbed him by my insistence on the Divine Office. I laughed as I said: "Gosh, that was my assignment. That was the topic of the conference." It soon came out that the master, in effect, had asked Tom what made me tick. When I heard the answer I saw that Tom not only had wit, that instantaneous presence of mind, but that he was witty, for Tom simply said, "He's Irish." Father Robert responded, "But so am I." Robert was even more Irish than I, and even had a bit of a brogue. My parents had lost every trace of theirs, so I was never exposed to it in my early days. Tom told the master that quite obviously I would rather argue than eat; that I enjoyed controversy; that there was that in me which had people saying the Irish slogan was: "Fight, you devils, I hate peace." It was a revelation to me, not only of Tom Merton's quick perceptions, but also of my own personality. I was unconscious of the impression I conveyed to others.

The master then asked me if he should allow Tom to read the Fathers, particularly St. Augustine. "By all means, Father. But can he read him in the original?" I was assured that he could, Tom having attended both Cambridge University in England and Columbia University in New York. My interest in the young novice grew. I think it was that first session which laid the foundation for the close friendship that developed between Tom and myself, and the high regard we ever held for one another. At any rate, I told Father Robert that St. Augustine and the other Fathers of the Church would make excellent spiritual reading for any of his novices. Perhaps that recommendation set Thomas Merton off into his study of those giants of the Church who led him into the discovery of the essence of our life: contemplation of God, and not the Divine Office as our sole work?

The Fathers of the Church, as we read them in the lessons in the various nocturnes, feed the mind, heart, and soul of the choir monk, and lead him ever more deeply into a knowledge of and a love for God, especially in His Christ. The old breviary held a miniature library of the Fathers, and I, for one, sorely regret the loss effected by the diminution of those readings after Vatican II.

Vatican II, however, confirmed me in my convictions expressed in the above conference. Look at what the Council said about us: "Members of those Communities which are totally dedicated to contemplation, give themselves to God Alone in solitude and silence and through constant prayer and ready penance." The Council went on to reiterate the doctrine of Pius XI by saying: "No matter how urgent the needs of the active apostolate, such Communities will always have a distinguished part to play in Christ's Mystical Body, where 'all members have not the same function.'" That last quote is from St. Paul, but the next few lines echo Pius XII in his Encyclical on the Mystical Body: "For they offer God a choice sacrifice of praise. They brighten God's people with the richest splendors of sanctity. By their example they motivate this people; by imparting a hidden, apostolic fruitfulness, they make this people grow. Thus they are the glory of the Church and an overflowing fountain of heavenly graces."

The Council went a step further when it dwelt exclusively on the monastic life. "In the East and in the West, the venerable institution of the monastic life should be faithfully preserved, and should grow ever increasingly radiant with its own authentic spirit. Through the long course of the centuries, this institution has proved its merits splendidly to the Church and to human society." Then comes the clincher. "The main task of monks," said the Council, "is to render to the Divine Majesty a service at once simple and noble, within the confines of the monastery. This they do either by devoting themselves entirely to divine worship in a life that is hidden, or by lawfully taking up some apostolate or works of Christian charity."

One did not have to wait for the Council, for the very rhythm of the life here at Gethsemani inevitably brings home to any thinking man that he is here to relive the life of Christ. I even question the necessity of the prefix "re" before the word "live," for I believe it was St. Bernard who summed it all up in the phrase: *vivere in Verbo* — to live in the Word. That is an echo of St. Paul's unforgettable and challenging line: "I live, now not I, but Christ lives in me."

While that model pertains to all Christians, it becomes a mandate for us monks. It is made quite simple by the rhythm of the liturgical year, which is lived to the letter behind these cloistering walls.

It is true that as religious and priest I had followed the liturgical calendar faithfully. Actually, I had done so from the time I had reached the age of the use of reason, for all Catholics who assist at Mass regularly have no other calen-

147

dar they can follow, since the Ordo knows no other. But what a difference in the modes!

I was not here a year before I realized that this very busy life, with hardly ever an hour you could call your own, was actually a life of *leisure*. As the years went by I recognized that this is a life of *luxury*, though no monk owns a thing, not even his own thoughts!

The leisure of the life came home immediately. I was free from every obligation save that of following the order of the day. There were no classes to prepare, no retreats to conduct, no missions to be given, no phone calls or doorbells to answer, no couple about to be married to be instructed, no couple already married to be counselled, no family feuds to be settled — nothing but *ora et labora* all day long, every week, every month, every year. As far as outside occupations were concerned, I had none. How else can one define leisure? But it was a leisure with a purpose, and that purpose was to live in, as, and for Christ Jesus.

That purpose could create a problem had we not the liturgical year to live, for we are human beings, and every human being has in his flesh and blood and bone that capital sin called sloth. Here is where I saw the wisdom, the prudence, and practicality of the supreme pedagogue we name Mother Church. She begins her year on the first Sunday in Advent. That is new year's day for us monks. I took it as a time to look over the past and to plan for the future; a time for stock-taking; a day for inventory; a day to draw up resolutions. But what a difference between this new year's day and that in the secular world and on the secular calendar. My focus was on eternity, not on time, for I had learned from Augustine that *quod aeternum non est, nihil est* — what is not eternal is not worth consideration!

I well remember one first Sunday of Advent, on which Holy Mother Church would have me turn over a new leaf, and it was the new page in my life's ledger. As I let my eye of faith look upon it, I suddenly realized it was not a blank page, but rather like a sheet of very expensive stationery. When stationery is flat on one's desk, it looks blank, but when held up to the light it is found to have a water mark, usually the name of its maker imprinted into it. Turning over the new leaf in my life's ledger this new year, I held it up to the light of faith, and saw it had two words deep in its being: *donum Dei* — a gift from God. God was giving me more time. My theology had given me the axiom: *Nihil frustra dedit Deus* — God never gives anything without a purpose. What was the purpose in this latest gift of time? The answer was to be found in the liturgy, in both the Office and the Mass.

Whenever I came across that word *nunc* in Latin, which means now, my mind would always race back to my study of time in cosmology. What a mystery! A second is right now; then it's gone, and will never return. We are always looking for the next second to come. We tell ourselves that we have all the time in the world. That's a lie. The truth is we have only this present moment. That is why we find real wisdom in the popular saying that "there is no time like the present." That is all the time we ever actually have. God allows us only the present moment. That is why Paul's words: *Nunc est tempus acceptabile* — Now, right now, is the acceptable time — have always haunted me, especially on the first day of the liturgical new year. It could not be otherwise when the Office and the Mass have Paul saying: "Now — right now — is the hour to arise from sleep. Your salvation is nearer than when you believed." Advent after Advent, on its first Sunday, I have been combining these two texts of St. Paul as my "new year's resolution: Now, right now, is the acceptable time to put on Christ. That is precisely what the liturgy teaches. As repetition is the mother of studies, again and again, in Office and Mass, that insistent, imperative word "now" is heard. She makes one keenly conscious not only of the passing of time, but of its infinite preciousness and eternal importance.

This idea of time so impressed me that I used to enjoy teaching canon law to young monks on their way to the priesthood. I might begin one year by daring anyone in the class to give me the exact time. When they'd read it off the clock on the wall or the watch on their wrists, I'd say: "A monk in New York or Carolina would not agree with you, neither would any monk out in Utah or California." We were on Central time in those days, and the references I had made were to the foundations we had made from Gethsemani. The fun would begin when I asked them just what time was. Another year I might tell of the letter I had received telling of a girl of seventeen, who could not even be taught how to tell it. When given an intelligence test, she had come out with a rating of 54. "You know, of course," I would then add, "that 40 to 60 marks the moron. Of course there is no one in this room with an IQ that low. But is there anyone, no matter how high his IQ, who can give me the exact time?" When they looked at the clock I insisted that not only the clock, but every clock in the world lies, for every one was man-made, whereas true time is God-given.

I would quote the old saying: "It is later than you think," and prove it by showing them what a wobbly world we live in, and inform them that its apparent uniform motion around the sun was neither apparent, nor uniform. While it is true that our earth spins on its axis to give us a day, it also revolves around the sun to give us our seasons each year. Yet, while spinning and revolving, it was also wobbling. For it is like a wheel on an ill-fitting axle. It looked as if the pins through our poles were not fast-set. That is why we had to snap on our headlights at a different time every evening, and why we marked December 21st as the shortest day in the year, and June 21st as the longest, even though each was clocked at exactly twenty-four hours.

Most were amazed when I insisted that the clocks on our walls were practically always slower or faster than God's timepiece, the sun. I insisted that it was not easy to tell time

150

exactly. An IQ of 54 won't do it. An IQ of 100 will find it difficult. To make it all the worse, an IQ of over 154 will find it doubly difficult to tell you exactly what time is. Even St. Augustine, who had an IQ a bit higher than most of us, used to say: "If nobody asks what Time is, I know. But were I anxious to explain it to some one who would ask me, plainly, I know not."

It would have been cruel to leave them there. So I'd go back to Aristotle and Aquinas and give my students their definition of time: "The measure of motion according to before and after." The complete revolution of the second-hand of the clock gives us one minute of time. The revolution of the minute hand gives us one hour. The revolution of the hour hand gives us half a day. However, all these divisions into hours, minutes, and seconds are purely arbitrary. We could just as arbitrarily, and just as logically, divide the day into twelve hours, the hours into 120 minutes and the minutes into 120 seconds, couldn't we? What are we to conclude then: that time is a mere figment of man's mind, a pure fabrication of man's intelligence, an *ens rationis*, as the schoolmen would say? Does all our wrestling with this idea lead us away from God to whom all time belongs, from whom all time comes, to whom all time is to be given — and given in Christ Jesus, and as Jesus Christ?

Time is measure, Aquinas said, but measure is only in man's mind. That is not the whole of the definition, for time is a measure of motion, and motion is outside man's mind. So Thomas and most of the schoolmen with and after him, said that time was an *ens rationis cum fundamento in re*, which means that there is some foundation outside the mind for the mind's conception. In the case of time, the foundation for the mind's measurement was motion; ultimately, all motion is to be traced back to the Prime Mover: God.

"Would there be time in a completely depopulated city," I would ask. "Is there time on a desert island that is

151

truly deserted?" If a negative response came too quickly, I'd pester them with: "Well, the sun will rise and set over them. Why wouldn't that mark a solar day? The stars, in all their silver majesty, will move across them. Why not a sidereal week? The moon will wax and wane above them. Why not a lunar month?" You see how fascinating this topic was to me. I was telling you about the leisure and luxury of this life because it is led according to the calendar for the liturgical year, and I have contradicted myself. When stressing the leisure, I said I had no classes to prepare, yet I have just dwelt on the classes in canon law. I did teach here for some years, but those were the middle years of my forty. Those classes have ceased to be, for Dom James Fox, the successor to Dom Frederic Dunne, did what I had urged Dom Frederic to do. He sent our bright young students to Rome and even to the Jesuit Gregorian University. I will miss them, for I love to teach, and know that God has endowed me with ability to educate. But I also know that God knows what He is about.

I see now what He was about in my soul as He tantalized me with this concept of time, and also filled me with wonder and gratitude for the leisure and luxury of the Cistercian way of life. He, the First Cause, works wondrously well through His secondary causes, us men.

Newman once said: "The work of Christ includes two things: what He has already done for all men, and what He is now doing for each man; what He did once for all, and what He is doing incessantly; what He has already done for us, and what He is actually doing in us right now; what He has done on earth, and what He is now doing in Heaven; what He has done in Person, and what He is now doing 'per Spiritum' in human persons." St. Augustine said: "The Mystery of Christ is the mystery of ourselves. For Christ only lived His life on earth in order to live it over again in us." Hence, we have not begun to really live, until we have begun to live in Christ Jesus.

Christ was living in me, but was I living in Christ — *consciously?* Each first Sunday in Advent saw me renewing my resolution to seize the present moment, and to "wake from sleep" by never going to vest for Mass without realizing that Christ would offer that Mass in me, and I would offer it in Him. Never would I go to choir to sing to the Father without realizing that I would be doing it in Christ Jesus, and trying to do it as Jesus Christ. When at manual labor, I would be working in Christ Jesus, and Jesus Christ would be working in me, with me, and through me.

Of course, it is one thing to make a resolution, quite another to keep it. As has been said: Resolutions? Yes, we make them, not to keep them, but to break them, for we're only poor weak mortals after all. In my leisure here I came to realize that we were anything but poor, and anything but weak, when we spent time the way it was given to be spent: living in Christ Jesus.

I had the leisure to devote the entire day and night to developing the spirit of the season. I knew the devil's strategy has ever been to divide and conquer. The one counterattack is unification or integration. Hence, all I had to do was to follow the lead of Mother Church given in her liturgy of the Hours and the Mass. In those I would be one with the Prophets, the Patriarchs and the People of God of old who incessantly cried to the Lord to come. *Veni, Domine — Noli tadare — Excite potentiam tuam, et veni — Visita nos — Ostende faciem tuam.* Those bold imperatives, addressed to God, begging, yet commanding Him to Come! — Don't delay — Use Your Power, Stir it up, and Come! — Visit us! — *Show us Your Face!* — Are what one hears from the past and uses in the present, as he chants his Advent Offices and offers his Advent Masses.

After the night Office, filled as it was with figures and types, prefiguring and typifying Him who was to come, I was impelled to turn to Micah, Isaiah, and Daniel, those Prophets of God who had told the place of His birth as man,

153

the time He was to come, and the guise under which He would appear. During the day I would not neglect such types and figures as Abel and Joseph, Abraham and Melchizidek, David and Elias. The Paschal Lamb and the Brazen Serpent told me why He would come, and what He would do. Then the Office was but a fire that blazed higher day after day to reach its climax in those wondrous O Antiphons of the last seven days, antiphons that are poetic splendor and rhetorical gems: "O Wisdom" — "O Root of Jesse" — "O Key of David" — "O King of Nations" — "O Sun of Justice" — "O Lord and Leader of Israel" — to climax on the 23rd of the month in an antiphon which gathers all the luminous grandeur of the preceding to fling it across the horizon of the thinking man like so much fire: "O God with us. . . ." That is Advent here — a season of wonder, warmth, even of vehemence that approximates holy violence, and in which the "violent carry the Kingdom of Heaven" away in their hearts, for they look steadily in the ever approaching face of God.

Despite what I've said before, a monk in Gethsemani has all the time in the world to enjoy his leisure as he employs it to experience God. With the leisure that is ours we are able to spend Advent with all these characters out of the past, and very especially with her who was carrying Him in her womb as she made her way towards Bethlehem and the birth of Life.

She is the one who will show you the *luxury* that is ours. In the midst of Advent, we celebrate her Immaculate Conception, which came to pass because He was to be born of this woman! Dom Frederic would have us prepare with a novena made in community. The day itself began with the vigil in her honor and then moved on from the dark of near midnight (we rose at 1:00 A.M. on such a feast) to the dark at day's end (7:00 P.M. for Gethsemani's "children of Mary," her "other sons"). Every hour of that day was bursting with song, honoring God who spared her from all stain of sin, and honoring her who was to bring forth Him who would free us from all sin!

The night Office for the feast would run from 1:07 A.M. to 4:30 A.M., for everything was sung, especially those moving responses after each lesson. By 5:30 A.M. we were back in choir for Prime which was followed by the matutinal Mass at which the entire community was present as offering priests. At the conclusion of that Mass, we would move into the chapter room to hear a sermon in her honor. Breakfast would hardly be over before we would again assemble in church to chant Tierce, then offer the solemn high abbatial Mass. Thanksgiving would be made by singing Sext. At 1:00 P.M. we would be chanting the hour of None. Two hours later, we would be assembled for Vespers, which would be followed by benediction of the Blessed Sacrament. By 6:00 P.M. all would be in the chapter room to listen to some reading before we moved into church to sing Compline which always closed with the *Salve Regina.* What luxurious living of a feast. The day was saturated with song, and we would be filled with wonder and joy over God's goodness in giving His Son and us such a mother.

So you see I have reason to call this life both *leisure* and *luxury.* You should also see why I say that bold, black legend over the entrance door — God Alone — tells the whole story of life at Gethsemani. But because it was with, in, and for God alone, we were burdened with the weight of the world of men — those for whom He came through Mary! Yes, we were and are Atlas, and we can never shrug our shoulders. We carry the multitude of men on our shoulders, for we are Christ!

8

I Enter the Upper Room . . .
and the Heart is Laid Bare

†

There are a hundred and one different ways of describing the Trappist life. Yet it can adequately be summed up in one word: *Fiat*, which means "Thy Will be done," understanding, of course, "by me" and "in me." It is a perfect summation, for that one word sums up perfectly the life of Christ. Every individual life, like all life, especially that of any and every religious life, is a mystery. It can be described as paging through an album which Mother Church has placed in our hands, and finding on each page the face of Christ. That album is the liturgical year, and it is apt not only for us monks, but for all Catholics — in fact, for every human being who has breath, or who will ever breathe. What are we but a gnawing hunger for God? He shaped each human heart and set it beating. He was its origin, and He is its ultimate object. Hence, our life, and every human life can aptly be described as a beating heart whose systole is but the cry: *Vultum Tuum, Domine, requiram* — Your Face, O God, I seek. And whose diastole is the last cry of the Bible: *Veni, Domine Jesu* — Come Lord Jesus! That is true of each of us not only in time, but for all eternity, for what will heaven be but the vision of God!

As I look back over the forty years behind these walls, I wonder if the tragedy of life does not lie in our failure to listen to our hearts, and thus learn what life is all about. The romance of all living lies in the truth that while there is life, there is hope! We can yet listen, and listening, learn! We still have time.

Time is utterly priceless, yet something we all squander with a recklessness that must make angels weep. It is a creature we clasp within tightly closed fists, but is always running out the cracks between our fingers. It is as omnipresent as the air we breathe, yet as elusive as the wind; as unstable as quicksilver, yet as steadfast as the pyramids and the sphinx; as relentless as a tyrant, yet as resourceful as a lover. About it, can't we adapt Omar Khayyam's lines and say:

> The Moving Finger [of time] writes;
> and having writ,
> Moves on; nor all your Piety nor Wit
> Shall lure it back to cancel half a Line,
> Nor all your Tears wash out a Word of it.

That shows the tyranny of time, but not its resourcefulness as a lover. For, though some say it is an overrated physician, it is still true that there is no wound that time cannot heal. Truly, it is a commodity that all crave, yet few use wisely. Who is there who is not always saying: "Give me time?" The ambitious cry for it, so that they may attain position and power. The avaricious cry for it so that they may garner wealth. The artists cry for it so that they may finish their masterpiece. The sick cry for it, so that they may recover health. Even the dying wanton cries of it, saying that he will then live worthily. What wouldn't Dives in Hell give for a moment of time, or that rich man to whom Christ said: "You fool! This very night your life shall be required of you." Don't we all cry, "Give me time"? It is given, second after second, by God, "the Usurer," who passes on every tick of time, saying, "Trade till I come," and He demands doubling each talent of time when He does come!

157

Therein we see the Lover in all His resourcefulness, and come to understand why my old professor of poetry, Fr. George Johnson, when reading the *Rubaiyat* in Edward Fitzgerald's exquisite translation, would pause after almost every stanza to say: "Ah, beautiful — but vicious." Just look at the last line in my quote: "Nor all your Tears wash out a word of it," and think of Mary Magdalene washing the feet of Christ with her tears, and washing out a whole life of wanton living!

Now there is the intriguing element in this gift from God called time: it is ever coming and always going. We, who know why time is given to us: to put on Christ, to glorify God, to become a saint, act as though we had all the time in the world, even as we realize we cannot guarantee ourselves the next tick of the clock! When we think at all, we see the truth and the falsity in that saying of Teresa of Avila: "All things are passing." Even as we nod in agreement, we hear in our deepest selves that nothing passes, for there is an eternality to every tick of time, and we will be held responsible, not only for every idle word, but for every idle second! Once we fully realize time's elusiveness and its eternality, then we listen to our hearts and learn not only what life is all about, but also how to live it.

That is the beauty of this leisure to love God that is the Trappist life. We have all the time in the world to leaf through that album filled with the face of Christ.

As we turn the last page of the Advent season, we look upon the face of the Babe of Bethlehem. After seeing Him circumcised, and following Him into Egypt, we come back to Nazareth and study the *face of the Boy*, watch Him learn His foster-father's trade. Soon we are looking on those captivating features as He gives His Sermon on the Mount; see the compassion in the *face of the Man* Christ as He gives the widow of Naim's son back to her after lifting him from the bier; watch the light of love rise in His eyes as He looks on little children; see those same eyes flash fire as He indignantly rebukes scribes and Pharisees, and angrily scourges moneychangers out of His Father's house. All too soon, with Him, we turn our faces toward Jerusalem, and know the same fear the Apostles knew as we watch the *face of the Man of sorrows* take on a seriousness we have never seen before and hear His predictions of that Passion and Death which awaited Him in the Holy City.

The study of that face in this all-hallowed album of the liturgical year, slows, deepens, strikes into one's very heart, as the page after Holy Thursday is inexorably turned as time marches on, and we have to look long and lovingly on the *face of the Criminal* before Pilate — blood-spattered from the precious, mighty price He is paying for us, which trickles down from the crown of thorns; bruised from the beatings that took place in the dungeon. Good Friday is a very long day liturgically, a day that drains one as he looks on the *face of Christ crucified*, then at the ninth hour gazes upon the *face of the Corpse.* Yes, it is a very long day, but somehow not near as long as is Holy Saturday, during which there is no Mass! Oh, what an emptiness. God is dead!

Yet, at midnight, we turn another page in that priceless album, and look upon His *face in Glory!*

We relive the greatest story ever told year after year. It has tremendous impact, and yet so many different impressions, for time does march on! We go to the tomb with Magdalene and the women, and find it empty! We run with Peter and John. We linger with the Magdalene and watch her mistake Him for the gardener, and then fall at His feet in love. We go to Emmaus with the two who hope, listen to Him as He opens the Scriptures, recognize Him in the breaking of the bread, and rush back to the cenacle only to learn He has already been there. Next Sunday we watch Thomas put in his fingers and fall down saying: "My Lord and my God!" Hear our beatitude for not seeing, yet believing, then stay in that same cenacle until the fall of flame.

Then comes the Acts of the Apostles, and the life of the

159

mystical Christ begins! Peter, who so cowardly cringed before a servant girl, speaks out so boldly that he is thought to be drunk, but he wins three thousand converts after sounding that wondrous word: *Metanoia.* The Baptist used it by the Jordan. Christ used it at Galilee. Peter uses it now in Jerusalem. In the old Douay version, it was translated as "Do penance." In the newer Kleist-Lilly, which is a translation from the Greek, *metanoia* is rightly translated as "change your minds." Mind is meant in the Augustinian sense of the whole soul and the real human individual!

St. Paul, thanks to the Holy Spirit, gives a much better bit of advice, which a Trappist takes to heart. Paul tells us to "redeem the time." Kleist-Lilly rightly translates that as "putting every opportunity [i.e. every tick of time] to good use," and again "making the most of the opportunity." So in this life of leisure I turn the leaves slowly in the beautiful album, this book of true beauty, and stare long and lovingly at the face of Christ, then turn to the soul's mirror and look long and hard at myself!

Then the mystery of religious life and the soul's life deepens. One asks: "Is it my will that is slowing the process? Or is it the will of God?" The latter, quite possibly. At Gethsemani we realize that nothing, absolutely nothing, in this wide, wide world happens but by the will of God: directive, positively permissive, or preventive. He respects the freedom He has given me, and allows me to use it and, may God forgive me, even to abuse it. That is why I say the most important word in any language is *Fiat:* "Thy Will be done, O God." It is the sanctifying doctrine of abandonment reduced to a word. My sanctification, and consequently, my salvation and glorification depend on my doing the will of God. Why am I white and not red, yellow, or black? Why am I living in the twentieth and not the twelfth century, or even in any century before the coming of Christ? Why am I of Irish descent, and not German, Russian, Japanese, or Jewish? Why am I one who has Christ as

160

my focus and not Confucius or Mohammed; Jesus as my Master and not Gautama? Why a Trappist and not a terrorist? The answer is obvious: God's will for me. So you see why I look into the album Mother Church gives me, then into the mirror of my soul, and wonder if the discrepancy is due to my perverse will or the permissive will of God.

This is a mysterious life, and a dangerous one. How well I remember one Sunday afternoon when I was making a day of recollection, which we did on the first Sunday of every month. I was in the cemetery — not meditating on death, but because, in those early days, the cemetery was the only place we professed religious were allowed to walk. Well, I was peering into my soul, and I was literally uptight. My whole mind and being was as tight as a drum from striving too hard. Real strain is not sound spirituality, even as it is very dangerous for one's mentality. I see now that it was God who stepped in to save me from a break. I thought then that it was I who was wise in catching myself before I broke. Will we humans ever learn? Will we ever be truly wise? Will we ever remain satisfied with God's ways and God's will? Will we ever arrive at that tranquillity of soul which comes from the realization that a life's work is done only in a life's time?

It slowly dawned on me that the most necessary virtue a religious has to acquire is not poverty, chastity, obedience, stability, or that *metanoia* called for in his vow of conversion of manners. Those are all necessary, but the one virtue most necessary for the acquisition of any of the above is *patience*. Yes, patience with self, and above all, patience with God. "He knows what He is about," Cardinal Newman once said. Frequently, it is only on looking back that we see how true that is.

To enable me to arrive at the heart of the matter, God sent along a translation of a work by a French Jesuit Fr. Desplanques on the Mass. What a revelation that turned out to be! What a turning point in my spiritual life.

161

I knew the theology of the Mass. I had always loved the Mass, even before ordination. At Gethsemani, I had two Masses every day, my own offered privately, and the conventual Mass offered by the community. On Sundays, feast-days, and days of two Masses, we offered this august Sacrifice three times. One might conclude that Mass was the focal point of the day, and the monk's absorption. That is true.

Yet, as I look back, I can account for Fr. Desplanques' work igniting me as it did, by my realization that we gave so many hours to the Office during the day, and so much attention to preparing ourselves for the proper discharge of that Office by chant classes, private study of the Psalms and the lessons, that, though the Office is actually the setting for this gem of all gems, Christ's Sacrifice, I must have been too intent on the setting, and not attentive enough to the gem.

My appreciation of what I thought I appreciated quite fully deepened immeasurably. Who should have had a clearer perception of Christ's Mass as our own than those monks who had planted, cut, shocked, carted, thrashed, stored, turned — all by hand — the very wheat from which the hosts for the Sacrifice were made. We did that at Gethsemani back in the late thirties and throughout the forties of this century. What sweat there was in the long process, but what beauty, what contemplation. How often I mused on Father Len Feeney's poem, which he titled "A Field of Wheat." Hope I can recall his lines accurately now, for to the best of my knowledge this poem was never published:

> " 'tis starlight and the prairie owl is watching
>   the tall sheaves,
> Those tireless, ever-twisting, swishy silences of
>   grain,
> All tangled and wind-laced and fluttering their
>   leaves
> And murmuring and moaning in their pain.

" 'Some of us,' they whisper, 'shall ripen in the
      Spring
and feed the hungry multitudes beyond the
      land and sea,
And some of us shall tremble on the Table of
      the King.
Ah, which of us, dear brothers, shall it be?

" 'And which of us shall falter when the wagon
      load is high,
And fall from heavy harvest when the men are
      hauling in,
And trampled in the darkness of the furrows
      shall we lie,
And dream forevermore what might have been!

" 'O Sacred Bread, O Mystic Host, O Snowy
      Gown of God!
O dream of every blade of wheat that flickers in
      the sun —
O shall we rise up beautiful and fragrant from
      the sod
To be raiment for the Holy One!'

" 'tis starlight and the prairie owl has let his
      eyelid close
For tired heads must droop at last that birds
      may slumber sweet;
But the waves rise and the waves fall, and only
      the wild wind knows
The everlasting restlessness of wheat."

It would be next to impossible for any monk of Gethsemani, who had the slightest bit of imagination and intelligence, not to think of his Eucharistic God as he worked
on Gethsemani's wheat. He could be out in the fields,

163

breaking open the shocks after a spring rain, or putting them together again after the June sun and wind has done their drying work. He might be choking in the hayloft as the borrowed thrasher hurled up the golden straw, down at the mill turning over the golden grains, under that all but melting tin roof in steaming July or coughing and sneezing from the almost invisible dust as the stone wheels mercilessly ground the grains into the flour.

We were looking constantly on God in the making, God in embryo, His flesh being formed in our fields. The same is true of His blood. We could have watched the Mass being prepared from the days we had to prune our vines, on to the tieing up of the same, through the cutting of the bunches, to the crushing of the grapes, and that gradual fermenting of the wine for our Mass. We could have, but I am quite sure now that I did not do it consistently. It may have been because that wine was anything but palatable!

How could I have been so insensitive? You should have seen us priests enter the sacristy after the night Office, wash our hands in rotation, see the laybrothers, usually, and some few choir novices line up in back of us and help us vest. Everything was meticulously prescribed. Even the servers had their rubrics for helping us to vest. Woe to anyone of them who did not observe them scrupulously, for they would hear about it in the next chapter of faults. We priests had our own chapter of faults for the rubrics of the Mass, both prescriptive and directive. No one was allowed to be unmindful of those rubrics here at Gethsemani.

What a picture of recollection, dignity, reverence, we made as we stood, fully vested before those long vestment tables, with our servers in back of us, with the missal precisely before his breast, awaiting the clap from the abbot which would send us all bowing in unison toward the crucifix, turning together, and pacing slowly toward our individual altars. I am sure that some, today, would scream, "Regimentation!" It was. Better than that, it was reverential awe enfleshed in men who had been called by God to "Do this in memory of Me." I miss such regimentation. I really think it is because I miss such community awe and reverence.

Before I leave our old surroundings, I must tell you that once we had grown in numbers, we had to use what was called the back sacristy for some of our private Masses, and it was in this same back sacristy that I was made vitally conscious that I was offering Sacrifice, and that I was part of it. There was no heat in that back sacristy, and in January it can get really cold here in Kentucky. How well I remember the day the good laybrother presented me with the cruets at the Offertory and I found the water had turned to ice! That must have been the same day our abbot told me to start work on the new bakery. That was January 25, 1940. Out I went alone with a steel chisel, a few steel wedges, and an eighteen- and twenty-pound sledgehammer. My admiration for our founding fathers grew, for I found that they had built the foundation of the monastery four feet wide! I had to bang my way through from the outside, and it was 22 degrees below zero. I got through, but let me tell you getting that first stone loose was work! They did not use cement, as we know it today. They used some sort of plaster well-laced with hairs of some sort. Once I got that out, and the first huge stone loose, it was not so difficult.

I wrote the introduction to the translation of Fr. Desplanques' work. I am going to give it to you in its entirety because it is a soul-sincere and heart-deep recommendation for you and all your living — just as it has been for mine.

††

In 1910, Gilbert K. Chesterton wrote *What's Wrong With The World?* His biographer, Maisie Ward, tells us that Gilbert was still asking that question while writing his book. In 1940 Father Desplanques answered it. *We* are the answer! Especially we Christians; more especially, we Catholics. We have been, and yet are on the road to Damascus, the road to Emmaus, and the road to Jericho. Small wonder, then, that the world is on the road to disintegration.

Do understand me: there is nothing wrong with any of the roads we are on, provided we are knocked from our horse outside Damascus, have our eyes opened at Emmaus, and allow a Samaritan to pick us up half-dead by the Jericho roadside.

Now while it is true that we Christians, and especially we Catholics, have not been riding toward Damascus breathing out threats of slaughter, it is, alas, too true that we have been as ignorant as was Saul of that world-revolutionizing, because self-dignifying and self-destroying, doctrine that Christians and Christ are one. We have not been walking to Emmaus with hearts heavy because of hopes dead, but somehow or other, our eyes have been held so that we have not recognized the Stranger who joins us on the way — not even in the breaking of the bread! That we have fallen among robbers on our way to Jericho, that Materialism, Secularism, and modern Skepticism have left us half-dead, is all too obvious even to the least observant.

The Good Samaritan is at hand, however, not with oil and wine, but with something infinitely better — bread and wine! Out of that twenty-centuries-old revelation of revelations, Father Desplanques has made a new revelation by showing us that we have not remembered those few things we should never forget. One is that "the Mass is the supreme expression of the Love of God." Another is what the Son said of His Father: "*Pater mea agricola est* — My Father is a husbandman." — "Alas, O God," exclaims the Jesuit author, "Thy children, little and great, forget it. To an ever greater extent we find people who have never known it. School-books no longer teach it. Since the beginning of the Twentieth Century some even pretend that Thy wheat grows by itself, and that the mills turn better without Thee. Result: the barns are bursting, the granaries are cracking under the sacks — and the poorest of Thy children go without bread." Perhaps our greatest sin of forgetfulness lies in the fact that we have not remembered that the midmost moment of all time was the ninth hour on the 14th day of the month Nisan — and that that moment is eternal! Father Desplanques makes that moment as intimate and as personal as it was and is by saying: "Yesterday, on the 14th day of the month Nisan, at the ninth hour — we say at three o'clock in the afternoon — Thou sawest me just as I am now, occupied in writing . . . or in weeding my garden . . . or in sewing . . . or in laboring . . . or in suffering, perhaps. And Thou didst love me with an ineffable love. . . . To me Thou didst dedicate Thy last sigh, the last drop of Thy Blood . . . in one great cry." Oh, if we had only remembered that! If we will only remember it now, how different the world will be!

So as not to mislead, let me say that Father Desplanques gave no thought whatsoever to what was wrong with the world. His one concern was to set the world right. With a wisdom that is more than human, he shows us how to do that by giving us as solution for our every problem exactly what the Omniscient God gave us. Father Desplanques gives us — *Christ!*

To many a Christian that will not sound like a new solution; to the non-Christian it will not sound like a solution at all. Yet, it is the only solution that is sound. Father Desplanques does not say what has so often been said, namely, that the world needs Christianity. What he says is that the world needs Christ! Sad to say, there is a difference between the two. It is the Christianity of old that can save us, and only that. We modern Christians must walk not "in the fiery footprints left on the earth by the saints," but in the blood-red footprints left on the road that leads to Calvary by the Saint of saints. What Father Desplanques has said is that we must make *the Mass our life, and our life a Mass.*

Throughout his work his insistence is on what is most ordinary in the ordinary life of the ordinary man, and he shows how all this fits into the Ordinary of the Mass, and how the Ordinary of the Mass fits into it. There, precisely, is the new revelation he makes out of the age-old revelation of revelations. It is really a revelation of our own divine destiny, our sublime dignity, and of our one duty; a revelation of all we are, and all we have, and of all we can, all we must do for God, ourselves, and our neighbor, as we go our ordinary way in the ordinary circumstances of our ordinary lives. It is also a revelation of how deaf, dumb, and blind we have been all our ordinary lives — especially of how dumb!

As we search the unsearchable ways of God, it seems most patent that His Providence has reserved a rediscovery of the doctrine of the Mystical Body of Christ for our day of dictators and destruction. Abbe Anger was among the first to show that this truth is the white heart of the Kohinoor which is Catholic dogma. But it awaited Father Desplanques to bare for us the heart of that heart. He opens to us the center's central core when he reveals the truth not only that Catholic laymen and laywomen are priests, but that the lives of all Catholic laymen and laywomen can be, should be, and must be the life of the only Catholic high priest. He does this when he shows that, like Christ, the Catholic has only one thing to do — *offer the Sacrifice of the Mass!*

"I have a Baptism wherewith I am to be baptized," said Christ, "and how I am straitened until it be accomplished." We know it was a baptism of Blood. We know it was a Death, Resurrection, and an Ascension. What we have not known, and what Father Desplanques teaches us, is that we have the same baptism wherewith we must be baptized, and that we shall live in straits unless we accomplish it. The tragedy of this tragedy is that we have all the elements at hand, yet we do not inform them; we have the body, but we do not inject the soul. His Passion — our passion — is being renewed again and again, but mankind is not being regenerated simply because we are not Mass-conscious, Christ-conscious, God-conscious, divinely self-conscious men and women. We have not realized that we and Christ are one. Hence, we know little of our worth as persons, our wealth as Christians, nor the weight of our obligations as members of Christ Jesus.

How we need to pray to God with the author for "this ardent conviction: that not a hair falls from our heads without Thy permission; that in Thy hands emperors and dictators are as pawns, even as am I, or any poor fool . . . and that behind the curtain of appearances week by week, day by day, minute by minute Thou controllest the whole scenario of the centuries and the years. . . . Yet, despite all that, for the Grand Drama of Love, Thou claimest from Thy child his two arms, his two feet, his whole soul, his whole heart even to its last pulsation."

What he has written cannot be read. It can only be pondered in wonder, awe, and love — reflected upon with deep, deep sorrow, and ever-mounting joy. Its every thought stops and stimulates, gives both pause and impulse, generates thought and inspires hope.

What the genesis of his book was, he does not say. In his preface he cites *Miserentissimus Redemptor*, the encyclical of Pius XI in which the priesthood of the laity is stressed. In the same preface he makes mention of Catholic Action; and, thank God, we are coming to realize that *the* Catholic Action is the Mass! But perhaps Father has indicated the real source of the work when he so pithily and penetratingly says: "We have mediocre Christians because their Mass is mediocre." Never was a condition more accurately traced to its cause. We Christians are, in great part, the real causes of our world's sad condition, and the cause of our very real condition is our ignorance of the interrelation and the interpenetration of the "ordinary of our lives and the Ordinary of the Mass."

How Catholics need to know that the priest at the altar has need of *their* fervor; that

169

Christ is expecting something from them; that
souls, whom they love, are *depending* on them;
 that
Everywhere, silently, they are beseeching:
"Come! *Collaborate!*"

How our Catholics need to know that Christ, the Divine
Poor Man, is crying:

"Give Me what is still wanting to My Passion!
Give Me the painful labor of *your* hands! the
 suffering of *your* heart!
Your tears! *your* flesh and blood! Give Me *your*
 life"

How often have we heard the cry for the Mass in the
vernacular so that people could understand what was going
on. Well, here it is! But instead of helping us understand
what is going on, it makes us alarmingly conscious of the
fact that we must carry on for Christ, with Christ, and in
Christ. How often have we heard discussions on the necessity for, and of the ways and means of, bringing our Sunday
religion into our workday, weekday life? Well, here is how!
A priest cannot go into a workshop, a machine shop, or a
factory in chasuble and alb, not even in his cassock. You
laypeople, you priests by baptism and confirmation, you
other-Christs, "without any other ornament than your
working clothes, can offer up to God, through the Christ of
the Mass, all the work, all the activity, all the human labor
which must not be lost. Christ, in you, will transform all
that into acceptable adoration and love."

I know there are some who will say that this book is not
for the ordinary run of people. These are the ones who
would have said the same thing about St. Paul's Epistles to
the Corinthians, the Ephesians, the Galatians, and the Colossians at the very time Paul wrote them. These are the

ones who are wiser than the all-wise Holy Spirit under whose direction — I almost said dictation — Paul wrote. Thank God that the much wiser Catholics are now admitting that God did not reveal the doctrine of the Mystical Body bootlessly; that it is a truth, a revelation, that is most pertinent to our times. Whenever this question arises, I like to ask what Emile Mersch asked in the introduction to his monumental work, *The Whole Christ:* "Is it to be regretted that God should have given us a union with His Son which transcends our own limited views? . . . Are there truths in our Religion that are dangerous? truths that must be avoided? truths that, by their very nature, are capable of engendering only false notions and vain discussion?" What I prefer to asking those questions is to point out to our very enlightened age the nature of the audience to which God the Holy Spirit addressed these letters and this doctrine. The Church at Corinth was anything but an aristocracy of intellectuals! It was made up then, as Christ's Church has ever been, and shall ever be, of peoples from all ranks and all classes; but the bulk was, as the bulk is and ever will be, not from the schools, but from the stores, the docks, the shops, the streets! They understood those Epistles and this doctrine. Can't we?

Father Desplanques thinks so, for time and time again, he addresses "the sweeper with her broom, the seamstress with her needle and scissors, the stenographer with her notebook and pencil, the housekeeper with her market-bag . . . this rich man, this laborer, this servant, this society lady . . . those with a brush in their hand, or a shovel, a pickaxe, or a fountain pen, a broom, a pair of scissors, or a fork . . ." — just exactly the audience the Holy Spirit addressed through Paul! This Jesuit priest has seen what that intrepid Apostle saw, namely, that the life of a merchant, manufacturer, banker, lawyer, doctor, artisan, or simple laborer, is not life . . . unless he becomes a Christ-merchant, a Christ-manufacturer, a Christ-banker, Christ-lawyer, Christ-doctor, Christ-artisan, or a simple Christ-laborer. He sees that the whole purpose of life is that if we cannot reduce to zero the number of the damned, we can, at least, each day increase the number of the blessed. He sees that man was made to serve God our Father, to serve all our brothers and sisters in Christ, and not simply to serve himself! With a rare clarity he sees that "the Cross is the axis of the world, and this planet the Repository for the Host." Pascal never thought deeper thoughts, nor did Claudel express them more beautifully.

But the point at issue is the practicality of such thoughts and expressions. If anyone will think a moment on the revolution this doctrine has effected since Christ first spoke of the vine and the branches, and Paul first wrote of the Head and members; if one will see how the society of the ancient world slowly changed from a society in which, literally, slaves were countless, into a medieval society, in which the slaves had become serfs, and serfs were rapidly becoming freedmen — all because we are one in Christ; if one will think of the numberless captives made during those ages when war and insecurity filled prisons much as our modern dictators have filled concentration camps, and then think of the religious orders, such as the Mercedarians and the Trinitarians, established just to ransom those captives — all because Christ said: "I was in prison and you visited Me;" if one will think of how the poor in Apostolic times were cared for by the rich in Jerusalem, and how the poor in the Roman Empire and the poor down to the time of the Protestant revolt were cared for by the Church; if one will think of how in the Middle Ages they were cared for by those who erected and conducted orphanages, homes for the aged, and guest-houses in every monastery; if one will remember that the Papal States were called the patrimony of the poor just because the revenues from them went to the poor. If one will awake to the fact that from the fourth to the sixteenth century not a sermon on charity, nor an appeal for funds was ineffective simply because they were based on the truth that "whatsoever you do to these . . . you do to Me!", then one might cease to question the practicality of this most practical of all practical doctrines ever given to man. If we are to believe the words Christ spoke about the Last Judgment, we get to heaven, or we go to hell, precisely because we have lived or failed to live this doctrine which says the Christ and Christians are one!

In our day practicality is recognized only when it shows social, political, or economic results. That is why I like to call attention to the fact that hospitals were unknown in pre-Christian times. The first modern hospital — truly a medical center — was erected by St. Basil of Caesarea in 369. The great medieval orders of knighthood, such as the Knights of St. John, the Knights Templars, and the Teutonic Knights, worked in hospitals, and the motive behind all this was: "I was sick, and you visited Me."

In our day we have seen altogether too much of racism and nationalism. Too few of us, however, have seen that the Catholic Church has always opposed racism, that St. Peter condemned it in the First Council of Jerusalem, that St. Paul was tireless in his insistence that "there is neither Jew, barbarian, or Scythian, for Christ is all and in all." That is the doctrine of the Mystical Body.

The Church could not stop the fall of the Roman Empire. The dry rot had set in before the Empire was Christianized. But what she could do, and what she did do, was to prevent all Europe from lapsing into barbarism after the Empire fell. She did that by taking all human tribes to her bosom, breaking down the barriers of race, language, custom, and law, and teaching them to love one another, since they were all members of the one Body!

The same work is before the Church today. So are the same means. It is worthwhile noting that the Holy Roman Empire was based on the doctrine of the Mystical Body of Christ, and that true democracy rests on no other foundation. Surely no one is going to contend that all men are created exactly equal, when faced with the fact that no two men are ever born physically, intellectually, socially, or economically equal! Our equality comes from the fact that we are persons, and persons who can be incorporated in the Holy Trinity's Second Person. It is on that base, and on that base alone, that we can ever hope to erect a sound and effective supra-national institution which is calculated to safeguard the liberties of the world. Just as, in the final analysis, it is seen that our present-day chaos is the result of the denial of this doctrine, so it will be seen, by those who see ultimates, that the one remedy for our situation, and the one sound hope for the future, lies in a reaffirmation of this doctrine — an affirmation not in words, not in slogans or songs, not in placards and parades, but in the ordinary of our lives translated into the Ordinary of the Mass, and the Ordinary of the Mass made the core of our ordinary lives!

Since work and wages make up the ordinary of most of our lives, let it be said that even in the economic field this truth is fundamental. In his *Quadragesimo Anno* Pius XI said: "Then only will it be possible to unite all in harmonious striving for the common good, when all sections of society have the intimate conviction that they are members of a single family, children of the same heavenly Father, and further, that they are one Body in Christ and everyone members one of another."

A reflective reading of Fr. Desplanques' work leads inevitably to the conclusion he expressed somewhere, namely, that "nothing but God is of importance any longer in my life." He has brought God near, made Him more intimate than your father, mother, or best friend, more important to you than your own breath or heartbeat. "Teach me to pray!" has been the cry of every soul created. Father Desplanques teaches us as Christ taught us. He shows that we are syllables in the Word, particles of the Host, the drop of water in the wine to be transubstantiated into His Blood.

174

Having shown us that, he has shown us how we can save mankind. As he put it: "The sanctification of a single soul is one of the major elements in the reconstruction of the world."

To enter into the spirit of this book is to enter into the very presence of God, with the consequent eruption of fear that presence inspires and the ebullition of love it inflames. The author has made time stop and has given us a sense of that perpetual present which is eternity, for he links the Mass now being offered by you and me and the entire Mystical Body of Christ, not only the first Mass ever offered in the Upper Room, but those said in the dark of the Catacombs on the still warm bodies of the latest martyrs, those magnificent Masses of the later centuries said by the pope or a bishop with twenty to a hundred co-consecrating priests, and the last Mass to be said ten hundred, ten thousand, or a million years from now just before the trump of doom. It makes one think that the ancient Greeks, in demanding the triple unity of time, place, and persons in their great dramas, were foreshadowing the triple unity in the world's greatest drama, wherein time was caught up by the timeless, the universe by its Creator, and all persons in the Godhead's Second Person.

It has been said: "It is the Mass that matters. After going through Father Desplanques' book, one cannot escape the conclusion that nothing else really does matter.

†␣†

This mystery of faith had always intrigued me. As a mere stripling serving Mass in the dark of winter at 6:30 in the basement of St. Peter's Church in Dorchester, I awakened, I won't say to the mystery — I was too young — but certainly to the mysteriousness of the action. I memorized the Latin responses, but had no idea what they actually meant. Yet, even then, I found music and mystery in the words. Our curates offered prayerful Masses. We were blessed by an exceptional group of priests who inspired rev-

175

erence and awe during and for the Mass, even in fidgety altar boys. So, in all truth, I can say that the Mass was central to my life from earliest youth. When I got to theology and entered into the depths of the different theories on the Holy Sacrifice, I was truly in my element.

Granted that there is some truth and beauty in each theory presented by able theologians, I found the most truth and beauty in Father Maurice de la Taille's, S.J. So I adopted it as my own, and have never ceased to teach it. Of course, we can never forget that the Mass is the mystery of faith; consequently, it can never be fully understood by any finite human being. At the same time, however, we finite human beings must always remember what Father Len Feeney wisely insisted: "A mystery is something we cannot know everything about, but it is not something we can know nothing about." We do know, at least we should know *much* about the mystery of faith, and I delight in putting the essentials of what we do know about the Mass on the five fingers of one hand.

Number one: the Mass is *not* some thing; it is *Someone!* It is Jesus Christ, the Second Person of the Blessed Trinity made Man. Number two: The Mass is Jesus Christ acting as *priest and victim*. Number three: There are three principal parts in every sacrifice. In a bloody sacrifice there has to be an *Oblation*, or offering of the victim; then *Mactation*, or slaughter of the victim offered; finally, and most importantly, there has to be *Acceptation*, or sign from God that He has accepted the offered and slaughtered victim as sacrifice.

In Christ's Sacrifice, quoting de la Taille, "the Oblation was made in the Upper Room on Holy Thursday Night when Christ took bread, blessed, broke, and gave to His disciples saying: 'Take and eat. This is My Body which will be given up for you.' Then taking the cup of wine, He said: 'Take and drink . . . This is the Cup of My Blood — which shall be poured out for you.' The *Mactation* took place

176

Good Friday on Calvary — when that Body was given, and that Blood poured out. The *Acceptation*, the most important part, came on Easter Sunday morning when God showed His approval of that Oblation and Mactation by sending the Fire of Life back into the Corpse of Christ and we had the Resurrection." (See how the Passion, Death, and Resurrection form one indivisible act!) We have the three principal parts in the re-presentation of His Sacrifice in the Offertory, double Consecration, and Holy Communion in the Mass.

With my fourth finger I ask: Why this Sacrifice? and give the four purposes of the Mass: adoration, reparation, thanksgiving, and petition. What of the little finger? That's us, for we are His members! Then joining the little finger to the thumb, I say: united with Him we must act, in Him, with Him, and through Him, as priests and victims, offering ourselves, dying to ourselves, to be accepted by God. We do that in order to *adore*, for we are creatures who owe Him adoration; to *repair*, for we were born sinners, and have sinned since; to *thank*, for we have nothing that we have not received from Him; and, finally, to *petition*, for self and for all others.

Those same five fingers talk to me all the day long, every day, telling me who I am, why I am, and what I have to do for God, self, and others so long as He, our Great High Priest, gives me life.

That my one purpose on earth was to make His Mass my life, and my life His Mass, simplified and unified all life and living. As a creature I simply must *adore* (and I had come to look upon life behind these walls as adoration). As a sinner I am bound to *reparation* (and that was the impelling attraction to and basic motivation for entering this Trappistic way of life). As an unmeriting recipient of all that I am, and all that I have from an ever-generous God, I owe Him immense *gratitude!* Finally, as a member of the human race, and a member of His Mystical Body, I must *plead* con-

177

tinuously for mercy upon myself and all other human beings. How can I do any of these effectively save in Him, with Him, and through Him in the Holy Sacrifice of the Mass?

Now you can understand why, for me, Holy Saturday is the longest and emptiest day in the entire year, no matter what the clocks may register, nor what time the sun rises or sets. For on that day there is no Mass. All Souls Day and Christmas Day are the shortest, for on those days I am allowed to offer Mass thrice! How I loathe to leave the altar after the third Mass! How I long to be able to go on lifting paten and chalice, and saying: "This is My Body . . . This is My Blood."

Indeed it *is* the Mass that matters, and little else does!

We were placed in Christ Jesus by baptism. That wondrous Sacrament marked our birth. But it is not enough to be born; one must grow. Just as the human infant must grow and grow in order to become a man, so we Christians must grow and grow in order to become *Christ*. That is the exalted and exalting reality of our existence. How frightening, and utterly frustrating it would be had not Christ said to His Apostles: "Do this in memory of Me." Were more meaningful words ever spoken?

One day, in one of our eastern cities, a street reporter pushed a microphone before a young man who was passing by and asked him what he considered the most important words ever spoken by any man on earth. For the best part of an hour this reporter had been putting this same question to passersby. Varied indeed were the responses he had received. Little did he, or anyone listening in, expect the profound reply given by an unidentified young man. He took one look at the reporter, gave a quick glance at the mike, and without a moment's hesitation said: "This is My Body. This is My Blood," and passed on.

What instantaneous presence of mind that young man had. As you ponder the purpose of life and the meaning of your individual existence, you may find other words Christ

178

spoke that are personally more meaningful to you than those which effected the first transubstantiation of bread and wine into His Body and Blood. However, how would you ever become holy with the holiness of God; how would you ever worship with an act worthy of your God; how would you ever be able to offer yourself as an acceptable sacrifice to God, had not Christ gone on to say: "Do this in memory of Me." Had Christ not made Mass possible for us, we could never answer the plea St. Paul put to the Corinthians: "We entreat you, in Christ's name, make your peace with God. Christ never knew sin, and God made Him sin for us, so that in Him, we might be turned into the holiness of God." Where are we more in Him than in the Mass?

With that before you, you should appreciate why Bossuet once said: "There is nothing in the universe greater than Jesus Christ; and nothing in Jesus Christ greater than His Sacrifice; and nothing in His Sacrifice greater than that last sigh and precious moment which separated His all-adorable soul from His all-adorable body." Undoubtedly he had in mind what theology teaches as the essence of the Mass: the double consecration, which so dramatically symbolizes the Death of Christ. His description is excellent. While we thank God for having undergone death for us, we must thank Him even more for reuniting that all-adorable soul with that all-adorable body, and making that precious moment so admirably described by Bossuet, unending, even as it is rendered, in its re-presentation, differently.

Christ did all that by rising from the dead. He did it also by saying to His Apostles, and through them to their successors: "Do this in memory of Me." For with those words He instituted both the Christian priesthood and the Christian Sacrifice, without which this wondrous world of ours would indeed be a vale of tears, you and I naught but wanderers in a land without water, and all our accomplishments, no matter how stupendous, naught but ashes for the wind. While Blaise Pascal was right when he said: "Outside

179

of Jesus Christ we do not know what life is, nor death, nor God, nor ourselves," he would have been more right had he said: "Unless you are 'in Christ Jesus,' you neither live, nor die, nor find God, nor know who and why we are."

The men of our day are making fabulous discoveries, achieving goals once thought to be only the stuff dreams are made of, conquering realms deemed beyond all human reach. Yet, what are all these accomplishments, achievements, inventions, and discoveries compared to what you can do by fulfilling that command of Christ, as far as in you lies: "Do this in memory of *Me*"?

The late John XXIII, in his short reign as pope, managed to change the whole atmosphere of Christendom, filling it with an irenicism that promises well for the ecumenism he so dexterously encouraged. Barriers that had stood for centuries, and were thought by many to be impregnable, he broke down. Unquestionably, in this century of outstanding pontiffs, he turned out to be among the most outstanding. Yet, had he succeeded not only in reuniting Christendom, but in converting the world to Christ; had he been suddenly endowed by God with power enough to implement every section of his masterly encyclical *Pacem in Terris* and bring true peace with real justice to our embattled world; had he been enabled to have nations do away with their stockpiles of bombs and actually disarm, all that would have been as nothing compared to what he did every morning in the privacy of his chapel as he vested as practically every simple priest vests, and said what every simple priest says the world over: *Introibo ad altare Dei* — I will go unto the altar of God — and offered Mass.

That is not rhetoric. That is reality. Hence you may well ask what would you have been, what could you have become, without Christ and His Mass.

The thirteenth chapter of the First Epistle to the Corinthians is known as the hymn to love. It is one of the most beautiful passages in all Scripture. To bring this chapter to sharpest focus for you, to give you the clearest realization of just what Mass is, and what it means to you, we will change the word "love" in St. Paul's lines and substitute for it the name of Him who is Love, and who is the Mass, and have that famous chapter read:

> If I should speak the languages of men and angels, but am not in Christ Jesus, I am no more than a noisy gong and a clanging cymbal. And if I should have the gift of inspired utterance, and have the key to all secrets, and master the whole range of knowledge, and if I should have wonder-working confidence so as to be able to move mountains, but am not in Christ Jesus, I am nothing. And if I should distribute all I have bit by bit, and should yield my body to the flames, but am not in Christ Jesus, it profits me nothing.

> One in Christ Jesus is long-suffering, is kind, is not envious; one in Christ Jesus does not brag, is not conceited, is not ill-mannered; is not self-seeking; one in Christ Jesus is not irritable, takes no note of injury, is not glad when injustice triumphs, is glad when truth prevails. One in Christ Jesus is always ready to make allowances, to trust, to hope, to be patient.

Borrowing again from St. Paul, we take what he used as preface to his magnificent hymn in praise of love, and use it as climax to what we have made into pointed praise of Christ, which proves conclusively that in all truth, He *is* our life, our way, our all. We now say: "Be eager always to have the gift that is more precious than all the others."

We have just shown you what that gift is; namely, life in Christ Jesus. You will never live in Him more fully, nor

181

more fruitfully, than by living in Him conscious of His priesthood, His victimhood, His sacrifice — in other words, conscious of His Mass. For it is in Mass that you meet Christ as Sacrifice, Sacrificer, and Sacrificing. It is also in Mass that you find yourself for what you are, and what you are ever to be: the priest who offers, the victim who is offered, and the sacrifice that is being offered; for, in Mass, you are in Christ Jesus, to be and to do as He is and He does.

Heretofore you did not get all you should have out of Mass because, perhaps, you failed to realize that Mass is an act of love — God's and yours; that Mass is that *admirabile commercium*, that wondrous exchange, which changes all life; that in Mass God the Son places Himself in your hands to be offered to God the Father in the unity of God the Holy Spirit as perfect honor, praise, and glory, and you place yourself in the hands of God in Christ Jesus to be offered to the same Godhead for the same sublime purposes.

Heretofore you may not have become as holy through Mass as you should have become because, perhaps, you did not realize that holiness is a share in the very nature of God, which can be had only in and from Him who shared our nature, and became the font of all holiness for men by becoming the Lamb of God offering His Mass, and making it possible for you to offer Him and yourself in that one, same Mass.

You will get more and more out of Mass, and become holier and holier through Mass, if you will try to be ever conscious of the truth that Mass is Someone and not something, and that you, thanks to your share in His priesthood, have that Someone in your hands to be offered to God, even as you, as victim, place yourself in His hands to be offered through Him, with Him, in Him that God the Father in the unity of the Holy Spirit might have all honor and glory.

9

Times Are A 'Changing

. . . and So Am I

†

I have already lived a long life. Seven and a half decades is a long time in anyone's measure. Yet, as I dwell on it now, it seems to have been a very brief life; shall we call it present consciousness? Intellectually, it has been a tremendously stimulating and very full life. It has been filled to the brim, and even overflowing emotionally. Socially, though forty years have been spent behind these walls, it has run the gamut. Yet it has been, as all life should be, *simple*.

Can you imagine that from a man who has lived through two world wars, the Depression, Korea, the Cold War, Vietnam; has watched things change from horse and buggy to landings on the moon, from telegraph to telephone, television, and satellites? Can you fail to question his sanity, let alone his sincerity, when you know he has watched our mores and morals change to such an extent that a thoughtful man has reason to question if he is living in the same country in which he was born and has grown up? Marriage, the family, home, schools, and even the Church, in some respects, have so changed that our society in the last quarter of the twentieth century no more resembles the society into which I was born in the earliest part of this same century, than black looks like white, or night resembles day.

When I was a boy there was one divorce within my, admittedly, limited society. The attitude toward the woman, I believe, was quite general in our entire country. She was ostracized. I grant that was not very charitable, hence, not at all Christian. But the rationale behind that attitude of mind was most certainly Christian and basically human. The basis of all society is the family, and a family is constituted by the moral union of parents with children in a home. You cannot have children without a father and a mother, so society was protecting itself when it was insisting on the permanent union of married couples. Divorce, then, was recognized as destructive of society.

I begin with conjugal society because that is where domestic, civil, national, and international society begins. I have not exaggerated when I tell you that the difference between the mores and morals of my youth and those of my advancing old age is as drastic as that between black and white, or night and day. Further, I am showing you how God led me into the realization that life is simple.

Let us look at contraception. When I was a boy, Margaret Sanger spent many of her days in jail for advocating — and that not too openly — birth control. Today pharmaceutical companies seem to be competing with one another to produce and sell newer and newer contraceptive devices, while our own government seems overanxious to distribute them worldwide.

As a boy I, with other boys, not to mention grown men and women, openly laughed at suffragettes! Today, do you think anyone running for elective office, be it that of local sheriff or anything lower, can disregard the women's vote? Who laughs at those pushing for the ERA? The "Women's Lib" movement does occasionally cause a laugh by some of the antics and statements of members of the movement, but who cannot look at them and agree: "You've come a long way, baby!"

I am not trying to say there was only one divorce in my

town or in my time, nor that contraceptive devices were un-known until the advent of the pill. Nor am I contending that women should not have the right to vote, that they are not entitled to equality before the law. I am saying that they and our entire society have gone too far, demanded too much, and demeaned themselves almost beyond the recognition of their innate dignity, which always called forth real reverence. I dare say that unless women use their vote, their equal rights, and their God-given superiority to change our mores and morals, they may find that respect for their own lives has vanished from their world as the third step is taken as contraception and abortion lead on to euthanasia.

It is not a very pleasant prospect for any of us, since we are all growing older! But it is a reality that all must look at, stare at, until we actually see it! What hurts, what actually depresses a thinking person is that the solution is so simple, so obvious! Let all, especially women, simply accept and follow the startlingly, simple plan anyone can read in the very nature of each individual. Women are women, and men are men, made so by that *ens Simplicissimum* — that simplest of all beings: God the all wise!

Now I am clearly back to my original proposition: Life is simple. I insist on that truth despite the truly bewildering changes I have lived through, and in the midst of which we are still living. You see, I would not want you to labor under the utterly false idea that, because I have been cloistered behind these walls for forty years, I am unaware of what is going on, and consequently, have been led to believe the absurdity found in the statement: *Life is simple*.

There is profound truth in the remark that the only permanence we know is change. I can't find many of the countries, let alone their capitals, I learned as a boy. Yet the continents and the oceans surrounding them remain the same. But let me come quickly to the particular history I have had to review these forty years.

In one of my earliest efforts concerning us Trappists I

made the statement that we Cistercians of the Strict Observance (Trappists, is the popular designation for Cistercians of the Strict Observance) are the Benedictines of the
Benedictines. I still hold that, much to the chagrin of Benedictines and the other branches of the Cistercian Order.
The point I am making is that I had to get back to the fall of
the Roman Empire if I were to get back to the roots of my
order. Hence Edward Gibbon had to be read. Were things
changing in those days? Huns, Vandals, Goths, and Visigoths changed "the glory that was Greece, and the grandeur that was Rome" to shambles. But one thing remained
— the one thing Gibbon could not understand: Christ's
Church. He recorded the fact. He was striving to be something of an historian, and facts are stubborn things. A good
historian does more than record facts; he accounts for their
cause. And God is the Cause that explains Christendom
fully. Gibbon, of course, did not admit that, but wrapped in
pompous phrases his hollow attempt to explain the obvious,
without giving the obvious explanation. Thus did he afford
John Henry Cardinal Newman marvelous matter for an
easy, but thorough, refutation. A later historian did better
than Gibbon when he wrote: "She (the Catholic Church)
saw the commencement of all the Governments . . . that
now exist in the world; and we feel no assurance that she is
not destined to see the end of them all." That concession
could not have given Thomas Babington Macaulay, who
had his own particular bias, any great delight. But he went
as far as he dared when faced with the evident indestruc-
tibility of the Roman Catholic Church.

Here I am, just over a century later, seeing how exact
Macaulay's premonition and prediction were. More than
two-thirds of the ruling dynasties of his day are no more.
Russia has no czar, Germany no kaiser, Austria-Hungary no
emperor, France no king; for that matter, neither has Spain,
despite Carlos being the heir to Franco. I could make the
list longer. It is not change so much as stability that con-

186

cerns me and, I hope, you. Where do we find it? Look to Rome. As she has done for two millenia, the Catholic Church, even as she watched crowns drop, even as many of the heads dropped with them, has gone on crowning pope after pope. That's stability. That's permanence. That's God.

I was born just as Leo XIII, successor to Pius IX, died. I learned that Leo, along with his predecessor and his three successors, was prisoner in the Vatican, thanks to the hostility of the Italian government under Victor Emmanuel. But just as I was turning into full adulthood, I saw Benito Mussolini restore Vatican City to my sturdy mountain climber of a pope, Pius XI. How well I remember the sage remark of a Frenchman who was watching the "black shirts" marching in triumph into Rome. As wave after wave passed him with all the swagger which accompanies such triumph, he quietly said, *"Il passera."* We know how prophetic he was! But the papacy remained after the Fascisti had gone.

That triumph and that march was but a passing episode to the Eternal Church, who has witnessed so many similar crises, but who always survives. Yes, there is permanence in this ever-changing world.

Even Macaulay saw this. "When we reflect on the tremendous assaults She has survived (and he reviewed those assaults both from without the Church and within her) we find it difficult to conceive in what way she is to perish." Indeed, it is difficult, for she is imperishable! I do not say that on my own authority, but on that of one whose promises are always fulfilled, and whose predictions never fail. Christ is my authority! The millions who fill St. Peter's year after year can look up to its majestic dome and read for themselves the very words Jesus Christ used: *"Tu es Petrus, et super hanc petram aedificabo Ecclesiam Meam, et portae inferi non praevalebunt."* If the very Powers of Hell cannot prevail, what chance have weak human powers?

So you see there is permanence in this ever-changing world. There is *the* Church. There is Christianity, that permanently changing, and that changeless permanency! There is Christ! Because of Him, His Church, His Kingdom, there are monks. And the brilliant Father Lacordaire once said: "Monks, like oaks, are eternal." Of course, you and I know that there is only one truly Eternal — the Creator of both oaks and monks. One of the greatest historians of monasticism, Count de Montalembert, echoed Lacordaire about the eternality of monks.

Montalembert, a member of the French Academy, had to make this confession. "Have we not all come forth from College knowing by heart the list of the mistresses of Jupiter, but ignorant even of the names of the Founders of the Religious Orders which have civilized Europe, and so often saved the Church? In all the course of my education, domestic or public, no one, not even among those who were especially charged to teach me Religion and History, no one considered it necessary to give me the least conception of the Religious Orders. The first time I saw the dress of a monk — must I confess it? — was on the boards of a theatre, in one of those ignoble parodies which hold, too often among modern nations, the place of the pomp and solemnities of Religion."

That the past century has not bettered the situation in the field of higher education is evidenced by a passage from *The Emancipation of a Freethinker*. Dr. Herbert Ellsworth Cory writes: "I am ashamed to confess how abysmal was my ignorance in my early Harvard days and long after. . . . To me the solitaries of the Fourth Century and after were morbid, monkish visionaries, selfishly turning their backs on their fellows to cower in filthy caves and mortify the worshipful body."

Don't blame Dr. Cory. He got his ideas from a source as reliable as the one whence Count de Montalembert got his first view of the monk's garb. My research showed me clearly that history had been false to monks, and literature unfair. It saddened me to read the works of so capable a man as Dr. G. G. Coulton and recognize whence he drew his material. One can only feel pity (not sympathy, note!) for the coloring of this man's vision and the warping of his mind. His hand actually shakes with passion whenever he pens a passage wherein the Catholic Church, a monk, or monasticism figures. What astounded me was to find this otherwise careful historian taking Chaucer's *Canterbury Tales* and Langland's *Piers Ploughman* as his main sources when delineating the medieval monk. That is as logical as it would be for me to take Sinclair Lewis' *Elmer Gantry* as my source book for a portrayal of the Protestant clergy in twentieth-century America. Lewis wrote fact; he gathered newspaper accounts of actual happenings. But Elmer Gantry is no more representative of the Protestant clergy than Benedict Arnold is of the American officers of the American Revolution. Sinclair Lewis wrote a libel, a dastardly lascivious lampoon. Dr. G. G. Coulton often does the same, actually drawing caricatures when he means to delineate characters. A person of passion and prejudice should never turn his hand to history. Truth is too chaste!

Sir Walter Scott with his *Waverly Novels* has been the active agent in the production of many misconceptions of the monk. His Knight Templar and his Friar Tuck in *Ivanhoe* live. They are drawn with such mastery that they all but breathe. Therein, Scott has been a cartoonist, not an artist, for an artist selects characteristic details and heightens them, whereas a cartoonist picks out some salient defect and sets it in bas-relief. Sir Walter's abbots, monks, and nuns are as representative of monasticism as Pontius Pilate is of fearless justice, and Judas Iscariot of unswerving fidelity.

One day Count de Montalembert stood at the foot of the Grand Chartreuse, on the brink of that bounding torrent which, once seen, is never forgotten, and there, at the entrance to that wild gorge, met his first monk. The surprise and emotion which stirred his soul at the sight of what he called a vanished world stayed with him as a sweetness the

189

rest of his life. He knew then that the stage was no place to garner true ideas nor ideas of truth. He knew then that literature had been unfair. He later learned that history had been false. His three volumes on *The Monks of the West* are his valiant effort to do justice to those who had been pilloried. Gallantry had called to gallantry, and gallantry responded.

It is sheer joy to read his refutations of the defenses that did not defend. Too often, and too long has grace been demanded for monks in the name of the services they have rendered to science, to letters, and to agriculture. Montalembert showed the inadequacy of all such defenses. But even his brilliant apologia did not vanquish all attacks or attackers. He dedicated his monumental work to Pius IX in 1860, but in 1902 a fellow Frenchman showed that his mighty words had not taken full effect. In that year, Clemenceau, the Tiger of France as I came to know him in my lifetime, was little more than a cub. But he was tiger enough to show his claws and the sharpness of his intellect. In that year he turned to some Trappists and said: "I know that in the past you monks rendered important services. At a time when the Country was ruined by invasions, when Science was nonexistent, and Agriculture in its infancy, you covered France with your Monasteries and fostered a taste for industry and peace. . . . But today the whole Country is cultivated and civilized. We have our schools, our colleges, our universities. Our social life is thoroughly organized. I do not see what useful purpose you now can serve."

The monks went, for a time. So did Clemenceau. What of the France he regarded so highly? Today the monks are back, so Lacordaire was much more correct than the snarling tiger. They do seem oaklike, do they not?

In my researches into monasticism I came upon a spirited plea, written in 1939 by a Louis B. Ward. He titled it *Back to Benedict*. One passage read: "Early Benedictinism gave to Europe the three field system of agriculture, it contributed the staining of glass, the illumination of the manuscript, the development of music, gothic architecture, schools and the progress in craftsmanship that distinguished the Thirteenth from the Sixth Century. Early Benedictinism, through its emphasis on the dignity of man, and its peculiar emphasis on the obligation of manual labor, was all important in winning the battle for human freedom. Some poetic minded writer tells us that when Benedict first raised the axe to cut down a tree he not only chopped down the tree but struck at the manacles, the fetters, and the shackles of the human slave. It was Benedict who created the first free labor market in Europe."

In 1941, Dr. Cory went further than Louis B. Ward when he wrote: "I did not know that the cenobitical Benedictines were not content with mere prayer and the preservation of ancient learning, but also went out into the fields to teach the people the use of the plow and to organize market places, which, if emulated today, would go far to annihilate the price fixing of avaricious capitalists. I did not appreciate how St. Benedict prepared himself and his followers for all this by retiring for a space from a civilization as degraded as our own period of wage slaves, capitalists, communists, Nazis, voluptuaries, indifferentists, and militarists, only to save this disintegration from turning into a perdition — from which only such saints today will be able to save us."

The Freethinker who was emancipated then goes on to tell much about the fifth and sixth centuries and the corpse of what had once been the grandeur of Rome. He finds Italy "a country of grinding taxation, divorce and birth-control, a country wherein the gluttonous and lascivious plutocracy depended upon hordes of barbarian mercenaries. It was this civilization," he says, "so like our own today that was inundated by Alaric and his Visigoths . . . by brutal Huns under Attila . . . by Vandals . . . by Alamans and by Lombards, who for half a century devastated all

191

Italy from sea to sea. This was the chaos which Christian monks turned into a cosmos, which was to reach its climax in the Thirteenth, 'The Greatest of the Centuries.' "

Christopher Dawson, historian, sociologist, political scientist, and able critic, has written a substantial book on this very theme, titling it: *The Making of Europe.*

Now, of course, it is tempting to lay such "flattering unction to our souls." However, while all these men tell truth, the impression they leave is untruthful. The monks did make Europe as Dawson states; they did bring a cosmos out of chaos as Cory points out; they actually civilized the barbarians and emancipated the slaves, as Ward has proven. Unquestionably, they did preserve the ancient classics, gave us doxologies in stone through their Gothic cathedrals, and wrote Sacred Scripture in glowing stained glass windows. Unquestionably again, humanity owes a debt to monks which it can never fully repay. Yet, what is due to monks is not due to monasticism. What Benedictines did, was not done by Benedictinism. What was actually achieved by ascetics and mystics, was not achieved by their asceticism nor their mysticism. In other words, I must insist that these many appreciations do not really appreciate, nor do these attempted *apologias* actually defend.

When Benedict of Nursia fled from the schools of Rome, the farthest thing from his mind was the preserving of the classics, or the idea of reconstructing the fast-falling European civilization and culture. He went to Subiaco for the same reason he would later go to Monte Cassino. It is the one, same reason men still come to Gethsemani. Benedict did not write a Rule to produce empire builders or world civilizers. He did not plan to raise a family of literateurs, scientists, nor sociologists. His monasteries were not to be abodes for artists and architects. No indeed. His one aim, his single purpose, his simple object was to produce men whose sole aim was *the glory of God*.

So you see where my research led me — to the simplicity of life and living. If the word "simple" can be predicated about any man, without the slightest qualification, that man was Benedict of Nursia. He had but one idea. By that one idea he was dominated; in it, he was totally absorbed. That one idea was not the world, not civilization, not even self. That one idea was — God. So dominant was this idea that it keeps peering out at one from the most unexpected places. For instance, in the fifty-seventh chapter of his Rule, Benedict provides for the talented in his communities. He will allow them to employ their skills only when the abbot permits it, and only so long as the artist or artisan is not puffed up with pride over his skill. He then goes on to say that the product of such work may be sold, but warns: "Let not the vice of avarice creep in; let the goods be sold somewhat more cheaply than is done by seculars, that *in all things God may be glorified.*" See what I mean? How could anyone, save a man totally absorbed in God, find in vulgar commerce, in the everyday buying and selling of goods, a means of glorifying God?

I really believe it was right here that I discovered the truth that life is simple, and that it is only we humans who rather unintelligently complicate it! I saw clearly that while Benedict wanted his monks to give themselves to agriculture, he never wanted any of them to become agriculturists. Had that been his aim, then Clemenceau was right in expelling the Trappists from France in 1902. If Trappists existed only to drain swamps, clear forests, cultivate the land, and foster a taste for industry and peace, if their end was civic, social, educational, or economic, they no longer served any useful purpose, as His Excellency so barbarously pointed out. A sophomore in any agricultural college in the country could teach the whole Trappist community how to farm. But Clemenceau's assumption is false. Horribly so. Benedict's prime purpose is religious. That these countless benefits accrued to mankind through the instrumentality of Benedict's monks is only a proof that religion is no separate sphere in any thinking man's life. It penetrates and even permeates his sociology, economics, arts, sciences, and civics. Religion is no mere appendage to life; it *is* life and real living. Truly it is more practical than Pragmatism; much more useful than Utilitarianism; and ever so much more matter of fact than Materialism. But that is not said to show that Benedict was a sociologist, scientist, or economist. Never. Benedict was a saint. You see, Dostoevsky was anything but wrong when he defined reality as the "relation between man, God, and Satan." Religion is very real and Benedict was an utter realist. Life, you well know, is real. Benedict would have his men live it. That is why he insisted on simplicity.

It was such analyzing that had me differing even with such great apologists for monasticism as Count de Montalembert and John Henry Cardinal Newman. The Count had refuted, much in the same manner as I have done above, those who thought we were to be praised for what we had done for man, saying that no founder of a religious order or legislator for religious life ever assigned the cultivation of the soil, the copying of manuscripts, the progress of arts and letters, or the preservation of historical monuments as the specific aim for his disciples. He then said that institutions that were simply human and powers that were merely temporal could, perhaps, confer the same, if not greater, temporal benefits upon society. But then he came to his real defense of monasticism and the religious life by insisting that orders with their rules do for men what no merely human power can ever do: they take the man wasted by sin and recreate him into virtue. They do that by disciplining not only the body, but the soul of man, transforming it by chastity, subduing it by obedience, elevating it by sacrificing self and acquiring humility. Thus do they produce those prodigies of evangelical perfection we call saints. But then, to my way of thinking, he fell into a slight error when he spoke of all this as "ecclesiastical *self*-devotion." It is the first part of that hyphenate that I dislike.

Cardinal Newman was even more direct when he spoke of "*self*-salvation." In his *Historical Sketches* he has a magnificent passage describing us. "The monk," he says, (and I put "Benedictine" or "Cistercian" as modifier to that noun) "proposed to himself no great or systematic work beyond that of saving his soul. What he did more than this was the accident of the hour, spontaneous acts of piety, the sparks of mercy or beneficence, struck off in the heat, as it were, of some religious toil, and done and over as soon as they began to be. If today he cut down a tree, or relieved the famishing, or visited the sick, or taught the ignorant, or transcribed a page of Scripture, this was a good in itself though nothing was added to it tomorrow. He cared little for knowledge, even theological, or for success, even though it was religious. It is the character of such a man to be contented, resigned, patient, and incurious; to create or originate nothing; to live by tradition. He does not analyze; he marvels. His intellect attempts no comprehension of this multiform world, but on the contrary is hemmed in and shut up within it. It recognizes but one cause in nature, and in human affairs; and that is the First and Supreme; and why things happen day by day in this way, and not in that, it refers to His Will."

That is a beautiful passage and an accurate analysis of character, done only as a Newman could do it. Yet I claim that the masterly analysis is marred by that opening sentence. Both the Cardinal and the Count would have avoided the imperfection in their works had they been conscious of the careful phrasing Ignatius of Loyola used in the first line of his Spiritual Exercises. There we read that "man (that means every man) was created to this end: to praise, reverence, and serve the Lord, his God; and by doing this, to save his soul."

Both Benedict and Ignatius are saying that man's prime purpose is not to save his soul, but to give glory to

God. There is a close connection between the two, I admit, but I also strongly insist that the salvation of one's soul is a consequent, not an antecedent. If a man, or a monk, praises, reverences, and serves God, he saves his soul. But as one illustrious general of the Jesuits, and a very learned commentator on the Exercises, Fr. Roothan, pointed out: "It is only the infinite goodness and liberality of God that has so united His own praise, reverence and service with man's greatest good that the one necessarily follows the other." But you notice he says "follows." That simplified life for me. It is dogmatic theology at its base and pinnacle. All orthodox Catholic theologians teach that the *finis primarius creationis*, the very first reason God created, was His own glory. The creature's good is the secondary, or the *finis secundarius*. That is precisely what the First Vatican Council meant when it so absolutely decreed: "If anyone says the world was not created for the glory of God, let him be anathema." (D. 1805)

The practicality of the distinction lies in the fact that it answers questions that should never be asked, refutes objections that should never be raised, and clarifies concepts that should never be obscured. It actually simplifies all life and living, as it says explicitly that monasteries are made not for men, but for God.

Viscount Francois de Chateaubriand made a very dramatic and very touching appeal for monks and monasteries when he said: "If there are refuges for the health of the body, ah! permit Religion to have such also for the health of the soul; for that is still more subject to sickness, and its infirmities are so much more sad, more tedious and difficult to cure." That plea is touching, but it is based on a false premise. Monasteries are not spiritual health resorts, not infirmaries for spiritual invalids, not sanitoria for the soul-sick, not psychopathic hospitals. They are houses for God.

Thomas William Walsh, in his monumental work, *Teresa of Avila*, did both God and man a favor when he set

196

forth the truth that this valiant woman, after making a new foundation, rejoiced, not that there was another convent opened for women, but that there was another house opened for the praise of Almighty God. That is why Gethsemani has stood behind these Kentucky knobs for over a century, not primarily for Americans, nor for America, but solely for the God who made America and Americans.

Again and again I was coming across the query: What do you cloistered contemplatives mean to man? Such a query manifests a gross misconception, not only of the purpose of contemplation, but of the very purpose of creation. Let me illustrate. A very capable, and quite well-known Anglican writer, Miss V. Sackville-West, was captivated by two Carmelite women, each a saint in her own right: Teresa of Avila and Thérèse of Lisieux. She gave us the result of her captivation in a study in contrasts which she titled *The Eagle and the Dove*. Toward the end of the book, despite her evident admiration for the commanding Spanish woman who was Teresa of Avila and the very winsome French girl who was Thérèse of Lisieux, Miss Sackville-West has a page which, if not indicative of her own skeptical attitude toward contemplatives, is most certainly a perfect externalization of the skeptical mind of many a modern. She writes:

> There are many, indeed, amongst those 'living in the world,' subjected to its grind, its difficulties, its anxieties, its tangle of ethics, its wearying exaction in the performance of duty, its claim for the sacrifice of self in the care of others, its demand upon our sympathy and our practical helpfulness at cost to ourselves — many who have no patience with the contemplative life. It appears to them as a form of escape from reality; almost as a form of self-indulgence, of selfishness, of evasion of responsi-

bility, a withdrawal from the unpleasantness of the world which, nevertheless, is everyone's charge to help, within our own range, to run. About the teaching, or the nursing, or the missionary Orders, they feel differently. That is a thing that can be readily understood and respected; for it approximates more closely and even in a recognizably nobler degree to the calls made upon our own humanity and daily obligations. The applied heroism of a Father Damien or a St. Peter Claver is admirable to all. To the people of this mind — and they are the large majority — our duty to our neighbor is more urgent and immediate than our duty towards God; the one duty does not and should not exclude the other; but God should be served through the medium of devotion to our human brotherhood, not through the quiet of a taperlit chapel or the isolation of a cell. Estrangement from the burden of life is no part of our common citizenship; the prayers devoted to the evil of the general soul would be better translated into the care of the general body.

Isn't that magnificent writing? Unquestionably she has expressed fully the modern mind — even that of many in the Holy, Roman, Catholic, and Apostolic Church. But, actually, all she has asked by that long paragraph is: What do you mean to man? How can one give a right answer to a wrong question? I am not going to right now, for while Miss Sackville-West seemed to dissociate herself from the mentality in that paragraph, she really contradicts herself in the next few lines wherein she exposes her own mind. She goes on with: "Quarrel as we may with the apparent waste of energy, the waste of potential usefulness, the waste, as we see it, of virtue involved in a living burial; indignant though

198

we may grow over the desertion and even the heartbreak of those who see themselves abandoned in a cold world as the door of the cloister shuts finally on their faces; irate though we may be over the loss of competence in a society which so grievously needs it, the loss of talent applied to cogent ends, the denial of usefulness where usefulness should surely be given. . . ." Then she relents a bit as she goes on to add: ". . . none of these arguments or resentments can or should apply if once we accept the, to us, strange but powerful principle that the mundane and material values can be turned utterly upside down."

The authoress all but exhausted her stock of synonyms regarding exasperation and anger as she tells us of quarreling, being indignant, irate, and resentful toward contemplatives. Her animosity has been aroused because she says there has been a waste — a waste of energy, usefulness, and even of virtue! There has been a loss of competence and talent. Society has been defrauded and the world robbed of real ability. What has she really said more than what was heard twenty centuries ago? All her angry cry comes down to is: "Why this waste?" That indignant query was first heard at a banquet when a practical man saw a loving girl break an alabaster box of precious ointment and pour its priceless contents over the head of Jesus Christ. That man angrily exclaimed: "Why this waste?" John the Evangelist tells us that man's name was Judas Iscariot and goes further when he informs us that "He did not say this out of concern for the poor, but because he was a thief."

That is rebuttal enough for the thoughtful. For the modern mind one must be much more explicit. Mary Magdalene did not waste the ointment she poured out on Jesus Christ, as He Himself, at that same banquet, explained. Neither are the contents of the alabaster boxes which contemplatives break and prodigally pour out before God ever lost, and they contain ointments more precious than that the Magdalene used!

199

You can see how complex many moderns make what is so simple. A cursory glance at the objections presented by Miss Sackville-West suffices to show they are pragmatic, utilitarian, humanistic, and materialistic. Man is crying to man for help from men. A little closer study shows them practically atheistic. The tenet that our duty toward our neighbor is more urgent and immediate than our duties toward God is hardly theistic, and most certainly not Catholic theology! It is a sentiment that might sound applaudable before a Rotary Club, but hardly presentable before a Roman rota or a Roman congregation. It smacks very much of the exaggerations of what some are presenting these days as the social Gospel. It is simply untenable, for it is to rewrite the tablets of Sinai, the Gospels of Jesus Christ, and even the Natural Law imprinted on every human heart by the Maker of every heart that is human.

Expressly and quite explicitly, Miss Sackville-West, and many like her in the modern world have put man before God, body before soul, and implicitly, at least, denied reality to the One truly real.

If that young lady, and many like her, could only be taken through the door I first entered at this monastery and read that startling, bas-reliefed command, GOD ALONE, then led along Gethsemani's dark cloister to the door of the abbatial church and study the two words emblazoned over that entrance, *Venite Adoremus*, she might realize that we monks have not come here to escape reality, evade responsibility, indulge in selfishness, but only to advance ever closer to the source of all reality, to pour out self in utter selflessness as we shoulder man's prime, preeminent, and all-important responsibility — *adoration*.

Man was made to adore. That is every man's prime vocation. It is precisely for that God made him. Therefore, the only human life ever wasted on earth is the life without adoration. Fr. Teilhard de Chardin saw this and made what appears at first as a startling statement when he said: "The thinking man has only one option: adoration or suicide." A moment's thought shows how true that is. Since there is a God who made man, and since He made him for His own glory, it follows ineluctably that man should adore his Maker. Of course, if a man is stupid enough to deny the existence of God, he is doubly stupid to stay in what so many call the rat race. We monks know who made us, and why He did so. We realize the human heart is in exile, and is athrob with a yearning for a far-off happiness it knew when life was young and it walked with God in a Garden. How exact St. Augustine was when he exclaimed: "Thou hast made us for Thyself, O God; and our hearts are restless until they rest in Thee."

Yet, what I have said of myself, I can say about Augustine: The ancients stole all his new ideas. Centuries before Augustine, the inspired Psalmist wrote what many look upon as the most beautiful words in the Old Testament; namely: "For what have I in heaven? and besides thee what do I desire upon earth? *For thee* my flesh and my heart hath fainted away: thou art the God of my heart, and the God that is my portion for ever."

With that before you, it should be evident why I claim the two words over the entrance to the monastery proper, GOD ALONE, plus the two over the entrance to the abbatial church, VENITE ADOREMUS, tell the whole story of the life lived here at Gethsemani. Talk about simple! How could one complicate it? Well, it can be done, and it has been done. That is why I borrowed the slogan my good and ever-witty friend, Jim Maginnis, had taken for himself in his business of selling life insurance: K I S S, which means Keep It Simple, Stupid, and made it something of a rule for life and living.

†

In one of my next sermons after this discovery I shared it with the community. It was on the Feast of Christ the

King. I claimed the rule was but the call of Christ the King to battle. I cried for men with souls as keen and uncompromising as a sword; for men with wills totally committed to the cause of Christ; men who will be monks in the root and real meaning of that word monk. *Monos* does not mean men who will live alone, but men who will live for God alone. *Monos* in the Benedictine sense does not refer to hermits, not to solitaries, but to cenobites who serve *sub Christo, pro Christo, et in Christo. Monos* means men whose wills are *one* flaming passion, whose minds are *one* blazing idea, whose hearts flame high with the fire of *one* unquenchable desire: Christ and His Kingdom. *Monos* means men who are single-eyed, single-hearted, single-souled; men who are perfectly integrated individuals fully and firmly incorporated in Christ — the real *Monos*, the *sole* Son of God, the *One* and *Only* Word of the One and Only God.

I went on to say: let us realize that the call of Christ the King is a specific call. Christ has not called a single man in this room to be a monk. Never. No, not one! He has called each and every one of us to be a Cistercian monk of the Strict Observance. Now we are at the heart of the matter, and I dare say:

> Clasp of this truth its central core.
> Hold fast that center's central sense.
> For one split-atom there
> Will yield you more
> Than realms on Truth's circumference!

That is the center's central sense of our call: the *specific difference!*

That is truly the heart of the matter for us, especially in these days of adaptation and renewal for there is grave danger that many may adapt but never renew, and that could be fatal!

202

We need precision in our thinking these days of confusion, and greater precision than any computer can give. We need sharper focus than any of the latest pinpoint focalfinders of the day can grant us. I say God has given us that precision and that focus by pointing us to the *specific difference*. This difference does make all the difference in the world.

We must not be mere monks. We must be, and ever and always be, Cistercian monks, and even more specifically, Cistercian monks of the Strict Observance, or we will be nothing! We must ever have, and continually cultivate our own specific, definite, determined, distinctive, and distinguishing *esprit de corps* — our family spirit, our legitimate family pride, our family characteristic, or we will never be the men, the monks, the mirrors of God, and the members of the Mystical Body God meant us to be, and Christ called us to be.

The stress is on the *specific*. Just as the Franciscans know their Francis and their characteristic spirit — poverty; just as the Jesuits know their Ignatius and their characteristic virtue — obedience; just as the Dominicans know their Dominic and their specific call — preaching; so we must know our tradition, our distinctive virtue, our characteristic spirit, and our specific and specifying work in the Kingdom of Christ. That means we must know our Robert, Alberic, and Stephen; our Bernard, Aelred, William of St. Thierry, and Isaac of Stella; our Largentier, de Lestrange, and de Rancé. We must know our forefathers and our family. We must know, love, and live our tradition. That means that we must be souls of *simplicity!*

Not simple souls, mind you, but souls of simplicity. For that has ever been, and, please God, it will ever be the characteristic virtue of the Cistercians of the Strict Observance. That has ever been their distinctive and distinguishing spirit. Consequently, we follow Christ the King as Cistercians of the Strict Observance, or we do not follow Him at all, for we will not be answering our specific call. We answer not that generic call to deny ourselves, take up our cross daily, and follow Him, but we deny ourselves the Cistercian way, take up the Cistercian cross, and follow Him in the Cistercian manner. When I say Cistercian I mean the Strict Observance, for Pope Leo XIII, in approving our union back in 1892 and 1894, said we are the *true* Cistercians. The point is that there is a Cistercian way of living, a distinctively Cistercian way of loving, a distinguishing Cistercian way of being — and they are achieved, day in and day out, by *simplifying* everything. We are men of simplicity, or we are not Cistercians of the Strict Observance.

Our prayer is *simple*. Our work, our meals, our dress, our day, our whole manner of living, loving and being is *simple*. All that simplicity is attained by being men of one idea: the glory of God in, through, and with Jesus Christ, the glory of God in our Office, the glory of God in our Mass, the glory of God in our manual labor, the glory of God in our *lectio divina*, the glory of God in our contacts with the world, or our lack of such contacts, the glory of God in our reading, writing, breathing, being, the glory of God in the very beating of our hearts — all that in, through, and with Jesus Christ. For we are men of one passion — *Christ*; men of one purpose — the peace of Christ in the Kingdom of Christ. Christ within us! Christ without us! Christ above us! Christ below us! Christ on our right side, and on our left! Christ all about us!

It is the Person of Christ, and specifically as king, sole ruler, sovereign, only Lord and leader — the Person of Christ is the whole inspiration of our living, loving, and being. Like Him, we have come into the world for one, sole purpose: to give, not to get — to give glory to God the Father. For that were we created; for that we were called by baptism, confirmation, and some by holy orders, and all by the one same call of Christ the King to be Cistercians of the Strict Observance. That is a call to *kenosis*, not to *pleroma*

— to an emptying out, not to fulfilling! If you give, I assure you, you will get; if you empty yourself for God, God will fill you; if you succeed in *kenosis*, you will experience *pleroma*. For our God is a grateful and generous God.

"Let this mind be in you which was also in Christ Jesus," says St. Paul. What was that mind? The Father! Let this will be in you which was also in Christ Jesus. What was that will? The Father's glory attained by doing the Father's will. "I do always the things that please Him," said the Lord, and He was talking of His Father. "In the head of the book it is written of me: I come to do Thy will, O God." The last chapter of that book was written in Gethsemani when He cried: "Let this chalice pass . . . yet, not My will, but Thine be done!" Christ's *kenosis* was final on the Cross. His *pleroma* followed fast: His Resurrection! And we must be Christ, or be untrue to all that we are.

In choir we must be the *labia Christi* — the lips of Christ — glorifying the Father, and getting grace, which is Godliness, for all the sons of the Father. On the farm, in the fields and in the farm buildings we must be the *manus Christus* — the hands of Christ — working with energy for the Father's Glory. When we read we must be the *oculi Christi* — the eyes of Christ — taking into our deepest depths the truth, the light, the life, the love of the Father as revealed to us fully in the Christ, for we must read the specifically Cistercian way so as to assimilate that truth, light, life and love into our own being. Do that, and we can sing our hymn of Terce with utter sincerity, for our "Flesh and lips, our heart and mind Will sound forth our witness to mankind, As Love will light up our mortal frame Till others catch the Living Flame."

There is your description of a true Cistercian of the Strict Observance: he is a living flame of love, made so by Christ who, in all truth, was naught but a loving flame who lived for one purpose only — His Father and His Father's glory. Like Christ, then, we will burn on and burn on until, like Him, we burn out. Our *kenosis* will then be complete, and we will be ready for the *pleroma*, which will be none other than God Himself — the *Agios, Iskyros, Athanatos* — the All-Holy God, the All-Strong God, the Ever-Living God.

††

I began this chapter to tell you of the external changes in my monastery, and consequently, in my monastic living. There were seventy-two in the community when I arrived in 1936. That had grown to eighty-two by 1937, to ninety-six by 1939. By 1940 we passed the one hundred mark. By 1952 we numbered 279! Growth was steady and none too gradual.

Yet, I must not go too quickly, lest you miss God's wily and wise ways. Were you to look down on the physical plant of the monastery in 1936 and again in 1952 you would see what I mean by things that change ever remain the same for the outline of the main monastery has not changed one iota since 1853 when the first monks began their construction. Yet, in this, my fortieth year, there is not a single place or thing in the monastery that has remained the same!

Allow me to anticipate just a bit as I add that were you to look down on the monastery today you would find two exterior changes from the original outline. One is a roof-garden atop the north wing of the building. Dom James Fox had that put in either in the late fifties or early sixties. It was to give us some place to walk when the early spring thaws and rains had made the grounds muddy. I use it more in the fall to view God's glory on the sides and tops of the surrounding knobs when He has splashed this world with golds, greens, russets, reds, yellows, and scarlet that looks like flame. It is beauty that takes the breath. The other change is the lack of a spire atop the Church.

Let me show you some of the changes in my environment which led to my changing. Let us begin on the ground floor. Just before I came here the toilet facilities were brought in from the outside of the house. Primitive? Well, we are situated in the backwoods! Since I have been here, those facilities have been changed three or four times and really brought up-to-date. When I was a novice, it was necessary to approach the abbot, kneel before him, and ask for the key to the shower. There was only *one* shower for the entire community. Today I can count almost forty separate showers in the different facilities around the monastery. None of them is ever locked, and there is no need for a key to the shower. Today, too, the washrooms are really plush. Where one caldron stood, and to which we had to approach individually to procure a tin basin full of water, then, after washing, turn to two or three roller-towels, there are terrazzo floors, tiled wash basins, hot and cold water, and individual towels. There are even mirrors! In the old days we never saw ourselves in a glass. You may think we have gone soft, but I say we have only become clean.

One assignment I could be sure of every week was shaving. I was given a pair of hand-clippers, which barbers used before long hair came in, and with them shaved all the choir-monks once a week. (The laybrothers all grew, or attempted to grow, beards.) Once a month I would be assigned the job of cutting all the choir-monks' hair, and giving each of the professed monks a "corona." That is, I left about a three-quarter inch of hair around the top of each head, if they had not gone completely bald! I was the barber for the choir-monks all during Dom Frederic's abbacy and for some years into Dom James Fox's term. It was he who one day shocked us by saying we could have a razor and shave ourselves once a week. We were getting cleaner! And all that began before Vatican II had been called, let alone before that Council had called the entire Church to aggiornamento, or updating.

I've told you how I had to break through the four-foot wide foundation to begin work on a new bakery underneath

207

the monastery proper. Well, that process was repeated year after year until we had an entire new floor to the abbey without adding an inch to its height. After that bakery there came a kitchen, scullery, various storerooms and a boiler room. That merits mention, for when I came here we had "psychological heat" in the abbatial church. What I mean is there were two rather large radiators that began to clank about the time we were finishing Matins about 3:15 A.M. But it was only psychologically that I felt any heat from those radiators. I saw my breath as vapor many a wintry morning as I sang to the Lord. I well remember how a Frater Alfred from Brooklyn had his big toe frozen in the church, how it gangrened, and how we buried him before he had reached his twenty-eighth year of life. In all truth, those were primitive days, and we were penitential monks!

Now I can count thirteen major works that were completed while I was under Dom Mary Frederic Dunne for thirteen years. We began with that lake in the woods, and went to building a corncrib, pig house, chicken house, garage, and greenhouse. We changed the entire front yard, and almost the entire backyard. Then, we erected that famous wall, the horse-barn, and the carriage-shed, which we turned into a laybrothers' novitiate. We erected a water tower — all that while we were farming over eight hundred acres and living off the produce from our own vegetable garden.

Under my second abbot, Dom James Fox, we hollowed out the entire monastery, literally! We left the old shell, so solidly built by our predecessors, the original founders of Gethsemani, but inside that shell we built a fireproof steel and concrete monastery, as modern inside as this morning's newspaper, while outside it is as ancient as early Citeaux.

Dom James ruled me, and the rest of the community, for almost twenty years. During that time he not only refurbished, I should say actually built, a new monastery within the shell of the old, but added a ladies' guest house, which has a motel as modern as Holiday Inn, for our female blood relatives, plus a men's guest house for male relatives and men seeking God through midweek and weekend retreats. He had us monks do practically all the work! Now you know why I became a jack of all trades, save electricity.

My third abbot, Dom Flavian Burns, carried on that change by having us build private rooms for each monk. My old "hotel" is no more. The facade is there. You can still see where it was on that second and third floors of the old monastery, but the high-ceilinged, spacious rooms, with the old furniture is only a memory and an outline. In their places stand what the old monks would call luxury apartments!

My present abbot, Dom Timothy Kelly, has seen the old novitiate, where I learned the ropes, demolished, along with the old infirmary. In their place a very modern infirmary and new novitiate, wherein the present-day novices live in private rooms, have been built.

Still I say that with all these changes nothing has really changed in the life we lead, and the living that is leisure to love God and man! Now you'll be calling me what I have been calling myself: Rasputin, the Mad Monk.

I adopted that name after God had given me the other side of my calling, that of victimhood, which *is* the other side of the priesthood of Christ Jesus. Before I tell you about that, let me insist that I took the name Rasputin before the book *Nicholas and Alexandra* had been read in the refectory — hence, long before I knew just how mad a monk the real Rasputin was.

10

A Third Vocation

Reacquaintance with the World

†

God did give me another vocation within the Trappist vocation, and it did lead me on to reacquaintance with what we religious call the world. But the vocation was not, by any stretch of the imagination, given by God for that specific purpose. No, indeed. For it was most personal, and had nothing to do with the world directly. Before we get into the essence of this third vocation, let me orient you fully so that you can understand the reacquaintance with the world.

For the first thirteen years of my life here at Gethsemani, I went outside the walls, that is, I left the precincts of the huge spread that is Gethsemani proper only once. It was after a porcelain crown which had kicked up in my mouth that Dom Frederic told me to go to Bardstown. I was the most surprised man in the world. Dom Frederic was most hesitant to allow any of us go to a hospital until we were almost in *rigor mortis!* Fr. Francis chaufeurred the only automobile we had — a Paige that must have been nearly my own age. Without a word, or even a sign between us, he drove me up what was then called the Green River Turnpike — a gravel road which stretched between Ball Town and Gethsemane Station. As a novice I used to look over the wall around the sawmill every afternoon as I chopped wood, to view a school bus passing at about 4:00 P.M. — just to convince myself that there were other humans on earth besides the seventy-two monks amongst whom I was living. But now I was riding along that turnpike! I inhaled deeply that morning, and they were inhalations of a strange freedom, after being closed in behind those walls for thirteen years! It wasn't that I wanted to get out from behind those walls; it was simply a new experience, similar, I now suspect, to that which a man feels when he is first freed from a long incarceration.

I did not leave the grounds again until early January of 1949. But before we come to that enlightening and definitive happening, I must tell you some of the exceptional happenings between my first and my second exodus.

The phenomenal growth from 1936 to 1952 does not give you all the facts, nor any explanation of the phenomenon. I tried to provide that not long after I had received my third vocation and just as I was becoming reacquainted with the world. I stated apodictically: "Gethsemani, Kentucky, is the wonder of the modern world." My proposition read: "The unbelievable is happening, and of all places, it is happening in America. . . . For the first time in over six hundred years, a Cistercian monastery has a community of over two hundred and forty monks. That monastery is the Abbey of Our Lady of Gethsemani, Trappist, Kentucky. It is the marvel that has set much of America wondering."

It was my second vocation that had filled me with historical facts, and enabled me to speed along with my proof. I knew that back in the heyday of monasticism, the twelfth and thirteenth centuries, it was ordinary for Cistercian cloisters to hold three, four and even five hundred men. In 1153, when St. Bernard of Clairvaux died, he was mourned by a community of seven hundred monks! Then came the decline, and when de Rancé took over La Trappe in the late seventeenth century, there were not five real monks in his abbey. The regime he inaugurated, in which he returned to the principles and practices of early Citeaux, gave him notoriety and his followers a name, but it did not fill monasteries. At his death, at the dawn of the eighteenth century, not one hundred monks mourned him.

Yet he gave birth to what seems deathless. Even that tidal wave of irreligion called the French Revolution failed to wash away the foundations he had laid. Slowly, up through the years, the Trappists have grown. From time to time, some enthusiastic historian of the Observance, graphing the growth, has dreamed of a monastic renaissance and has been bold enough to prophesy a second golden age of the Cistercians of the Strict Observance. Now and then, some monastery would show an influx which would lend color to the dream and give a shadow of substance to the prophecy. Aiguebelle in France, a hundred years ago, was one such, for in the mid-nineteenth century she had a personnel of two hundred and forty men. But, as always, the dream soon faded and the prophecy remained unfulfilled. But, today, Gethsemani, with her over two hundred and fifty monks, has broken the six-hundred-year-old record.

My research for *Burnt Out Incense*, the story of this house, indicated that as the nineteenth century neared its end, Gethsemani seemed to have already reached her end. In late 1895 Dom Edward Chaix-Bourbon, the third abbot of this American monastery, was forced to resign, whereupon her father immediate in Melleray, France, disowned her as a daughter in disgrace! That was practically an unheard of action in the order. But when both the general and the general chapter of the same order ignored Gethsemani completely for over two years, you can safely bet that most of the fifty monks in the abbey thought they were hearing the death rattle in the throat of their mother. Then came in January, 1898 the dynamic and colorful Edmund Obrecht as administrator *ad tempus*, having been appointed by Dom Sebastian Wyart, abbot general of the Reformed Cistercians (another name for the Trappists). By October of the same year this black-haired Alsatian was confirmed as duly elected abbot of Our Lady of Gethsemani. He put his abbey in the news almost immediately by celebrating in 1899 the golden jubilee of her founding. He did that in his always dramatic manner. Nearby Bardstown and the surrounding towns in these backwoods of Kentucky saw more pomp and pageantry on that occasion than they had ever seen before.

As the twentieth century dawned, Abbot Obrecht had sixty monks under his rule. Despite all his dash and drive, this powerful personality did not win much of a response from America or Americans. He did swell the ranks a bit, but he did so by picking up recruits as he travelled through Ireland, France, Germany, Belgium, Italy, and Holland on the many missions entrusted him by both the Holy See and the Cistercian Order. When he died in 1935, after having been abbot of Gethsemani for thirty-seven years, he left a community of only eighty monks, and half of these were Europeans.

Then the miracle began which was to astound not only twentieth-century America, but the entire Catholic world. Mary Frederic Dunne, the first American ever to persevere as a choir-monk, was elected the first American Trappist abbot. His regime opened in a deeper dark than had any of his predecessors, for a flu epidemic struck the monastery and carried off victim after victim. Before Dom Frederic's hand had gotten used to clasping his crozier, nine new iron crosses sentinelled mounds of "burnt-out incense." By the time of his abbatial blessing Dom Frederic could count only seventy men who had lived with him under Dom Edmund Obrecht. By 1939, less than four years after his election, Dom Frederic counted almost double the number that had played part in that election. Before D-Day in 1944, despite all his clever moves to enlarge choir, dormitory, refectory, novitiates, he found his monastery literally bursting at the seams, and he made the first foundation ever made from an American monastery by sending twenty-one men to Conyers, Georgia.

213

That was only a beginning. By 1946, less than two years after war had ceased, more than one hundred and fifty ex-G.I.'s had come to Gethsemani seeking admission as monks. Not all were accepted, and of those who were, not all stayed. Enough did, however, to force us to make three foundations: Utah, South Carolina, and New York State. In his comparatively short abbacy, Dom Frederic saw his community grow from seventy to over two hundred and thirty. Small wonder he so often spoke of God's miracle of grace!

Dom James Fox, his immediate successor, had even more reason to speak of miracle and of grace. When he was first made prior of Gethsemani in 1939, there were not three hundred Trappists in the entire United States, but by 1950, there were over three hundred and fifty novices in seven of our states, and because he was abbot of Gethsemani, he had some responsibility for practically all of them. Were he to gather all his monks into one house in 1953, he would have had more monks under him than the number who had mourned St. Bernard at Clairvaux in 1153.

Europe stood aghast at the spectacle of lively, luxury-surrounded young Americans crowding into cloisters for prayer and penance. Even Pope Pius XII gasped when Dom James told him he had more than a hundred novices in Gethsemani alone, and hence had to have them living in tents, since the abbey had burst its seams! We did purchase two large circus tents, and set them up in the quadrangle formed by the four sides of our huge abbey, and made cells within them for the laybrother novices.

Now those on the other side of the Atlantic know all about our ability to produce. They conceive the American character as a conglomeration of dynamisms and drives, so dominated by our impatience for results that we commit ourselves unquestioningly to unbelievable expenditures of energy, and keep our commitments. After two world wars they laugh at our lofty idealism. Our openhanded giving without counting the costs, our uncalculating generosity, they take as something inseparable from our character. Yet, with all their analytical genius, they have failed to analyze us fully. It was a Frenchman, Jacques Maritain, who after having been among us for some time, saw into our deepest depths. He wrote: "There are in America great reserves and possibilities for contemplation." Jacques went on: "The activism which is manifested here assumes in many cases the aspect of a remedy against despair. . . . To my mind, if in American civilization certain elements are causing complaints and criticisms, these elements proceed definitely from a repression of the desire, natural in mankind, for the active repose of the soul breathing what is eternal. . . . The tendency, natural in this Country, to undertake great things, to have confidence, to be moved by large idealistic feelings, may be considered, without great risk of error, as disguising that desire and aspiration of which I spoke."

That analysis and evaluation gave me hope for Europe coming to a correct understanding of us Americans, and precisely of the influx Gethsemani knew before, during, and just after World War II.

It was an exciting time for those of us who had come behind these walls before Hitler manifested his mad complex and compulsion to dominate the world. It made us wonder just what was going on. My conviction remains that true manhood is the full explanation. I know what every real thinker knows: Man wants God. Full manhood is reached only when Godhood is attained. As William of St. Thierry put it: "Man is a lover of the Divine," and again: "Man is most man when he is most like God."

I saw the influx of these ex-G.I.'s as America's awakening to true manhood. Leaving nothing of their manhood behind, save that which had ever unmanned them, their pride, I saw them overcrowd our cloister not because of what so many superficial cynics say, a lost love, but precisely that they might become lost in Love. They came not because the world seemed beyond redemption, but they came

215

to help save that world. It was not because they were afraid of life, but they came, with eyes wide open, that they might live life more fully. These veterans proved to me that American youth was becoming keenly aware of the Augustinian truth that man is a mind with a memory of God.

Once that memory is stirred, two truths stand out with all the vividness of flame wavering against waveless black velvet: Never in all time did man need God more; Never in all Eternity did God need monks more. The first is obvious. The second sounds blasphemous. Yet, it is age-old doctrine. In his Letter to the Colossians Paul taught that truth when he told about "filling up in my flesh those things that are wanting to the Passion of Christ, for His Body, which is the Church." Pius XII taught the identical truth in his Letter on the Mystical Body when he wrote: "Christ *needs* His members. . . . On the prayers and voluntary penances of the members depends the salvation of many." Between those two great teachers of truth twenty centuries lie, during which countless loyal followers of Christ have lived the chivalry contained in the definition of a Christian given by Raoul Pius, S.J., who said: "A Christian is one to whom has been entrusted the welfare of all his fellowmen." I have always completed the bedazzling definition by adding: ". . . and the Glory of God by the completion of the Passion of Christ."

Maritain's evaluation and the influx of G.I.'s had set me reevaluating our Trappist vocation. Actually, every entrant into this cloister has the same effect on me. I always wonder what brought that one, or this one, here to this life. Back in the late forties I saw how all these truths fitted into one another. Maritain said it was natural for us Americans to undertake great things. What could be greater than being a Christian in Raoul Pius' definition, that of helping save mankind? Or more idealistic than following the lead given by Pius XII and satisfying the stark, staring poverty of the Son of God who *needed* us to complete the work He inaugurated in the bareness of the stable in Bethlehem and climaxed in the naked cruelty of Calvary's Cross? A cry for help came from Omnipotence in helplessness. Red-blooded American youth answers that cry, with generosity.

That answer is more natural than, perhaps, Jacques Maritain claimed. It is as normal for a human to desire the divine as it is for a human to breathe. How could it be otherwise, since man is nothing but a breath of God in a vessel of clay? Water seeks its own level, and being seeks its prime source. The human heart is naught but a hunger for God; the human soul, a burning thirst for the Fountain of Living Waters; the human person, one throbbing ache for a love that will satisfy. No finite love can give final ease to that ache. That is why men come to Gethsemani.

I make no apologies for contending that Trappists were living in tents here at Gethsemani in the late forties and early fifties because so many ex-G.I.'s heard the cry of Christ: "Give Me your lips, that with them I may yet go on praising My Father from earth. Give Me your hands and your heads that I may fold the first like so many Gothic spires pointing to Heaven as I bow My head in prayer. Give Me your hearts, that with them I may love other children than those My disciples one day tried to turn away; other sisters than those whom I loved at Bethany; other sinners than the one of Magdala's streets, the woman taken in adultery, and the one by Jacob's Well. Give Me your bodies, that in them I may yet be scourged for the sins of the flesh, nailed to a gibbet for sins of avarice, crowned with thorns for the awful sins of pride. Give Me your lives, that day after day, year after year, until the sun burns out and the stars fall, I may die that the last straggler of Humanity's long caravan may live forever."

That is the fact St. Paul spoke of to his Colossians, and the fact that Pius XII stressed in his *Mystici Corporis*. That is the truth Trappists strive to incarnate from the dark of their vigils, unto the dusk of their Compline, day after day.

That is the "active repose of the soul breathing the Eternal" that Maritain depicted.

They may not have perceived all that clearly before they entered, but soon after coming behind these walls they learned that they had to make an all-out effort to be the men God made them to be. Here they found they could live life fully, because here they could be fully in love. Here they learned, slowly perhaps, but surely, that a man becomes a monk, and a monk gradually becomes a mystic, a Christian fully conscious of himself — conscious that he has a work to do for God, and a work to do for his fellowman; keenly conscious that he has a specific task assigned to him from all eternity, which must be done in a specific span of time; conscious that he can do it, that he must do it through Him, with Him, and very specifically, in Him who made the first Gethsemani immortal by agonizing there for mortals. Thrilled by this consciousness, American youth comes to serve, to sacrifice, to suffer. He comes to *love*, even if he has to do it in tents!

Now just as there is a boy in every man, there is also a chivalrous knight in every monk. Hence, besides a cause, a commander, and a campaign, there is a call for and from a Lady Love! We have both in Mary Immaculate.

From earliest youth I had a true and tender devotion to Mary, the Mother of God. As a Jesuit I ended every litany of the saints with a cry to Mary, Queen of the Society of Jesus. Daily, as a Jesuit, I had recited her rosary, so you can imagine how much at home I felt when I came to Gethsemani and learned that every single Trappist monastery as well as every single Trappist monk is named after her. That is what the "M" before my name Raymond stands for. We opened every single day with a salute to her, and closed every night with our world-famed *Salve Regina*. It was heartwarming to learn that it had been at Citeaux that the Immaculate One had been first named *Notre Dame: Our Lady* — and that it had been at Clairvaux that St. Bernard, the mellifluous one, had earned his title of Citharist of Mary. There is nothing that I have written that does not contain many references to Mary. Call it romantic, but I well know that when a child is afraid, it will run to its mother. But when a child is in danger, it is the mother who runs to the child. Now even the blind can see that the Christ Child, who lives in the Mystical Body, the Church, is in grave danger these days. That is why, during the past century and a quarter, we have had so many personal appearances of the loveliest Lady of heaven or earth — our Lady of the Sacred Heart. That is why, on each occasion, she has had one message: Save the world for the Heart of my Son. She has used, practically speaking, but two words, prayer and penance, and has urged mankind to the one great work, reparation.

In 1830 at Paris, her message to Catherine Laboure was: "Pray!" In 1846, high in the French Alps at La Sallette, she wept as she pleaded for penance and prayer. In 1858, little Bernadette Soubirous heard "the lovely Lady" ask her to pray and do penance. In 1870, the same lovely Lady blazoned the sky above Pont Main with the words: *Donc, priez mes enfants!* In our own lifetime she has appeared again and again at Fatima in Portugal; at Banneaux and Beauraing in Belgium, at Heede and Pfaffenhofen in Germany; outside Tre Fontane in Italy, and more recently in the Philippines. Each time she has asked for what is the Trappist life: penance and prayer. That is why I say she was behind our purchase of tents in the late forties and fifties and behind each entrant's approach to the grey walls that surround this monastery.

Those tents have been gone long since. But this ladyhouse still holds more than a hundred Americans intent upon being true sons of God and children of Mary.

Please do not look upon that as an aging monk's garrulity, nor as a rhetorical writer's digression. It is neither. It is simply the further baring of my soul, mind, and heart. I hope to discern for both of us God's ways with this monk.

219

Dom Mary Frederic Dunne died in 1948. God took Dom Frederic from me August 4th and gave me Dom Mary James Fox August 23rd. Such is the continuity, the eternality of the monastic life, in which Fr. Ryan's lines about "nothing lives but something dies, and nothing dies but something lives 'til skies be fugitives" are more applicable than they were when he wrote them about nature.

Dom James commissioned me to write the life of Dom Frederic. I took the title, *The Less Traveled Road*, from Robert Frost's poem, "The Road Not Taken," which ends with the lines:

> Two roads diverged in a wood, and I —
> I took the one less travelled by.
> And that has made all the difference.

I have just scanned that book's foreword, and see another Frenchman gave me my lead and my enlightenment. Father Raymond Bruckberger, one of the most heroic figures of World War II, had exclaimed: "America is astonishing!" That cry came from a man who was a member of the fearless French commandos, then, when France fell, chaplain general of those even more fearless men in the Resistance. In 1951 he came to America and was not here but a few months when he became truly enthusiastic, so much so that he ventured into the prophetic. First, he found a convent of cloistered contemplatives in, of all places, Hollywood. He learned that it was frequented more and more by those whom he called "stars from a lower heaven," and that this was but one of more than ten such convents of cloistered Dominicans here in America. Being a Frenchman, he was amazed. They have some rather peculiar ideas about us Americans, especially about Americans as possible contemplatives! So astonishment drove Father Raymond Bruckberger to learn as much as he could about cloistered contemplative life in America. He was particularly anxious to ascertain whether this kind of life was cultivated as much among males as it seemed to be among females. I understand that mentality, for it is quite universally true that women have been more generous with the Lord God than have men. They seem constitutionally more unselfish, and consequently, more ready for the kind of sacrificial love that is called for by the cloister. You can imagine Father's astonishment when he discovered that America held more Trappist monks than any other country in the world. "This flowering of the contemplative life seems to me as important here as atomic research." He prophesied: "Some day the prayers of these children of God will burst on the world like the bomb of Bikini."

Since I had become so well acquainted with the French mind, I could understand this brave priest's reaction. He was, for the first time in his life, in this land of crass materialism and multimillionaires, where seventy million people admit they have no church affiliation whatsoever, yet he was finding that religion in its highest flight and purest form had suddenly assumed an ascendency which it had already lost in the so-called Catholic countries of the Old World. Here he was in a land where ninety-five million radios blare jazz and jungle music night and day; yet the silence of the cloister was exerting such an attraction for youth that they were actually overcrowding certain cloisters. He was observer enough to note that as many as seventy thousand people thronged into stadium after stadium to watch a big league baseball game, while up to a hundred thousand would cheer themselves hoarse over capers on college gridirons Saturday after Saturday. Yet utter solitude and complete seclusion were winning recruits in such numbers that Father Bruckberger noted that "the Trappists, each year, have to send some to other Orders, simply because they cannot keep them all."

I insist that there are no accidents with God, and call this commission from Dom James a gift and grace from

God, given me to deepen my appreciation for life behind these walls, and, as I now see it, as preparation for my "third vocation."

First of all, I had to explain that the Trappist life, for almost a century, had attracted very few native-born Americans. When I entered, it consisted of a handful of Frenchmen fighting for existence down here in Kentucky, a few Irishmen doing the same in Peosta, Iowa; and in the Blackstone Valley of Rhode Island, a group of French-Canadians engaged in the same fierce struggle. Extinction seemed ever imminent, and was staved off only by securing replacements from the mother houses in Europe and a few recruits from foreign lands.

After World War II, all changed. The three monasteries, which for decades had about them the atmosphere of death and decay, were suddenly astir with buoyant, vigorous life. Grizzled and bent monks still made their way, slow-paced, about the cloisters, but at every turn one was met by youngsters abounding with energy. Buildings which had merited the slur of Renan, because of the "vastness, emptiness, and lack of solidity," were suddenly found filled beyond their capacities. Communities, which had had to plead the possibility of another French Revolution, with its consequent expulsion, as an excuse to continue their meager existence in this pagan land, suddenly found themselves faced with the necessity of making foundations of their own, or allowing American vocations to go unanswered.

It was quite a phenomenon, but how was it to be explained? Some pointed to the dust clearing away from Hiroshima and to the Iron Curtain creeping so relentlessly over Europe and Asia. Others offered the blasting of our "brave new world" by the bombers of World War II. Still others claimed it was the cringing fear of the annihilating potentialities of atomic fission which had gripped our civilization.

I recognized all these as contributing factors, but proved that they were not real causes by directing the gaze to what was going on in the other five continents of the world. They were all much more cognizant of the ruin left by World War II than America would ever be. Further, each had much more reason to shudder because of the threat of annihilation slumbering in the implements lying ready for the next world war, for they well knew who would feel the impact first. Yet, on none of those continents were cloisters being crowded, nor the contemplative life being cultivated, as they were here in America. It was a startling phenomenon, for here we were, the most modern and progressive people on the earth, startling the world by our return to the monasticism of the Middle Ages, and building what looked like a second Thebaid. What was the explanation?

The ultimate answer, of course, was God. For He is both the Seeker and the Sought, the Prime Mover and the Ultimate Rest, and it was He who had given that desire which is natural to mankind for the active repose of the soul breathing what is eternal. God, the First Cause and Creator of all, uses creatures as secondary causes, and anyone who would attempt an explanation of God's inexplicable ways must focus on those secondary causes, who are creatures. That is what I did as I wrote Dom Frederic's life. My thesis was that it is practically self-evident that American youths were not being pulled into contemplative cloisters by the cords of Adam, but that they are being held there by the Cross of the Second Adam. This can be made manifest by drawing up a memoir of the man under whom this startling movement began, and during whose short abbatial reign it neared its apex.

Of course, God used countless and varied instruments to bring these many recruits to Gethsemani. The chivalry contained in the gift of one's life to God moved some. The challenge to be as Christ-like as humanly possible attracted others. Still others were moved by what I call salutary selfishness. These wanted to lay firm hold on the surest means available to insure the salvation of their own immortal souls. Then there was the altruism that prompted many to lay down their own lives, and give every moment of every day, so that others might be saved. Yes, practically every means under the sun, from success to failure, from sanctity to sin, were used by God to bring these young men to Gethsemani. To keep them here, He used men, and the man He used most was Mary Frederic Dunne.

God had written His signature in clearest calligraphy over every year of this man's life. I had always admired him, and came to love him more deeply and more dearly every day I researched his life. I soon saw that God had put that signature of His in italics, and even underscored it during every week of Dom Frederic's brief abbatial career. God's signature is the Cross.

I do not hesitate to borrow from an unbeliever, especially when he tells a truth. Mercius was to Confucianism what St. Paul was to Christianity. With something very close to a Christian insight, he once wrote: "Whenever Heaven wants to confer a great work on anyone, it first drenches his heart with bitterness, submits his nerves and bones to weariness, delivers his members and his whole body to hunger, reduces him to the most extreme indigence, thwarts and upsets all his enterprises, and by these means wakens in him good sentiments, fortifies his patience, and communicates to him what has been lacking." I call that true insight into Divine Providence, and proved it to be an accurate outline of the life of one of Christ's closest followers: Mary Frederic Dunne. I borrowed an aphorism from the same Mercius to epitomize my first abbot. It ran: "The great man is one who has not lost the heart he had when a child." Edwin Arlington Robinson said: "The world is not a prison house, but a kind of spiritual kindergarten where millions of infants are trying to spell God with the wrong blocks." Dom Frederic had the right blocks, and was always spelling God correctly. How did I come to call this man who had been aptly summed up as "cold steel sheathed in silk" as like a "child in a kindergarten playing with blocks?"

Well, I think that such is the only characterization fitting for any true Trappist. This life inevitably produces those opposites in any real man who gives his all to living it to the hilt. It fibers the heart until it is that of a Viking, even as, in its simplicity, it recaptures for one the faith he had as a child, revitalizes it, and sets his soul vibrant with that faith which is childlike trust. That childlike trust can come only from a faith that flames. That conviction so gripped me that on more than one occasion I had Our Lady of Gethsemani saying:

> Send me the best of your breeding;
> Send me your noble ones —
> These I will clasp to my bosom;
> These will I call "My sons!"
> For I will not be won by weaklings,
> The subtle, the smooth, the mild —
> But by men — men with the hearts of Vikings
> And the simple Faith of a child.

It was not difficult to show that Mary Frederic Dunne was such. But I did get a laugh when Tom Merton came to me, after he had read the book, and said: "You certainly showed the penitential side of our abbot." I had thought that I had brought out Dom Frederic's mystical side! Tom's summation brought back to me my first remark to him about the necessity of being an ascetic for years before one could ever become a mystic. Either Tom was learning from my books, or he was teaching me by his kindly summation of the same.

Not long after Dom Frederic's death and Dom James' election I had to look into my interior life — the physical, not the spiritual. In late August I had to admit to an obvious malfunctioning of the gastro-intestinal tract. As the rule prescribes, I reported to Frater Vincent, the infirmarian and a full-fledged M.D. I took my medicine like a man, but nothing changed. I confess I was not greatly concerned, for God had blessed me with such a robust constitution that I usually threw off quickly any and every attack. But I could see that Frater Vincent was concerned.

In early October he had me see Dr. Greenwell from nearby New Haven. He prescribed. Again nothing happened. Then along came Dr. Philip Law from Chicago, a top-flight surgeon. Phil visited the monastery at least twice a year, and always saw the monks who had any ailment. He urged fluoroscopy and a colon-ray, just, as I learned later, Frater Vincent had suggested to the abbot earlier. Nothing came from either suggestion until mid-October. Then Dom James offered to take me to Louisville for an X ray. It was an offer, not a command. Since I was struggling to meet a deadline for P. J. Kenedy and Sons, I turned the offer down.

The morning of January 4th, 1949, however, saw a difference. I was on a ladder painting the ceiling of that little room into which Dom Frederic had taken me on the day of my arrival in 1936. Dom James walked in and commanded me to get ready to go to the hospital. I had no option this time. I had to obey.

The next morning I found Frater Louis (Tom Merton) and Father Odillo sitting in Senator Dawson's car, awaiting both me and Dom James. Soon he came along and got into the front seat with the Senator. I squeezed in between Tom and Father Odillo in the back. I say "squeezed" because good Father Odillo was anything but slim. What a ride that was! Dom James dug into his brief case immediately and began to read. In the back seat we three read our Office, said our rosaries — all privately — then looked out the windows at a damp, dreary, and sticky countryside. Not a word was spoken, not even by Senator Dawson.

An hour and a half after leaving Gethsemani, we drove into the porticoed entrance of St. Joseph Infirmary. Dom

226

James nodded to me. I grabbed my bag and followed him into this huge building, up a flight of stairs, and to the reception desk in the lobby. To the nun behind that desk Dom James quietly said, "This is Father Raymond."

The nun must have been trained by Dom Obrecht and Dom Frederic, for she kept silence as well as a monk! After a simple "Come," she led the two of us to room 139 on first east. Dom James gave me a blessing, and left. I looked about the room, then suddenly awoke to the fact that I had been left without a single word of instruction as to how I was to conduct myself.

Before I unpacked I sat down asking myself: What, in heaven's name, am I supposed to do? I'm a silent monk. I'm a strict vegetarian. I'm supposed to be cloistered. What shall I do? Should I speak? What should I do if visitors showed up? What about the meals? Should I insist on no meat, no fish, no eggs? Should I make signs? How *should* a Trappist comport himself in such surroundings? It was a quandary, but not for long. I very soon told myself to act as Christ would. That meant make no requests for any extraordinary services. Be human. Take whatever was offered. Be a perfect gentleman.

Then my door opened and in walked a white-capped nun who introduced herself as Sister James Marion, the supervisor of first east. I had never seen a Sister of Charity of Nazareth before. They were known in those days as the "white caps," for they wore the cutest little white bonnet that was ruffled or pleated beneath the ears. I took Sister James Marion in from tip to toe. All I could think of at that moment was Walter Baker's cocoa, for Walter Baker had a factory in Dorchester Lower Mills, not far from my boyhood home. On the wrapper around each can of cocoa was a picture of a lady in a white cap, garbed in a skirt that came down to the floor. James Marion looked as though she had modeled for that wrapper!

We had hardly become acquainted when in came Dr.

Fred Gettlefinger — all business. Doctor asked the usual questions, and scheduled X ray for the following morning, January 6, feast of the Epiphany. I referred to it as the feast of the wisemen from the East, and told all that I was from the East — Boston, Massachusetts.

That evening they began their prep for a colon-ray. It was my first introduction, not to "friend or enema" so much as to "nothing by mouth after midnight." They awakened me, if I had slept. I was on linen sheets for the first time in thirteen years. At home we had but one coarse sheet, and that of stiff sail-cloth. I lay my head on a soft pillow, certainly not like the straw pillow at home. I was in a warm room, not the chilly dormitory at Gethsemani.

Despite the "nothing by mouth" sign on my wall, they did allow me to offer Mass. I got my first sight of the chapel, which looked more like a fairly good-sized church. I entered the chapel just as a high Mass for the feast was ending. I found one side peopled with nuns. The opposite side held many more individuals, practically all in white uniforms. They were the nurses from the training school attached to the hospital, and others who were graduates about to go on duty for the day. It was quite a different sight from that of my community lined up in our monastic church.

I offered my Mass at a side altar with a huge statue of St. Joseph above it. Once I got before that altar I was at home. Thanks to God's great love, I was in heaven, literally, during that short half-hour. I was not allowed time for thanksgiving after Mass, but was hurried back to my room on first east and told to disrobe, put on the hospital gown that lay on my bed, then put myself in a wheelchair (which I resented, since I felt so capable of walking) and was taken to the elevator and whisked to the radiological department.

Dr. Syd Johnson was soon bending over me in the dark of an X-ray room, and palpating my abdomen. I soon saw he had found something amiss exactly where I had detected abnormality myself since late summer, and all through the fall.

The afternoon and evening sped. Sister James Marion came often. She intrigued me. One reason could have been that I had been so long away from females. Another was the strangeness of the habit and my ignorance of the Sisters of Charity of Nazareth. But deeper than either was the calm dignity, and the nice distance she manifested. I was edified and mystified. I admired the religious comportment, but I was curious about its source — the training these "white-caps" had received. So, I became chatty for the first time since my arrival.

Next morning, rather early, in came Dr. Gettlefinger. He had a very long face. He began, "Father, I have some bad news . . ." That's as far as he got, for I interrupted, "Not at all, Doctor. I've got cancer." It was really a guess on my part, but an educated guess and even a scientific one. My dad had died of cancer of the colon in 1935. My mother was even then dying of the same. Charlie, my baby brother's first child had died of leukemia. I had told Doc Law, in October, that I had either TB of the intestines or cancer of the colon. He laughed and said, "Good. You give an alternate diagnosis."

Dr. Gettlefinger's jaw dropped. He simply stared at me a moment, then said, "That's it, Father. All other tests were negative: lungs, heart, kidneys, liver. But X ray showed a growth near the sigmoid. I'll have Dr. Henry look in on you. Dr. Abell is out of town just now. When can you be operated upon?"

Sigmoid meant nothing to me then, and neither did the names Dr. Henry or Dr. Abell. I answered, "Right now, as far as I'm concerned, Doc. But I'm a monk. I must tell my boss."

Before I was able to tell my boss, Dr. M. Joseph Henry appeared on the scene, a dapper, white-haired, piercing-eyed, keenly alert little man whom I liked immediately. I've come to know myself since then, and realize I am a gregarious individual who likes practically all people on first contact. But this liking for Joe Henry was different. It grew and grew until it became a real love for the man as a man, as a stalwart Catholic gentleman, as an expert surgeon, as a tremendous husband and marvelous father. We became truly intimate friends. But that day he was all sharp, rather abrupt questions and quick decision. He said he would operate Wednesday morning, January 12th.

Once he had left, I looked at the facts. I had four days to prepare for surgery. I had cancer. What was it all about? What was life all about? Was this the end? A few years back I had read how Fr. Miguel Pro, S.J., during the persecution in Mexico under Calles of the Catholic Church, had offered himself to God for the soul of Calles. After some brave work as Christ's priest and apostle, ministering to the persecuted, disguised as a cab driver, and I suppose many other disguises, he was arrested, tried, condemned, and shot. Calles repented on his deathbed. Those facts stirred me to the roots of my being. The chivalry, the romance, the man, well, please God, at base it was the Christ, the priest, the religious, that had me offering myself for Stalin.

How could I fail to imagine that this was it? That is the fact. In those days the word cancer was synonymous with death to me. So here I was, just forty-six years of age, sixteen years had gone to the Jesuits, almost fourteen to the Trappists, the other sixteen had been spent trying to grow up. It had been a happy life, and, as I thought then, long enough. Thirty years in religion, and sixteen of those as a priest. But then I faced the fact that I had four days, maybe, to prepare for the particular judgment. Although frightening enough in one way, it seemed like a pleasant prospect, until I faced all the facts. Then it became a very serious business.

I called my abbot. He had been my confessor for some time before he went to Georgia. I gave him the verdict of the professionals. When I mentioned cancer, I heard him catch his breath. I laughed. Then I asked if he could get in

230

Tuesday, as I wanted to make a general confession. He graciously granted the request. All that took up most of Friday. Saturday was a peculiar day. I tried to write an article for *Review for Religious*, but without much success, for I had other things on my mind. The biggest thing was preparation for the general confession. It is strange, and can be alarming, to find how sharp memory can be. So, as I say, Saturday was a peculiar day, and even a peculiarly hard day.

Came Sunday, and I thought my last Sunday on earth. That was the thought in my head and heart as I awoke. I offered a particularly thought-filled, and as I humbly hoped, an especially holy Mass, thanks to my recollection and concentration. That brief hour was the only time I had with myself and God alone that day. What a crowded day it turned out to be.

Before breakfast was served, Sister James Marion asked me to cross the corridor and meet a patient in Room 143. By this time I had taken as my one rule: accessibility. I had found Christ always accessible. The good, the bad, the indifferent never had any difficulty getting in touch with Him. A Magdalene could crash the gate at a banquet given in His honor, and hear those most consoling of all words: "Thy sins are forgiven thee." A Nicodemus could come to Him by night, and learn a lot about being born again. Blind Bartemeus could hold up a whole procession, be brought into His immediate presence, and make his request of: "Lord, that I might see." Lepers could call out to Him, and He would not only hear them, but cure them. Christ was always accessible, and I would strive to be Christ-like. So I gladly granted James Marion her request. Was I the fortunate man! She took me across to a Fr. Carl Miller, S.J.

He was only skin and bones. I learned why, when James Marion told me how he had been flown from India, where he had labored amongst aborigines known as Santals for over twenty years, for he had been diagnosed as having cancer of the pancreas. Dr. Abell opened him, and closed

231

him, for the cancer had spread too far. While his body obviously was being rapidly ravaged, the light in his eyes told me the person was very much alive. I had seen that same light in the eyes of Brother Paul when I first landed at Gethsemane Station, and again when I had first met Dom Mary Frederic Dunne. It was that light which made up my mind for me to stay. I had come to call such a light the light of God's glory.

This lively little man, whose eyes held such vivid light, fired question after question at me — first about why I had become a Trappist after all those years as a Jesuit, then about the nature of the Trappist life, about the work the Trappists did. Soon he shifted the questions to prayer, and very specifically to contemplative, and even to mystical prayer. In typical Jesuit fashion he made practical application. He wanted to know how he could become more contemplative when he returned to his very active life in India!

How does one reply honestly to such a query from a man in such a state? He saw my hesitancy, but he misread its real source. He thought I was afraid to tell him his actual condition, and the hopelessness of that desire of his to return to India. So he told me, even more plainly than had Sister James Marion, about his condition and the prognostications of his doctors. He knew they gave him only a few months, perhaps even only a few weeks to live. But then he told me his convictions about the power of Our Lady's intercession. He was facing physical facts fully, but he was also all but wiping them out as he stressed supernatural fact. He openly admitted that he was asking for a miracle, and added that he expected Our Lady to obtain it for him. I am a realist and as I looked at and listened to this skeleton of a man, I admitted to myself that I could echo Christ when He exclaimed: "O, ye of little Faith." To hear this man, who was so obviously dying, speak of living among his Santals again, and living as a contemplative, forced me to admit that I had not such faith. But when he covered my hesitancy with a request, which showed he had read my incredulity, with a petition that I pray that he give God whatever He asks, and give it cheerfully, promptly, and without reserve, I saw that while he had towering confidence in the power of our Lady-Mother, he had even greater confidence in the wisdom and love in all God's choices.

He had not read aright my hesitancy in answering his question about how he could become a contemplative and a mystic. When he repeated that query, I secretly thanked God for His Providence. The article I had been trying to write for the *Review for Religious* was titled "Contemplative Prayer and the Contemplative Life." It was meant to show they are not synonymous. I told Fr. Carl about Dom Lehodey and Jacques Maritain and their insistence that one could lead a mystical life without ever once knowing anything like mystical prayer, and argued that the same could be said about contemplative life and contemplative prayer. He listened attentively, but then repeated his plea that I teach him how to become a mystic.

Later that evening, when Sister James Marion remonstrated with me for not answering his plea, I said, "Sister, a wise man never carries coals to Newcastle, nor salt water to the sea." I had read, and even knew, quite a bit about both contemplation and mysticism. But I did not deem myself to be either. But I was somewhat weary that evening from an afternoon and early evening that had been amazing, amusing, embarrassing, thrilling, and tiring. For, from the moment I had left Fr. Miller's room in mid-morning until the moment Sister had come in with my night's medication and libation, I had not had a moment to myself. I was getting reacquainted with the world, all right, but all was not right with my world.

Yet, when I noted a shadow of chagrin pass over the usually sweet features of Sister James I chuckled and said, "Fr. Carl taught me more about mysticism than I could ever teach him, Sister." Her large blue eyes opened wide, so I continued, "A short while ago I read a single word, a hyphenate, which described a mystic perfectly. It's a word that may shock you, but it is one that satisfies me. The writer spoke of a man being 'God-intoxicated.' Now, don't frown, just think. When one delves into Scripture, especially the Old Testament, and then reads later spiritual writers, he will find much about inebriation — spiritual inebriation. They are really saying the soul is 'drunk' with, or on, God. Now, admitting that comparisons limp, I still maintain there is a good analogy there. You've seen, I'm sure, good-natured drunks. They love everybody. They are happy, carefree, good-humored, generous. They'd give their shirt away. Now apply that to Father Carl. Isn't he a happy, carefree, generous soul? Is there anyone he does not love?" When she smiled and had her eyes light up, I concluded, "That man is 'drunk with God.' Who but a drunken man would want to go back to those aborigines in India; back to that dirt and squalor; back to a foreign land to live among foreign people, who speak a foreign tongue, and whose very thought-processes are utterly alien to your own? Believe me, a man has to be filled with God, filled to the point of inebriation, to be like Father Carl now. So why should I try to tell him how to become what he already is? . . ."

"But . . ." she broke in.

"No 'buts,' Sister. Let us realize there is a mysticism of action, a mysticism of prayer, and a mysticism of suffering. The first is for the many, like yourself. The second is for the very, very few, and it is a pure gift from God — one that cannot be earned. The last, I am beginning to suspect, is for all of us."

I went on for some length after that, but when Sister had left me for the night, I could hardly believe I had heard myself aright. Had I been just multiplying words in my weariness, when I had said that mysticism of suffering is for all of us? Or had it been God opening my eyes to my third vocation — that of a *victim*? I was not in any pain at the moment, but surgery was only three days off, and I had no expectation of surviving it at that very moment. Weary as I was I gave the thought much mulling over.

What had made me so weary? People! I've already told you I love people, yet, here I am now telling you they wearied me. After thirteen years in silence, solitude, and seclusion, I had delegation after delegation of nuns drop in on me unannounced, ply me with questions about my diet, my day, my duties, even my dreams, and then ask for spiritual direction. Group dynamics and group therapy were unknown terms those days, but I found myself in the midst of both! Then there were the laymen and the laywomen who dropped in. Finally, and most surprising of all, there was the number of priests, both secular and religious, who found their way to Room 139!

Fr. Carl died before Tuesday when Dom James was coming in for my general confession. His passing made me acutely conscious of the possibility of my own passing. I would be insulting God were I to go over all my past life, digging up those many stupidities which were real sins, since He had said, and meant, "whose sins you shall forgive, they are forgiven." To the best of my knowledge, I had never made a bad confession. I suppose I might have made some poor ones, but never a bad one. So why repeat them? I told Dom James my conclusion. He was expert enough in such matters to follow the maxim: *Credendum est confitenti*, trust the sincere penitent, and heard my weekly confession, blessed me, assured me of his and the entire community's prayers, and left.

He was not out of the building before a telegram from Fr. Jack came in for me: "Grounded in Washington. Will arrive 10:30 A.M. tomorrow. Hold operation if possible."

About four o'clock that afternoon I met Sister James Marion as I returned from traipsing all over the hospital, seeing sisters in radiology, the lab, surgery, not to mention a few patients, especially a Fr. Gerry Garvey, S.J., whom I had known when I was out at St. Mary's, Kansas, studying theology. Sister was indignant. "Father Raymond, you should be in bed. Don't you realize you are to undergo surgery tomorrow at eight o'clock?"

I laughed. "So I hear, Sister. But you wouldn't deny me the joy of saying 'good-bye' to my friends." She did not answer my laugh. She was mad. We headed toward first east. Her very stride told me she was more than irritated. I tried to placate her by saying: "I'll give you a very special intention in my Mass tomorrow morning, Sister." She stopped dead, faced me and said, "You're not going to say Mass tomorrow; you're going to be operated upon." The blue eyes were flashing. Just then who should come along but Doctor Henry. Before he neared us, I quietly said to Sister, "Now don't say anything. Just listen." When the doctor stopped beside us I first asked when he planned to begin.

"First thing in the morning," he replied.

I then told him of Jack's telegram. "O.K." he said, "I have two others to do. You can wait."

"I'll give you a special memento in my Mass, Doc." He thanked me. Thereupon Sister James exclaimed: "But he can't say Mass before his operation, Doctor."

"I don't know any better way for preparing for it, Sister," was all he said, and walked away.

Sister James Marion was a good and wise nurse, and very expert. But I could see she was none too pleased with the permission Doctor Henry had granted me, nor the manner I had obtained it.

I offered Mass early the morning of the 12th. I was "high" spiritually and physically — spiritually, because Sister James Marion had come into my room the day before with tears in her eyes. When I asked the reason, she mentioned an article by E. Boyd Barrett that had been read at table, titled "Shepherds in the Mists." The moment I heard

236

the name I started, for it was back in the very early twenties that Father Larry Kelly, S.J., our novice master at Yonkers, New York, had given us points for our morning meditation with tears in his voice. He told us that E. Boyd Barrett, a brilliant Irishman, from the English province of the society, had just left the order. It was years before I obtained the whole story, but I began right then and there to pray for Boyd. Hardly a day in the next twenty-six or -seven years passed without some prayer for the wandering one. I had read his early book on the Jesuits and recognized the animus for what it was: a form of intellectual pride, that devilish thing which has caused the downfall of so many. But here was James Marion telling me about his article, filled with honesty, true compunction, and a deep-rooted sympathy for those shepherds, priests, wandering in the mists. Boyd was back in Christ's fold, though not in the Jesuit Order. I was elated over the fact, and, perhaps a bit presumptuously, believed my prayers may have helped a bit. At any rate, that news enhanced the thanksgiving element in my Eucharistic Sacrifice that morning. I was spiritually high, even as I thought this might very well be my last Mass, my last morning.

They gave me nembutal the morning of my surgery, which explains my physical high. It can affect one in such a way that he feels glorious, as glorious as anyone happily incandescent from alcohol! In that elevated state I was rolled out of my room just about ten o'clock in the morning.

About ten-thirty a man in surgical greens came up to me. Covered as he was from head to toe in those greens, I did not recognize this man who was pulling off his surgical gloves. But once he opened his mouth, I knew it was Doctor Henry. He asked if Father Jack had arrived as yet. When I gave him a negative reply, he said: "I have another case I can do. You relax. But I see I don't have to give you that advice. You seem to be having a good time." Off he went.

About a half-hour later, he was back again. "Where

did you say your brother was grounded?" When I told him it was at Washington, he looked off in space for a moment, then came back to my side and said, "My two daughters go to Manhattanville. They take that train home. It is always late." I sensed that Joe was restless, so I practically shouted, "O.K., Doc, let's go." Nembutal is powerful stuff!

Once in the operating room, Doc Henry appeared much more relaxed and pleasant. As the nurse was tieing his gown, he almost laughingly asked, "Would you like to watch this operation?" He did not know my love for surgery. I have often said that had I not become a priest, I most certainly would have become a surgeon. So I answered, "I most certainly would." That is why I was given a spinal, which numbed everything below the paps, but left my head clear. At least I thought it was clear.

It seemed to me that Doc Henry began cutting almost before the drapes were fully arranged.

It was not too long before I heard Doc Henry say, "There it is." Of course, I did not know what he was talking about. But, when a few moments later, he looked down at me and asked: "Do you want to see your cancer?" I replied, "Of course I do." He then held up a foot of intestines. I looked and almost shouted, "Now, Doc, you have scientific proof that I have guts!"

I remember little after that. They tell me I began to show signs of nausea, so they snowed me. I recall nothing of the recovery room. My next conscious moment came in room 139, on first east. When I awoke, I looked, and knew I was not in heaven, for there was Father Jack standing in the doorway which connected my room with room 140. "Hello, Bozo," I shouted as strongly as I could. Then I turned and looked to my right. In my armchair sat Captain Jim Kinnarney, with his rosary still in his hands. The last I had seen of Jim was when they were rolling me to the elevator to take me to surgery. Jim held his rosary high then, and said, "I'll be in the chapel, praying this until you come down again."

I greeted him, "Well, I'm still alive, Jim." Then I began to tell Father Jack about Boyd Barrett's article. He finally smiled and said, "You're talking too much. You sound as if you were drunk. Go to sleep."

It took no great effort. It was heavenly to see Jack, but it was not heaven. So I rolled over, puzzled more than anything else. What was God doing? What were His plans for me? I was in no condition to work on that puzzle. I slept until Sister James Marion or one of the nurses awakened me to turn me, or medicate me further.

Sister kept me strictly cloistered for the next two days. Fr. Jack was the only non-medical person allowed in my room. Even he was not allowed in for any great length of time. Thus I learned something of the loneliness of a hospital room, and how true it is that life looks very different from the horizontal. It was a very strange experience for me. I found God both distant and very near. I found prayer difficult and as natural as breathing. I found myself perfectly abandoned to God's will and ways, and yet fighting my way back to life and vigor. To tell the truth, I was charmed and disenchanted. I found people simply marvelous. I found myself brittle, vulnerable, weak, practically helpless before what is called disease. I actually got a clearer insight into creaturehood. It is a very fragile thing, and despite all the vaunted freedom and self-assurance one claims, it spells utter dependency. But that only gave me lucidity into reality's deepest depth, and there was God in all His glory. For I saw that creaturehood spelled origin from God; continued existence — God's *concursus* or continual creation; life's only purpose to be God's good creature and prove it by doing His will from moment to moment. I turned my priesthood over, and found in its other side, *victimhood*. I had found my third vocation.

How long it took me to see all that, I do not know. I do know that in two days I was sitting up. On the third day I, with assistance, walked the length of the corridor from my

room to the nurses station and back. Was I perfectly resigned and even anxious, after that walk, to get back in bed!
I was as weak as the proverbial kitten.

But it did not last long. Two days later Father Jack left
for Boston and work on the mission band. We had had the
most glorious visit in thirteen years, for the good sisters
showed they were truly sisters of charity. They put Jack in
room 140, with the connecting door between us. They
served our meals together. Hence, I saw more of Jack, and
talked longer with him than I had been able to do since I
joined the Trappists. But I was not the only one whom Jack
saw. He was always all-priest. I know not how many he
comforted, consoled, counselled, confessed, and directed.

The day before Jack left, Joe Henry removed the
stitches. As he patted my abdomen, it was evident that he
was not only pleased, but actually proud of the job he had
done. He said, "If you lived in the city, I'd discharge you
today. But, knowing Gethsemani as I do, I'm going to keep
you for two more weeks." To be honest, I had no objections
whatsoever. I was becoming reacquainted with the world,
and I found that world fascinating.

A week after my surgery, I was up and around. I was
being summoned here, there, and everywhere in that hospital: to break the bad news to this patient, to cheer this one
up, to prepare this one for death, to meet this other one's
parents, or this parent's children. Then there were the visitors! Of course there was curiosity about this strange person, a monk. But, more and more, I saw it was to meet the
author. Talk about surprise. I myself began to wonder who
this Father Raymond was! The accessibility I had adopted
proved to have its drawbacks. Privacy was not only invaded,
it was overrun! But before I bring this chapter to a close, I
must tell you about the most delightful part of that in-
vasion.

I knew nothing about Joe Henry's background or reputation at that time. That he had trained under the Mayo

brothers and was of international repute I learned later. But I could not fail to see, in those few weeks at St. Joseph's, that he was not only a perfect gentleman, a genuine Catholic, delightful conversationalist, but a very holy layman. Before I left that hospital Joe had not only introduced me to his wife, but had brought his two daughters to meet me. In his wife, Betty McKenna Henry, I met a true Kentucky blue-blood and a perfect Southern lady. She had everything: class, culture, refinement, all the social graces to an eminent degree, but above all, she was genuinely human, in the best sense of that word. As for his daughters, young Betty, or as I came to call her, Little Joe, was truly a chip off the old block, for she had all her father's qualities of mind and heart, his temper and temperament. She was a gem! Mary White, the younger daughter, was more like her mother. What a tribute that is!

Such was the rapport between us that they not only adopted me, but soon adopted my family, and even my friends. So much so that one day young Betty, in typical Little Joe fashion, blurted out, "This is no longer the Henry home, it is Father Raymond's hotel." She had reason, for not only my family, but the few friends who were allowed to visit me always stopped off, first and finally, at the Henry home, and that, not infrequently, meant overnight stays there.

I did not blame young Betty, or Little Joe, for, as a consequence to cancer, and to the name of being a writer, those visits and visitors increased. So did my visits to the hospital, for Joe Henry had laid down the law: "Every three months the first year. Every four months the second year. Every six months the third year. Then, if you are still alive, every year thereafter." That is how it came about that I not only renewed my acquaintanceship with "friend or barium enema," but with the world.

11

Characters

Famous People Who Have Met Me

†

This chapter subtitle, which seems to resound so loudly with conceit, is merely a play on words of the title of Maurice Francis Egan's *Famous Men Whom I Have Met.* The cancer I lingered over so long in the last chapter did bring me into contact with some famous men and some real characters.

Many of you will recall how the genealogies were given in the old Douay version of the Bible. The word "begat" is archaic, but it is a telling verb. My cancer begat Dr. Henry, and he, in turn, begat for me Mother Betty, "Little Joe" and Mary White. They, in their turn, begat the Maginnises, the Lawlors, the McKennas, the Schwartzels, and many others. That begatting is still going on.

Cancer had another stirps which began, where every family should begin in a way, up in surgery. Not only did I meet surgeons of different weights, heights, reputations, specialties, and abilities, but I also met the supervisor of surgery and her many capable aides, assistants, and nurses. That cancer begat Sister Margaret, the supervisor of surgery, who begat for me and my soma Dr. "Mickey" Maguire, Dr. Henry Asman, Dr. "Happy" Phingst, and Dr. Jack Hemmer, each of whom kept his hand in by wielding a scalpel somewhere on my anatomy. As for the surgical nurses, there were those who "scrubbed" and those who "circulated" for my many experiences. Some sought me out for consultation, some for refutation, and others just for socialization.

I chuckle as I think of Maxine and Christine Wheat who were identical twins I could never identify correctly! I recall the day I asked Max to what church she belonged. When she said "The First Church of Christ," I put out my hand and said: "Shake, Max. So do I."

"But, Father, you're a Catholic."

"Right, Max. That is and was the first Church of Christ."

"Oh, you," was all she said as she walked away. That incident, and there were many similar, shows me now, though I was utterly unconscious of it then, that I was on something of a "mailman's holiday" while I was recuperating at St. Joe's. If that's not understood, I'd better say that while you may take a monk out of his cloister, it is next to impossible to take the cloister entirely out of an old monk. I may have been unconscious of what I was doing for God those days, but I was anything but unconscious of what God was doing to me, or so I thought.

Remember we Trappists of Gethsemani were just about steeped in the doctrine of abandonment, whose first and fundamental tenet is: Nothing happens save by the will of God — directive, preventive, or permissive. Next, the whole purpose of life is to do God's will. But how do we know God's will from moment to moment? For me, with my cancer, there was no slightest doubt, let alone any real difficulty. For, you see, we do have to be constantly on the alert lest we deceive ourselves and consider what is actually our own sweet will to be the will of God for us. Yet when sickness strikes, we can be quite sure our own sweet will is not in the illness. A normal human being, in religion or out of it, does not ask God to put him or her on an operating table. So when I found myself there, I knew I was there by the will of God, and I was happy and able to say, "*Fiat.*"

Still, I had reason to ask: "Just what are you doing to me? You did not take me home by means of those 'wild cells,' nor, as yet, are you allowing me to go to my monastic home. So what are you doing? *Silence* — here in this hospital that is humming with excitement even in the dead of the night. *Solitude* — here where humanity seems ever in flux. *Seclusion* — when they come to me from all sides. *Cloister* — when every angle of every corridor opens out to newer contacts. I don't know precisely what you have in mind, Lord. But I do know that this mind of mine is simply bewildered." Still, don't let me deceive you; the bewilderment, which was real, did not detract from the very real enjoyment of it all.

Dr. Henry discharged me on February 6, Feast Day of St. Raymond of Fitero, Founder of the Knights of Calatrava, and my Cistercian Patron, and insisted that I report back for full check-up the first weekend in May.

Now, certainly, every Louisvillian, and I'd dare say almost every Kentuckian, knows that Derby Day falls on the first Saturday in May. But I was neither a Kentuckian nor a Louisvillian. So the date meant just that to me: the first weekend in May. I have heard so much about the coincidence of Derby Day and check-up since, that even I have wondered what was in the good doctor's mind other than a full check-up.

In I went on Thursday afternoon. As I stood at the desk of the nurses station on first east awaiting Sister James Marion, I heard this feminine voice behind me: "So this is the man standing between me and my happiness." You can bet that turned me around. There, in the doorway of the linen room, stood this dark-haired, dark-eyed, somewhat darkened-skinned nurse in a gleaming white uniform, her cap sitting so sassily on her head, and a tiniest curve to her parted lips. "Who are you?" was all I could ask of this wisp of a girl who somehow seemed atingle with energy.

"I'm Jimmie Maginnis' girl friend; and he told me he'd never marry me until I had met you."

All I knew about Jim Maginnis at that time was from hearsay. He was the nephew of Doctor Henry, had lost his mother when quite young, and had been brought up by the McKenna's of Old McKenna Bourbon fame until World War II, after which he lived at the Henrys's. He had quite a reputation as a wit and a storyteller. But that was all I knew. Why he'd insist on his girl friend meeting me I could not guess. So after she had given me her name, "Mickey" Lawlor, I said, "O.K. Get married. You've met me."

They got married all right. I have seen them through parenthood and on into grandparenthood; and the friendship, begun back there in 1949, has grown faster than any oak, and stronger.

I did not see Jimmie during this first check-up, but I did see Mickey a few times. In fact, I think I sent for her once to ask her where she was hiding all the time. All day long, it seemed to me, over the intercom I'd hear: "Calling Miss Lawlor. Calling Miss Lawlor." She appreciated my implicit charge, of course, then laid me out in lavender as she told me she was responsible for every IV all over the hospital, and how she'd like to watch me trying to keep up with her as she flew from floor to floor. Mickey and I have carried on just such an interchange for almost thirty years now, so if it be true that we tease only those we love, you know what exists between Mickey and me.

Well, when I got to my old room 139 I was delighted to learn I had a Jesuit as next-door neighbor. Fr. Marion Batson had come back from the Patna Mission in India for something like "R & R" for the service men. I believe "Bats" got plenty of recovery, but I know he got no rest.

Because I had been a Jesuit, and because she saw that Bats and I had hit it off immediately, Sister James Marion had all our meals served in my room. Thus it was that I learned how Marion Batson had gone to India shortly after

245

taking his early studies as a Jesuit in America, and how, in India had spent the rest of his life of thirty-two years.

I was wondering why God was bringing these Jesuits into my life, and especially Jesuits from the Patna Mission in India. I knew He had a reason, and I had an obligation to fathom that reason as far as I could. Already you have seen what I saw in Father Carl Miller, S.J. — God-intoxication! I envied him for it, with a holy envy, I hope, and even prayed for a like inebriation. I didn't even "get high on God," perhaps because I was seeking my own satisfaction and not my own sanctification, which connotes God's glorification? There is such a thing as spiritual gluttony, and I could have been guilty of it. Well, what was I going to get from Fr. Marion Batson?

I received a tremendous amount of entertainment, intellectual stimulation, and awe-inspiring history of his works in the Patna Mission. One moment he would be telling me of his shrine built at Mokameh. He could make it sound like the Taj Mahal. I am convinced that Bats put as much love into the erection of that shrine in honor of Our Lady as Shah Jahan ever put into the building of the beautiful mausoleum in memory of his favorite wife. The next minute Bats might be telling me of his sessions with Nehru. They were very close, and the Pandit did not hesitate to summon the Catholic missionary for consultation.

Perhaps the most interesting, and also the most frightening, report was of the time he was taken off a train by a group of anti-Nehru people and, as it seemed, was about to be murdered, when a group of untouchables came on the scene, formed a circle around the Jesuit, told him to keep on talking, as they rotated about him. He very briefly told of the caste system in India, and how these people who were rescuing him were what they were called untouchables. The arresting party dared not break that circle about the priest, who admitted he was sure his time had come, that he was scared, but also was preparing himself for death, even as he did what he was told, and kept on talking. Finally, another train came along, and he was lifted onto it by the untouchables who, quite obviously, had not hesitated to touch Father Batson!

Bats, as we all called him with the double entendre in the name, was in the hospital, but I never learned why. I did learn he had obtained Nazareth nuns for his work around Mokameh, and that was something of a miracle, for they had countless missions here in the United States. So it was only natural that Bats spent much of his R & R lecturing to the good sisters about his and their work in India. But that room next to mine was home base for the good father during my check-up.

You can be sure I did not retire, as Trappists did in those days, at 7:00 P.M. that Thursday evening. But I did follow orders for preparation for the colon-ray in the morning. Friday morning, early, I was up on fifth, and on the X-ray table. As Dr. Syd Johnson bent over my body, gently prodding the barium through my colon, he suddenly said: "That little Irishman did a superb job. I cannot even see the suturing." Syd had already told Sister Joseph Robert how Doctor Henry had claimed his contact with me had turned out to be one of the greatest spiritual experiences of his life. That set me wondering just what kind of other spiritual experiences Joe Henry had had, for all I seemed to be doing was prodding him into arguments!

At any rate, I was soon back in my room only to find a note pinned to my pillow: "Patient out of his room." No signature. No explanation. When Bats appeared I asked him who put it there. He was no help. Neither was Sister James Marion, but she did tell me I should let her know whenever I left the floor. That was news to me. The point I am making is that practically every time I did leave the floor, whether after reporting or not, I would find a note pinned to my pillow with the same message: "Patient out of his room" — and no signature.

247

Came Saturday morning — Derby Day — and when I came back from offering Mass, there was the note on the pillow, but this time the message read: "Be in your room immediately after dinner." When Bats appeared he was holding a similar note in his hand.

"What's this all about?" he asked.

"I don't know," I said, "but let's be here after dinner."

We were. Sister Mary Benigna knocked, entered, and beckoned me to follow her. I stepped out into the corridor to find her knocking at Bats' door. Same gesture. Same silence. She then started down the corridor. I lifted my shoulders in question to Bats. He smiled and lifted his shoulders in reply: "I don't know. Let's follow her."

Sister went across the corridor to a room wherein a Father O'Shea, a priest of the Louisville diocese, was lodged. He was in his mid-seventies, had cancer but did not know it, or would not accept the fact. Bats and I had dubbed him "cardinal," for he had an air of pomposity about him, was regal in his bearing, had a vocabulary that bespoke wide reading, cultured taste, and keen consciousness of word-value. He was disconcerted by the fact that he was hospitalized and out of his parish, and that some other priest was administering his parish in New Hope. He told me he was charging the archbishop with embezzlement of his parish! It was amusing to watch him trying to corner the archbishop who was almost a daily visitor to St. Joe's. I suspect John A. Floersch enjoyed the game more than I did as a mere on-looker. Well, Sister Mary Benigna knocked on the cardinal's door, made the same beckoning sign, and led the three of us along that corridor, across the huge lobby, along another corridor leading toward the chapel. I was dwarfed between Bats and the cardinal, each of whom stood at over six feet. Not a word had been spoken so far. As we neared the chapel Bats did say: "This is a solemn high something or other." In those days for a solemn high Mass you had to have celebrant, deacon, and subdeacon. We went past the chapel, and into the convent, which was off limits, if not officially cloistered, to all but the nuns.

Sister stopped at the door leading to what, obviously, was the recreation room for the sisters. She opened a little box she had and passed out slips to Bats, the cardinal, me and to Father Vince Osborne, the hospital chaplain, who looked as perplexed as we three felt. Sister Mary Benigna gestured us to be seated in front of the first television set I had ever seen. Before I could get my bearings fully, nuns began to come in and sit behind us. They were not silent. Being Kentuckians they were chattering away about the different horses in the Derby. Then I opened my slip and found Americana written on it. I heard that morning that this horse was the favorite in the run for the roses. I hardly had time to think, "If my abbot could only see me now," when the television screen lit up and a commentator began to tell us about this being the first time the Kentucky Derby had ever been televised.

I could not sink down deeply enough in my chair — a Trappist monk, in his black and white habit, sitting in front of a room filled with nuns, watching the Kentucky Derby! Bats sensed my embarrassment, nudged me, whispered out of the side of his mouth: "Be yourself. Sit up and enjoy it!" I was grasped by all the commentator had to say, and the pageantry displayed on the screen. It was in black and white, but my imagination colored the flowers on the lawn and on the hats of the women celebrities who passed before the camera. When the band broke out with "My Old Kentucky Home" I knew I was in Kentucky, for they all stood up as if it were the "Star Spangled Banner" that was being played. I suppose, to them, it is the National Anthem.

Soon the shout came: "They're off!" The excitement of the race gripped me. I was surprised at the brevity of it all. It was over in two minutes. The favorite did not win. As we were leaving the room Sister Mary Benigna sidled up and said, "I'm sorry, Father. I wanted you to win the jackpot."

The letdown after the event did not last long, for Sister James Marion, who was moderator of the sodality for the nurses, had a May procession with coronation of Our Lady at its climax scheduled for that evening. Now I knew why she had asked me to pray that the rain would hold off that morning. It did. I saw Joan Gasser crown Our Lady that evening, and later that same evening learned that Joan had just been found with Hodgkin's disease.

I wrote the thrilling story of that sterling character in *Your Hour*, just as I wrote the story of Father Carl Miller. So you see I did not come home empty handed from my hospital stay.

The story I have not told is that about little Jo Carter who was brought to my room by Sister James Marion. She was a plebe from Lafayette, Indiana. As she was introduced I noticed she was a bit shy and ill-at-ease, even as she displayed a definite self-composure and the professional air of a competent nurse. I accounted for this as soon as Sister told me that Jo was not a Catholic. The professional air was explained later when I met Marie Goben, her nursing arts instructress. Marie was a professional, in the best sense of that word, and she so instilled professionalism into her nurses that one senior in the school said she was "gobenizing" the whole place. That was a compliment, though the one who said it meant it as a condemnation. Little Jo held out a medal and asked me to bless it for her.

I liked the youngster immediately. Jo is that kind of a person and personality. When I learned that she had been a semi-professional ball player before she took up nursing I understood the self-assurance that radiated out from her. All capable athletes have that air. Well, Jo got over her shyness as far as I was concerned in no time, and every visit to the hospital found Jo visiting me and asking questions about religion.

Before my first year of check-ups was ended, Jo was under instructions about the Catholic religion. Before my second year of check-ups was half over, Jo was in the Catholic Church. Marie Goben was her godmother. I know not who stood up for Jo as godfather, but I do know she claimed me in that capacity. For almost thirty years now Jo has been addressing me either simply as padre or as godfather.

After a few years of nursing in Kentucky, Jo joined the air force, and wrote me from just about all over the globe, and each letter made me praise God the louder for the child He had in this former semi-professional ball player. She was a credit to Him, to St. Joe's school of nursing, and to Catholicity. I doubt if anyone in the medical branch of the air force outdid Jo Carter in the various survival trainings. She had "deep water," "jungle," and "arctic" to my knowledge. She survived them all! She saw duty in San Domingo, when there was plenty of gunfire in that republic. Jo flew casualties back to the States and told me how, once the craft was airborne, she was in complete charge and had all the responsibility for the entire planeload. Her heart was too large for her own good. She suffered with every boy, as she called them, in every plane. While not all of her boys survived, Jo did.

The next experience came when she called me from one of the Carolinas to tell me she had joined my club. I had formed my cancer club early after my first experience with those wild cells. The members were to offer their sufferings for every other member's sanctification even as they offered them for God's glorification. Like myself, Jo survived her experience. But she was heartbroken when her superiors grounded her after her surgery, for she loved to fly. They sent her to Germany where she had charge of one of the largest hospitals there. After three years there, they sent her to Vietnam where she was in charge of all the nurses in that theater of combat. She kept in closest contact throughout her stay, which lasted to the very end of our involvement there. By this time she was a colonel.

Jo visited me after retiring from the air force, to which

251

she had given twenty-two and a half years of her life. I found her practically unchanged from the lively, sassy, self-assured, yet quietly self-diffident youngster I met in 1949. As I looked at her and listened to her, I wondered just what God had recorded to her credit for those years around the globe as air force nurse. Uncle Sam decorated her frequently, and showed his appreciation by all those advances in the corps. But God, who sees the heart, and records every unselfish deed, must have a much longer record and fatter dossier on the swaggering young ball player He sent to nursing school at St. Joe's infirmary. Unquestionably she has been with the dying more often than I, and I am sure she has aided each as they neared the Face-to-face meeting with God. Just how many she helped find God and His Church is another query not even she can answer. But I know the number is high.

The most frequent query I had to answer during the first check-up had to do with the centenary we Trappists of Gethsemani were about to celebrate almost one year late. Many knew I had some part in the planning. Little did they know just how much! I had laid out the entire program before I went in for my surgery early in January. When I got back home in February I was aghast when I learned that not a thing had been done in my absence. I just about raised the roof. Within a week I had covered the hierarchy of the United States with invitations to attend on June 1st, 1949. During the next week I got a great lift from a Frater Joachim. What a character he was! As Eugene Everett he had joined the St. Louis Province of the Society of Jesus. During his regency he came down with tuberculosis. After some years of treatment, that was contained, but Eugene thought he owed it to the Society to leave. The First World War soon broke out and Gene, who was now a practicing lawyer, joined the Fighting 69th of New York. In no time he was commissioned a captain and assigned to "Wild Bill" Donovan's attachment. What stories he had about Wild

Bill. Wounded in battle, and gassed, Eugene found himself back in New York shortly after the armistice was signed. He listened to the famed chaplain of the Fighting 69th urging the boys to settle down by getting married and accepting responsibility. Eugene followed that advice, but, despite a small family, he always felt a gnawing inside him to become a priest. After his family was raised he began applying here, there, and everywhere. As a married man, with a wife still living, he ran into difficulties. Finally, Dom Frederic paved the way for him to obtain all dispensations necessary, and accepted him as a novice here at Gethsemani. Gene had made his simple profession by the time I was working on the centenary, and being an aggressive individual, worked his way into the committee. Thank God for that aggressiveness. He had so many more practical ideas than I could ever have excogitated.

He contacted the governor of the State, the state senators, the representatives and all such political dignitaries. He was in touch with the military at Fort Knox, and in no time had arranged for them to come and help us with traffic, setting up relief centers in case of heat prostrations, accidents, and policing the crowds. By mid-May practically everything was in order. I say practically everything for I was soon to learn that protocol, about which I knew nothing, must be followed, or else!

I was still staggering from that blow when Abbot James summoned me, and told me that since everything was so well organized, I need not bother my head about the centenary.

I believe I can recognize a "firing" when I see one. I was puzzled. But I really did not care by that time, for everything *was* organized sufficiently to insure a smooth running of a big day.

Big it was, especially for Gethsemani. Some ten to fifteen thousand people came to the open-air Mass which was offered out in St. Mary's field, adjoining the monastery proper. Over one hundred and eighty monks followed the crossbearer down the avenue from the front of the abbey, and they were followed by priests, monsignors, priors, abbots, more than a dozen bishops, our own archbishop, Cardinal Dougherty, our own abbot, and the abbot general of the order. Color there was aplenty, not the least of which came from the Knights of Columbus' honor guard, who ushered in the cardinal.

Monsignor Fulton J. Sheen delivered the sermon, which he titled "The Thunder of Trappist Silence." Crews from the television and radio stations were on hand, and they asked me to do the announcing over the loudspeaker system they had set up. I did that, but after the Gospel, instead of introducing Monsignor Sheen, I announced that "we will now profess our Faith in the Credo. . . ." Hands waved from all sides of me. Many pointed to Fulton Sheen, and I had to correct my announcement by saying, ". . . after we hear the ever-eloquent Monsignor Fulton J. Sheen."

Monsignor was his usual eloquent self and, as far as I was concerned, climaxed what I still call a triumphantly successful celebration of our centenary. He did mention the hundred years Trappists have been behind these Kentucky hills, but his address was pointed to those ten to fifteen thousand as he tried to explain why we lived in silence. He gave three reasons: first, in order that we might know truth; secondly, that we might be ravished by love; and thirdly, that we might atone for sin (as did He who is Truth and Love, and who one day became sin for us sinners). With superb oratorical mastery he proved each point in his proposition, showing how Christ, who is Truth, is the quest of our lives, and the closer one gets to perfect truth, the fewer words one needs. Therefore, when one is clasped by Christ, Infinite Truth, silence is the one response. The same with love. Profoundest love, even that which is human, is wordless and speechless. When we look into the mystery of the love of God, we find it expressed in a sigh, a breath, the Holy Spirit. Hence the silence of Trappists who have been ravished by Love. Finally, they are silent as Christ was silent in all His trials because He had taken the guilt of the world upon Himself. Trappists emulate their Master. He even ended, as he so often does, with a poem which he claimed could serve as autobiography for each of us. Its last lines were: "And so did I follow Him who could not move? An uncaught captive in the hand of Love."

The same year we had the artistic monsignor for eight full days as retreat-master. With three talks a day, we had up to twenty-four beautiful talks on God, His Son, His Son's Mother, and the spiritual life. Convinced as I am, after much exposure to other retreat-masters, that there is really only one retreat, the spiritual exercises, I summed Fulton's stay with us as a treat rather than a retreat."

An artist of a somewhat different color also came the same year, Dr. Albert G. de Quevedo. "Potch," as I came to know him, had been a Jesuit in the California province for about ten years. When he left the Society he betook himself to Hollywood where his brother was working in the Jesuit parish thereabouts. Potch was a handsome Spanish youngster who had ambitions to take the place of the late Ramon Navarro. He had the looks, ability, and drive, and went out himself to the studios. They saw the potential in this handsome young Spaniard and began questioning him. Could he ride a horse? No. Could he drive a car? No. Was he an able dancer? No. Well, they would school him in all three. He concluded it would take a bit too long, and as he was walking back to his quarters after his conference with the studio bosses he saw a sign advertising a free lecture on psychology by some woman. He attended, and concluded he already knew more psychology than the woman would ever know. He decided he would become a lecturer.

His account of his first experience should make a book! He hired a public relations man, put out colorful, catchy ads, hired a hall, and packed it. He gave his "free lecture," after which those interested could sign up for a course which would cost them money to take. According to his own account he had that first audience falling out of their seats because of their laughing at his humor, and then standing up applauding for his matter. No one signed up for the course, however. He finally concluded that he had given them too much matter in that one talk. Yet he was convinced that he had found his work. It would be lecturing on psychology to help people solve their problems.

Off to Berkeley he went to obtain his doctorate. When telling me of that experience he said: "Joe, any one of our Scholastics, after their course in fundamental psychology as taught in our Philosophates, could teach those profs out in Berkeley. But I had to go through the course to get that bit of parchment which allows me to call myself 'Doctor.'" Before World War II he spent much time in Europe — at Oxford in England, then over to France, Spain, and Italy — studying Catholic Action and its various developments. When he returned to the United States he began lecturing in California, then slowly crossed the country, giving his courses in the various big cities: Chicago, St. Louis, Cleveland, Washington, Philadelphia, and New York, where he packed Carnegie Hall.

From that triumph he came down to Gethsemani to see me. For some time he didn't, but it was Christmas week. With four major feasts we had something of a "vacation." In the middle of it, Dom James sent for me and asked what I thought of having Dr. de Quevedo talk to the community. What did I know about the doctor? Nothing. But I said it would not hurt. So into the chapter room went the community and this handsome man. What a sensation he produced! His announcements for his lectures listed him as humorist and psychologist. He had the community in an uproar of laughter and then suddenly silent as he made his application to everyday living. I saw immediately why he was so highly endorsed by Catholic universities, highly representative Catholic lay organizations, and commended by Clergy locally and nationally. The man was Catholic to the core, even as he was truly one of the outstanding personalities on America's public platforms.

After that first lecture I was allowed to visit with him. I was amused to watch the psychologist looking me over. Of course, as an amateur psychiatrist, I was doing the same to him. Very soon we both were satisfied with our respective appraisals. So, flippantly, I said: "What a fake you are, Quevedo. What a phony."

"Why do you compliment so?" he asked.

"Giving nothing but the Spiritual Exercises of St. Ignatius wrapped up in all the supposedly attractive wrappings of that jargon from the behavioral sciences, and presenting it as psychology for living."

His head went back as he roared laughing. "Touché. You caught me. You are right. But, tell me, Joe, what else is there to compare with them?" Then we got down to the facts of his life. He told me his long, fascinating story, and concluded: "I'd rather be a laybrother here, washing the kitchen floors, than the celebrated lecturer who filled Carnegie Hall. As I looked down from my hotel window, and saw my name in lights on Broadway, the heart of the world, the thought struck me: *Quid hoc ad aeternitatem?* And *vanitas vanitatem.* I tell you, Joe, you've got it made."

He lectured every night that week to the assembled community, and so impressed them that many went to the abbot to ask if we could not have Dr. de Quevedo give us our annual retreat.

Here I am, thirty years later, seeing and hearing him tell how he handled his deep depression by saying to himself: "Albert, let's go and plow." I suppose because we monks do so much farming, he chose that illustration. I hear him starting out in the early morning amidst the rising mists, harnessing his horses, and driving them to the field. I

257

follow him down furrow after furrow, hear him lament some lost love which was recalled to him by a falling leaf, see the steam rise from his laboring horses, listen to his thoughts about life as he goes on and on through the day. Then as he turns the last furrow, I look back with him over what he has accomplished: a field fully plowed and himself euphoric over his triumph. In psychiatry we would call it "substitution" and "occupational therapy." He simply kept telling himself: "Albert, let's go and plow." He was an artist, an actor, a teacher, and a therapist — all in one.

Things began to hum around Gethsemani as Dom James fell into the footsteps of Dom Frederic. The first thing I noticed was a change in the farm policy. No longer would we raise our own wheat. I used to thrill to the fact that everything necessary for Mass was off our own grounds. The host came from our own wheat, and had been baked right here at home; the wine, if we can call it that, was from our own grapes; the water from our cistern or lake. Now we turn our fields into alfalfa, our herd into a prize herd of Holstein-Friesan. It took years to do the latter, but we did it. For two years in succession our herd won the plaque given to the best herd in the U.S.A. by the Holstein-Friesan people. Our bull was named grand champion, and we had a case in our milking parlor literally loaded with cups, trophies, and ribbons. Much credit for this must be given to Brother Clement Dorsey, whom I rightly named a Connecticut Yankee. He had been raised in Connecticut, and had all the best traits of a Yankee. He knew cows, and knew how to build a herd. We had one of the best bloodlines in the country.

Then came the building program. A horse barn went up. A carriage shed was converted into a novitiate for the laybrother novices. A new guest wing, housing over eighty men, was built. A modern pig barn, with farrowing house that was as aseptic as a surgical suite, came into being. But these were only the beginning. Before he left office in 1968,

Dom James had refurbished the entire monastery. We left up the shell, on the original foundation, but the interior is completely new, all concrete and steel, absolutely fireproof. This stupendous accomplishment astounds one when it is recalled that when Dom James took office, Gethsemani was totally broke. No wonder Mike Barry, editor-owner of the *Irish-American* of Louisville, came to me one day in St. Joseph Infirmary and said in his own cryptic style: "Your abbot is a graduate of Harvard business school, and he shows it."

I was telling you about characters who had met me, so I go on now to relate a surprise. A note from the abbot, through his secretary, told me that I was to go up and visit with Sir Arnold Lunn, who was just completing a world tour and had come to Gethsemani, and asked for me. He was a delight. He had his eyes wide open during his world tour, and I found him very pessimistic about the immediate future. In fact, he was willing to wager we would have a third world war before Christmas of 1950.

What did I, cloistered as I had been, know about world conditions? I detected a real sadness as he said: "Think of it, Father: Here is America assuming the position Rome once had, the position England had only lately, and she is without a real leader." Then he suddenly asked: "What do you think of your President Truman?" What a question for a monk who hardly knew that Franklin D. Roosevelt was dead! I suppose I said something to the effect that I knew little about him. Sir Arnold summed up his estimate by saying: "He's a fine little haberdasher."

The one thing that gave him hope for our country was the attraction to the contemplative life was exerting on our youth. He could not escape that, for we were overcrowded at the time of his visit, even after making three foundations, with a fourth in the immediate offing. The monastery in New England and the one in Iowa were emulating us. They, too, had made foundations.

At about this time I had developed a thesis about Babylon and Nineveh, saying that the U.S.A. had a choice: to listen, as did the Ninevites, do penance, be converted, and win God's blessing, or be as foolish as had been the Babylonians. I gave it to Sir Arnold. He liked the idea, and it gave us some common ground on which to exchange ideas.

Not everyone who asked for Father Raymond was allowed to see him. I remember an Archbishop de Susa, who came from Nagpur, India to see me. His request was denied, but he was allowed to address the assembled community. I was in the chapter room early that evening. So was the archbishop. Before the abbot arrived, the prelate walked over to my place and asked if I were Father Raymond. I nodded. He shook my hand and said: "It is easier to get an audience with the pope than it is to see you."

So you can imagine my surprise one rainy Saturday morning when the guest master came to my office down in the basement of the monastery to tell me there was a Mr. A. Lewis Oswald awaiting me in the foyer. I took it for granted that the guest master had consulted the abbot before summoning me, so I went up to meet this man.

Perhaps the best summary I can give now is taken from a letter I wrote my brother after the meeting.

††

I met a Mr. A. Lewis Oswald, attorney-at-law, from Atchinson, Kansas. A handsome fellow of about five feet, ten. Weighing perhaps 185. Flawless complexion, strong, square jaw, straight, thin nose, firm mouth, facile tongue. He won me immediately with his striking sincerity and total he-manliness. Graduate of Kansas, post-grad from U. of Michigan; past Grand Master of the Masons, Mayor of his city when 35, President of the State Bar Association, etc., etc., etc. A truly successful man. Father of three grown children, two boys and a girl, the latter just recently married; all three Phi Beta Kappas.

Well, he came down from Columbus, Ohio, where he had some business, in the hope of seeing the author of *Burnt Out Incense*. He wanted to talk to me, tell me some of his experiences, in the hope that they might fire me to write more, and plead for more tolerance in religion. You would have liked him. I took him to the "rat-hole" (as I called my work room), so we could have more privacy. He told me how his first wife had contracted TB after the birth of their third child, how she bore it for twenty years, then died of cancer of the intestines. When she breathed her last, the sisters and chaplain said: "Well, she is proof that not all the saints are in the Catholic Church."

A. Lewis, himself, is a Presbyterian, but only last week, according to Lewis, Monsignor Ryan, pastor of the parish out there, accosted him and asked: "Lewis, what is this I hear about you?"

"I don't know, Father," said Lewis. "I've known him so long I can't call him Monsignor. But whatever you've heard, it is most likely true. What is it this time: arson, robbery, or rape?"

"Worse than that, Lewis."

"Hmmm. Must be pretty serious."

" 'Tis. I hear that you hear more confessions of my young men and women than I do."

You can see the guy was orientating me on his Catholic connections and leanings. Funniest thing in the world is that the book that won him first to the Catholic angle was none other than *The World, The Flesh, and Father Smith*. He has read it a hundred times, he says; for he can get more relaxation and enjoyment out of the humanness of Father Smith than out of anything under the sun. From that book he awoke to the fact that priests are human, and a little more than human.

Fortunately I had read the same book years ago, and remembered something of the story. So the exchange was lively. Then he came to *Burnt Out Incense*. That, he said, showed him something deeper; not only the human, but also the divine. He has read it at least ten times.

Well, time flew, and before I knew it, it was time for Mass. I then learned that his wife (second) was sitting out in the car, and that the guest master had persuaded him to stay for dinner. I said: "Let's take the wife into Mass. After it, I will sit with her in the car, while you eat." We did that. I learned that the wife is a Baptist, had never been to Mass before, Kentucky girl, graduate from U. of Kentucky, post-grad from Vanderbilt; dean of women in some southern university whose name escapes me. Very soon we were chatting animatedly. Darned if she doesn't bring up *The World, The Flesh, and Father Smith*, without knowing all that A. Lewis had told me. I found her an even more penetrating reader than her lawyer-husband. She has taught history for years, and through it, had come to the same conclusion that A. Lewis had when he became grand master of his Masonic Lodge; namely, that all their rites had come from the Holy Roman Catholic Church. Suddenly she said to me: "I know that Lewis is struggling with the idea of becoming a Catholic. As soon as he does, I will take instructions."

A. Lewis did come back — more than once. We discussed religion unendingly. He told me how, when he was taken off a train with a bleeding ulcer at Kansas City, the nurse bent over him and asked if he were a Catholic.

"More than half," was Lewis' reply.

"Why not all the way?" I asked.

He claimed that, since he was a master, and a past grand master of the Masons, he had entrée where no Catholic priest could ever go. Since he told the Catholic truths, he was doing more and better work for God than he could do were he a Catholic. I couldn't deny the part about the entrée, but I did say that someone in his audience could ask him: "If you are so convinced of the truth of the Catholic Church, why don't you join?"

262

He was unmovable. He told me that he had planned to see me or Fulton Sheen about the matter. I told him since he had seen me, he could now go to Fulton. When he got back home he sent a telegram to the monsignor asking for an appointment, and all but demanding an immediate answer by wire. Fulton did not telegraph. He wrote a letter saying that since both of them were very busy men, it would be wise if he would write out his difficulties, whether they be historical, dogmatic, or moral. Lewie replied in a three-page night letter to the monsignor, stating that he had no difficulties, but that he was more useful to the Church doing what he was doing. Then he gave the same reasons as he had given me about entrée, etc. When the monsignor wrote back and said exactly what I had said about someone in his audience. Lewie came back to Gethsemani to ask if Fulton and I were in cahoots. I assured him I had had no contact with the monsignor whatsoever about him and his case. It was not long after that that A. Lewis Oswald came into the Church.

To show you what a fighter Lewie was, I'll conclude this chapter with just one episode. It was law that all the government had to do was put an item in the newspaper telling where they were planning to put a highway. Residents on that terrain were then to file their claims. Out in his part of the world lived an illiterate son of a slave from Bardstown. When Lewie heard the government was taking his land, his fighting instincts took over. With no hope whatsoever for recompense, Lewie took that case to court. He lost in the lower courts, and appealed to the higher. He went to the State Supreme Court, and lost again. But that did not stop him. He carried the case to the United States Supreme Court — and won! He was very proud of the fact that he had changed the law of the land.

After describing the Oswald affair, I told him about some other visitors I had had, and then added: "So you see why I feel like signing myself 'Gethsemani Reception Committee,' or 'Public Relations Man.' " I am not too fond of it all. It eats into my time so, and it tires me physically and mentally (except in such an unexpected affair such as the morning with A. Lewis Oswald). I can but ask God to use me as His instrument, accept it as done to Him in them, and to them for Him. Frequently, visitors leave me saddened for both the mortals and the Immortal. However, I read a poem that solaces me: Jessica Powers' 'The Cedar.' It explained how she looked out one day and saw a cedar bending under a weight of snow, and reflected that from all eternity God, the Omniscient, saw this tree with its 'burden of beauty and its burden of cold.' So, she concluded, 'Whether the wood breaks or the branches hold must be His devising.' Then she turned to another tree, one deep in her intellect, similarly burdened, and rejoiced in the fact that God had seen this tree, too, from all eternity; that He knew 'what each tree, each twig could bear; for He counted each snowflake as it fell.'

"I believe He has a purpose in it all, and I pray that I fulfill it." That was my personal conviction. To some friends I might say: "It's hell to be famous." But, in my heart, after so many cases like A. Lewis Oswald, I saw that such constant interruptions of my cloister and my silence, could be heavenly, too.

Now that I've told you what cancer begat, I must add what John Greene Hanning, or the man who got even with God, begat.

12

Brother Joachim Begets Many

†

As I've already told you, my mail was very limited under Dom Frederic. Hence, I knew little of the impact *The Man Who Got Even with God* had had on the general public. True, my brother Fr. Jack would write telling me "it is still at the top of the best-sellers list." That meant little to me at the time, for I hardly knew what a best-sellers list was. It is also true that one of the priests here, in his sermon in chapter, one day said: "Brother Joachim has become a household word in America." Again, that meant very little, for I wondered what he knew about the households of America. But, once I got to the hospital, my eyes were opened.

First of all, there was my own community. They were allowed to write to me. Short notes for the most part. I suppose the word cancer seemed to say curtains, so practically everyone in the community did send a note. When over eighty percent of the men who had entered since 1940 confessed that they had been attracted to Gethsemani by the book, I could only sit back and say: "Strange, indeed, are your ways, O God!" The idea of getting even had been planted in my mind by Dom Frederic's opening words about Brother Joachim. It then meshed with St. Ignatius' thrust in his Spiritual Exercises. Ignatius urged all to be an *insignis* in the army of Christ. An *insignis* is one who stands out in the service, one who goes beyond the call of duty, and gives his all. No red-blooded individual could refuse to strive to become *insignis*, and that came down to following Christ most closely — in other words, emulating their Leader and Lord. That, in its turn, could be expressed in our readily recognized phrase as "getting even."

I saw nothing original in the idea, save, possibly in the popular phraseology. Yet, it had so caught fire with these many youngsters that they hied themselves to the monastery to strive to get even with God. I marvel at the way God could take what I considered ordinary and make such an extraordinary thing out of it.

Then came the nuns. They came in such numbers that I had to take a little black book and schedule the appointments. The black book became a joke around the hospital, as I suppose I did, too. One Sunday afternoon, after a rather huge delegation of Ursuline nuns left the room, there stood in the doorway a little woman whose hair, eyes, and lips spoke to me of dynamite. She did not enter, just placed her hands on her hips, and while a tiny smile did show around her mouth, the eyes, dancing though they were, puzzled me. Were they laughing or blazing? "I'm at the pitchfork stage," was all she said.

"Come in. Come in," I said. But she did not move.

Again she stated: "I'm at the pitchfork stage."

What in the world could that mean? I wondered. I knew what a pitchfork was, but a pitchfork stage? I insisted, "Come in."

She did take a step or two into the room at that, then, as the smile widened a bit, but the same puzzling light stayed in those eyes, she, for the third time said, "I'm at the pitchfork stage." Before sitting down she added: "I've been standing out in that corridor for three-quarters of an hour."

"Not really," I broke in.

"Yes, really. And I have to catch a bus for Owensboro

shortly. I'm John Greene Hanning's niece. My name is Lucy. And I want you to know those nuns put me at the 'pitchfork stage.'"

Only then did it dawn on me that she was referring to the man who got even with God, and the time he stood at the gate of the monastery with a pitchfork in his hand, awaiting the return of some brother with whom he was going to get even. The realization that I was talking to a kin of his startled me. As I looked at this wiry, little woman, with the red hair and the eyes that flashed, I could not escape the conclusion that heredity is a fact. I was looking at a chip off the old block.

Since I have always insisted that there are no accidents with God, and that what we call coincidence would more correctly be labelled Divine Providence, I must add here a note I just received, through my abbot, from John Greene Hanning's grandniece, one Nancy McDevitt Heath. It tells how her son David suffered a head injury in August, 1976, and lapsed into a coma, caused by what the doctors called a brain-stem injury. His mother remembered what her great-uncle Jack had effected in the case of her uncle Lester one afternoon in the rain, so she turned to him regarding her own son. She is convinced that her great-uncle answered when her son came out of the coma.

Similar reports have come in down the years since *The Man Who Got Even with God* was published. But that is not the begetting I had in mind when I began this chapter.

I was accounting for my silence in early 1950 to Fr. Jack. After listing four or five reasons, any one of which would satisfy the most demanding, I confessed: But the real reason is "heart trouble." Here are the facts: A genius in Gregorian Chant came here from Paris (he is a graduate from the Schola Cantorum de Paris) to aid us in the restoration of our original Cistercian plain song, and to improve our own choir. I became interested in him and his job. Marvelous teacher and indefatigable worker. Good thing, for

267

Dom James has him working from morn to night — literally! We have chant after Prime for all; after Terce for the schola; after dinner for all; in the evening for cantors and schola; in the evening for all. Well, when I learn he has a wife and ten or twelve kids in France and that he is as poor as the proverbial church mouse, I get more interested. So I have a brainstorm. I approach Dom James and speak to him about making contacts for Dr. Lefevre — that's the man's name. I told my good abbot that if he would write the various motherhouses in our area, they would jump at the opportunity, especially if he signed the letters. For some reason or other, he smiles and says: "You may write, if you want, Raymond." The response is immediate and enthusiastic. I tell Dom James. He says: "Go up and tell the professor. He's depressed just because of no contacts."

I go up. I find a madman pacing the floor of the bishop's room, ready to commit mayhem, murder, or suicide. The fellow was really raging. What revelations I receive. "Contacts" was part of the contract that brought him here. I resolve that that contract will be fulfilled. But the first thing I see is that it is necessary to get "Frenchy," as I now familiarly and flippantly called him, out of the house. He has been enclosed for six solid weeks, and, as I said above, working his head off morning, noon, and night. I tell him so. He is still raging, but rational enough to yell: "Where can I go? I know no one here." Then your ever-quiet, little brother says: "But I do," he did stop pacing and really looked at me for the first time.

I write the Henrys, and ask if they could not take him in for a weekend. What a response! They have been out here four times since; have taken "Mr. Music," as Doctor Joe calls him, into their home for two weekends; obtained a write-up for him in the *Courier Journal*; have made many contacts for him already; have him at this moment, and have been my right hand and my left as I plan a lecture-concert for Dr. Lefevre in Louisville around Derby time.

To make an end to what could evolve into an endless story, Jack, I'll simply say I have lined up almost twenty lectures for the guy and am getting anywhere from $75 to $125 for each appearance. Am sending him on a short western swing next Sunday: Cincinnati, South Bend, Chicago, Milwaukee, Dubuque, St. Louis, then back to Louisville. I've had him at Nazareth and Loretto already. Tonight he is at University of Louisville's Gardencourt, lecturing for the Alliance Francais in French. Tomorrow night he will be at the same university's school of music, lecturing on "The Place of Gregorian Chant in the History of Music." On May 4th, he'll climax that western swing with a lecture at the same university, telling the humanities department all about "The Culture of the Middle Ages" — and exemplifying it by music.

The original couple of hundred I had hoped to get for him will most likely be ten times that before the middle of next month. I've gotten him a contact with the Gregorian Institute of America — with a Summer School job in the offing, before he returns to France.

It's been work, time-absorbing work, but most refreshing. Pray I keep my intention pure enough to hear: I was a stranger, and you took me in; hungry, naked, cold — in prison, etc. Unquestionably *The Man Who Got Even with God* — one Brother Mary Joachim — is not only well-known, but well-liked from Kentucky to the Rockies and back again. This all began less than a month ago. I have little more than a month to go. It has all been done at breakneck speed. Do pray for that lecture-concert, which is to climax his stay. Then those ten or twelve 'Images of God' and members of Christ's Body will receive something worthwhile from their daddy's sojourn to Gethsemani. Now do you forgive my silence?

A month later I was again writing Fr. Jack: ". . . Do you see why I am so grateful to God? I began with the hope of making a few hundred for this man and his family. I'm

269

ending by making over a few thousand. Then the contacts: Notre Dame wants him for this summer. Their school runs for eight weeks. The doctor offered them eight days of intensive work. It is still hanging. . . . I told him to take it for the prestige and contacts. St. Mary's-of-the-Woods signed him for next year. Pius X School at Manhattanville has written. Dr. Bennett of the Gregorian Institute of America is after him. So, thank God and His Mother for me and with me."

My dear "Frenchy" had not left Gethsemani for any summer work, when Fr. George Donnelly came to my "rat-hole" unannounced. Fr. George had given me quite a story, which appeared under the title *God Goes to Murderer's Row*. Here he was now, looking for something close to the completed manuscript, and I had been working for the Music Man.

Briefly, Tom Penney was mixed up in the murder of Marion Miley, a nationally known golf star, in Lexington, Kentucky, when Tom, with "Skeeter" Baxter, and Bob Anderson, tried to rob the Lexington Country Club. They robbed it all right. They came away with a mere hundred and thirty dollars when they expected ten to fifteen thousand. Bad as that was, it was nothing compared to the fact that in the aftermath of their break-in: two women lay dead, Marion Miley and her mother.

Fr. George stumbled into the affair, but once in, he never left it until Tom Penney, as far as humans can judge, had just about stumbled into heaven. Fr. George had poured out the story the first time he met me in St. Joseph Infirmary. I was intrigued, for it really held a double mystery. With Fr. George's help, I probed the Miley murder mystery quickly and satisfactorily enough, but probing the mystery of Tom Penney was a white horse of a very different color. When Tom was apprehended, just a fortnight after the murders, he brazenly stated that "God was just a three-letter word to him; and as far as any influence in his life, those letters might just as well be x-y-z." Yet, a year and a half later, as this same Tom Penney walked toward the electric chair, he said: "My only peace is in God, and with God . . . until I am with Him, I am miserable. Since death is the only way to God, I am impatient to be on my way." It was not swaggering bravado, either. It was quiet humility, and true understanding of life, self, and God.

To unravel that mystery took much longer and more labor than the unravelling of the first. I urged Fr. George to have some lawyer friend look it over to see if there would be any grounds for libel from any of the individuals' families, relatives, or friends. The lawyers saw no grounds for any action, but suggested we get releases from both the Penneys and the Andersons. We did and the book was published. It was a best-seller. I was busy on Dom Frederic's life when Fr. George returned from a trip to Europe. After giving me his impressions of the various countries over there, he laughed and asked me if I had fifty thousand dollars. Of course I had that paltry sum! George then told me I'd need that amount, and added that he would, too. He then told me that we were being sued for one hundred thousand dollars by none other than the girl, Tom's own wife, who had signed the release for use of all Tom Penney's letters and all other materials we had.

I wasn't frightened, but I was aghast at the brazenness of the move. The release had been witnessed, notarized, and filed! Yet here she was saying that she thought she was releasing those letters for a publication that would be practically private. It was then that I smelled the rodent. Some shyster had noted the success of the book and decided to cash in on its popularity. He did not get rich, I assure you. As far as I was concerned, I would have fought it to the last ditch. The lawyers thought it better to pay Mrs. Penney a paltry sum and thus quash the case. I am glad she got that pittance. But I had earlier resolved to ask my abbot to give her much from the royalties. I sure did not ask him after hearing of her effort through those so-called lawyers.

271

Just about this time, too, I was amused by human nature's reaction to the success of an individual. In an interview, Leon Uris told how some critics will go after a writer who attains a certain amount of popularity. He found they were going after him after the success of his *Trinity*. I believe Leon has something there, for I recall how Tom Merton was attacked after his phenomenal success with *Seven Storey Mountain*, *Waters of Siloe*, and *Seeds of Contemplation*. A Benedictine priest called him, among other things, "a young man in too great a hurry." My own turn came after a third best-seller, and it was a Jesuit priest who did the job. Tom was put out by the attack of the Benedictine. I wrote a note telling him it would be good publicity for his books, and to forget the guy's remarks. I know I only laughed, after at first smarting, over the good Jesuit's animadversions toward my endeavors.

But it was not only the critics who aired their views. Tom let me know that people were saying that he "would never stay in the monastery," that he "was already out of the Trappists," that he was "seen in New York at the Cotton Club." I laughed when I saw that he seemed to feel offended. I made signs to him about St. Paul. He did not comprehend, so I got permission to speak with him. I told him how St. Paul had saved my heart, my head, my gastrointestinal tract and all my nerves by five words. The ever-alert eyes became more alert. I spoke slowly as I quoted Paul's line: *Deus est qui judicat me* — It is God who judges me. I then briefly insisted that that short sentence enabled me to sail along with never a worry about what anyone thought of me and my doings. Of course, Tom and I had very different backgrounds, and very different mental and spiritual trainings. He thought me both callous and careless. I told him he was allowing his artistic nature to assert itself too much; that he was over-concerned about something that was bound to happen, and bound to pass. He still thought something ought to be done. So did I. I thought we ought to laugh our heads off. When he said something to the effect that I could take that attitude because I had not been talked about as he had been, it was then that I did manage to get Tom to laugh, for I told him about an experience of my younger brother, Fr. Eddie.

Ed, as usual, had made his annual visit in early July. On his way home he stopped off at the novitiate of his province. Few of the youngsters knew Fr. Ed, for he had been on the road, giving parish missions almost all his life, and seldom did he preach in Massachusetts. Ed can talk, but Ed can also listen. This evening he was listening as his fellow oblates chatted in their recreation room. Towards the end of the evening he was startled to hear one of the younger men say that Raymond had left Gethsemani; that he himself was not surprised; that it was practically inevitable. Further, Raymond had been seen in New England recently, in New Hampshire, at some night club. Eddie grew more interested as the speaker went on, but never interrupted him during his long story. When recreation ended Eddie did sidle alongside the man and asked what night, what time, what club. He got all three, then very quietly said: "I'll have to tell my brother he has strange powers." The young Oblate looked at Ed and said: "Your brother?" Then Ed really enjoyed himself as he said: "Yes, my brother. You see, I was visiting my brother the very day and hour you say he was seen in New Hampshire. I'll have to tell Joe he must have the power of bilocation." When the youngster lifted a puzzled query in the one word: "Joe?" Eddie chuckled and told him that Joe was Raymond, and Raymond was Fr. Ed's blood brother, and that Fr. Eddie had been with Joe at Gethsemani the entire day and the entire Trappist evening of the night this youngster said he was seen in a New Hampshire night club.

We laughed over that amusing happening, but Tom still wrote his "Open Letter to the Public." I kept on laughing. When a nun wrote to me from Canada and begged me to put her mind at ease by assuring her that I had appeared at her bedside after she had undergone major surgery, and again reaffirming my conviction that she would live, I stopped laughing and wrote to her. I told her bilocation had always puzzled me, for, as a philosopher I knew that, while Descartes may have gotten "de carte before de horse," as Fr. Len Feeney had so wittily put it, there was truth in the person being conscious of himself. Further, I held with Boethius, that "incommunicability" is the very essence of personhood. Hence, I always wondered *where* the person was who enjoyed bilocation. Could he possibly be simultaneously conscious of being in two places at once? Then I very strenuously informed her that I had no consciousness whatsoever of ever having visited her before, during, or after her surgery. I was sorry to disillusion her, but I was finding it difficult enough to carry on my therapeutic works in one place at a time.

After telling my brother how I had seen Frenchy off to Washington, Scranton, New York, Montreal, and then France, I suddenly asked: "Did I tell you about Madame Zarina, the internationally famed ballerina? Well, I entertained her here at Gethsemani just last week. Fr. Joe McPherson told me, in his inimitable style, that the ballerina was to visit the monastery. I was relieved when I read that she was in Louisville doing Paul Claudel's *Joan of Arc*. Somehow or other I felt that was better than doing a ballet. Well, to make a long story interesting, Dom James called me the day she was to arrive and asked me to meet her, entertain her, and show her all I could of the monastery. Then the whole scenario was unrolled before me.

"Frenchy, I believe I told you, had us cut a record of our Gregorian chanting. That was done by and for the Columbia Records. Dom James had to go to New York to finalize the matter. While there he met the vice-president of the company, who told him that his wife, the famous Madame Zarina, would be playing Louisville shortly and had expressed an ardent wish to visit Gethsemani. What could James do? He invited her.

"Mother Betty was contacted. She would be delighted, as usual, to drive the Madame out. They arrived for None. Mother Betty had Pat Taffel, daughter of the owner of one of the big electric companies in Louisville, a Manhattan-ville grad, along with a Denis Murphy, daughter of the leading architect in these parts, with her, as company for the Madame. James and I went out after None. James stayed for only about fifteen minutes, then left me with that bevy! Mother Betty was at her best, and, as you know, that is plenty good! The Taffel miss has plenty on the ball. Denis was no slouch, either. But the Madame . . . artiste from flawless coiffeur to dainty toe-tops. Born in Berlin of a Scandinavian mother and a German father, she combines the blonde, blue-eyed German type with the flair of a Greta Garbo. And could she *think!* She believed in God with a very vital belief, but I think that is as far as her religion and religious practice goes. Her knowledge of art, drama, painting, music, and the dance came out with a simplicity and a spontaneity found, I believe, only in the European educated class. This mad monk had a delightful afternoon! Just to listen to her talk was entertainment. Music was in her every tone; enunciation, perfect and effortless; localization of voice something to be admired and envied; and when she got a bit excited, to watch those hands and arms go out in spontaneous gesture was a lesson in poetry in motion, rhythm, and balance. You would have loved it all. She had a TV appearance to make that evening, else I'd still be out there watching and listening."

It was not too long after that happening that I was calling Mother Betty for another favor. Eddie Doherty, the star reporter of the United States, and a feature writer for the very popular, but then defunct magazine *Liberty*, had come to Gethsemani to see me about writing something on Brother Joachim. What a character Eddie was, and what a life-story he had. He gave it to me quickly one Sunday morning. I've read it since in his *Tumbleweed* and again in his *Gall and Honey.* He touched the mountain peaks that Sunday morning, and I was mesmerized! Eddie was my kind of a man — not because he had been married three times, and rebelled against God, seen the depths of human anguish personally, then the heights in human love, but because he was never conquered, never even subdued. Eddie had the Irish fight, and despite his angry rebellion, Eddie had the Irish faith.

At the moment we were talking Eddie was a married man, with the vows of a religious, and told me how a Melkite priest, impressed one day by Eddie's genuine piety and obvious deep knowledge of the things of God, had said: "If I were a bishop, I'd ordain you tomorrow." Eddie was in his late seventies when telling me all this. He was married to Baroness Catherine de Hueck, a Russian emigré and refugee from the revolution against the czar. With her, Eddie founded Madonna House in Combermere, Canada, and had quite a pious association working in many places on our ever-whirling globe. It was a whirlwind of a life for this little Irish-American kid from the streets of Chicago. Eddie did get ordained in the Melkite Rite, did offer the Sacrifice of Christ for a few years before he went to live with Christ forever.

Looking at the smiling face of Eddie Doherty, thinking of the many places he had taken me and the many persons he had shown me in this hurried recounting of his life, thinking of the veritable kaleidoscope of people God had thrown before me since my surgery — the young, the old, the sick, the dying, the brilliant, the dull, the married, the single, the religious, the laity, the keenly God-conscious, the agnostic and almost atheistic — I finally grasped Gerard Manley Hopkins' lines: "Christ — Christ plays in ten thousand places/Lovely in limbs, and lovely in eyes not His/To the Father through the features of men's faces." That was it! Christ was coming to me in varied garbs, in different forms, from diverse strata, but always the same Christ.

When I asked Eddie where he would be going next, he told me he was on his way to New Orleans to gather material for a book which he felt he would title, "A Nun With A Gun." I laughed at the title and accused him of going back to his days in Chicago and the Al Capones. Then I asked him how he was going to get to Louisville. "That," he said, "is something I don't know." It was then that I called Mother Betty Henry and asked her if she'd like to meet Eddie Doherty. She said she'd be delighted. So early that same Sunday afternoon I met Mother Betty at the gate house before I brought Eddie Doherty down from his room in our hotel. Mother had her youngest daughter, Mary White, with her and a tall, slim, dark-haired, deeply tanned, brown-eyed girl whom she introduced as Mary White's very dear friend, Miss Dian Fossey.

I looked Dian Fossey over from head to foot, and saw a very beautiful girl. But I noticed a tiny bit of nervousness about her. When Mother got the opportunity, she whispered to me: "Dian is not one of ours. So don't say anything about religion." Her remark had me turning to this good-looking girl and saying: "I hear you are a Protestant." I could see that I had startled her. She very hesitantly and very softly replied: "Ye-Yes, I guess I am." When I then asked, "What are you protesting?" she was even more hesitant, and I fear just a bit frightened. When she finally managed to say "Nothing," I told her she was not a Protestant, for she had nothing to protest.

That was our first meeting, but far from our last. During my next check-up in the hospital, Mary White came in with her friend, Dian. As they were leaving Dian lingered behind a step or two to ask if she could see me alone some time. "Of course!" was the immediate reply.

The very next afternoon Dian was alone in my room. Some time later she told me how she had gone home, stood before a mirror, and practiced saying, "Father." Before she went to work that very morning she did the same thing. For never in her life had she spoken to a Catholic priest, hence had never addressed anyone as "Father." With that before you, you can imagine some of the hurdles I had to clear before I had anything like an open track.

She told me she was seeking, but that she had not been much of a church-goer. She had been "raised amidst powder, paint and perfume — by baby-sitters"; for her mother was a model. She had divorced when Dian was quite young. Hence, Dian had not seen her father in years. Her mother remarried, but Dian retained her father's name of Fossey. Originally she had planned on being a veterinarian. In her sophomore year one of the tests was to deliver a litter of piglets. She did that O.K., but the sow rolled over on her litter and killed one or two. Because of that, the professor refused Dian a passing grade. That, she thought, was an injustice, and next year she obtained a degree at Berkeley as physical therapist. After a discussion with her mother, Dian selected Louisville as her theater for operation. Kosair Crippled Childrens Hospital attracted her, and she applied for a position. She was astounded to find that Kosair did not have a real physical therapy department, so she set one up. By the end of the year her new department was rated first in the city, and second in the state.

The hesitancy and nervousness noticed in the first two meetings soon disappeared and she talked quite freely, but with culture, refinement, and lady-likeness. She got down to the real reason for her visit. How did I prove that God exists? If He is such a good God, how are the crippled children at Kosair explained? What can one know about the afterlife? I very soon realized I was dealing with a very sharp mind.

The next day she informed me that after leaving me the previous afternoon, she had gone directly to a Protestant doctor of divinity. She gave me his name, and I recognized it as that of the leading preacher in the city. She proposed the same questions she had given to me. When he did not answer as quickly, or as convincingly, as I had, Dian let him know it. So she was back to ask more questions, and finally to say she would like to take instructions.

Well, the young lady took her instructions, and was baptized, and later confirmed. In that Sacrament she took Mother Betty's St. Augustine's and my own St. Raymond's names for her Confirmation middle name, thus gaining them as her protectors and patrons. I had noticed that the Henrys had all but adopted Miss Fossey, and, to me at least, it was evident that Dian was assimilating much of the mannerisms and developing the character of Mother Betty, whom I always considered the perfect Southern lady.

While Dian took on much of Mother Betty, there was one area wherein they differed drastically. Dian loved animals, especially any animal that seemed to be hurting or looked lost. I suppose it was this affection for animals that had her first seeking her degree in veterinary medicine. While her professional work at present was with the suffering rational animal at Kosair Crippled Childrens Hospital, her para-professional life seemed bound up with the non-rational animal. If she spotted a stray, or a wounded dog, cat, or bird, her car would stop immediately, and she would be out after the animal. It came to such a state that Mother Betty finally, and very firmly, told Dian that she would no longer drive with her. It was delivered with a smile and even with a kind of accolade for her tenderness toward the dumb animal, but it did not change Dian.

It was an education in God's ways to watch the development of this girl. Because of her closeness to the Henrys, she was brought very close to me. I saw how exact Thomas Aquinas was when he said that grace builds on nature. Dian had much before she came into the Catholic Church. She received much more from that Church, and it all became manifest in what must be called character, in that arresting sense which bespeaks integrity, fidelity, loyalty, dependability, sincerity, and limpid honesty. It *is* arresting in this world of ours, isn't it?

When I was a boy there was a famous combination in baseball which executed a double play with high frequency and great finesse. It was known as the "Tinker to Evers to Chance" combine. That is what I think of now as I endeavor to account for what God did to this monk through Brother Mary Joachim. The play will be from Henrys to Forresters to Raymond. That middle name is not new to you; I mentioned it earlier. It represents a family in Rhodesia, to which I am closely connected and greatly indebted. I have introduced them to the American reading public in *The Silent Spire Speaks*. But what I had to say about them there has little or nothing to do with what I must tell about them now. Briefly, Franz Forrester, the father of the family, was an Austrian count. Peg Forrester, the mother of the family, was daughter of Michael Hartney, intimate friend and fellow soldier to Eamon de Valera. Peg's mother is the only Irish woman buried in the original I.R.A. cemetery. Peg and Franz had three sons: Franz Michael, Franz Alexus, and Franz Robert.

Young Betty, or as I called her, "Little Joe" had gone to Europe after her graduation from Manhattanville. Mary White was not to be outdone. She elected a safari in Africa as her graduation present. Since she was human, I wanted her to see more than irrational animals, so I suggested that after she had her fill of lions, elephants, tigers in Kenya, she go to Rhodesia and visit my friends, the Forresters. She did, and came back agog, not about the game preserves, but about one "Pookie," the youngest of the three Forrester boys. The following year Pookie came to America and, of course, to my family, the Henrys. Mary White took him out to meet her friend, Dian. Pookie liked Mary White, but he obviously liked Dian more!

The following year Miss Fossey decided to go on a

safari. Before she set out I received a letter from Alexie, the middle boy of the Forrester family. In it he told how his younger brother was quite excited about some American girl coming to Africa. Then he added: "All I want to know is: Can she plow. I am over a month behind in preparing a huge plantation for the season." Dian went over, and while in Kenya, she met Dr. Louis Leakey, then went down to Rhodesia and the Forresters. After a few days with Peg and Franz in their home outside Salisbury, Peg suggested they go see Lexie. They found Alexie plowing. Peg said the two just stood and looked at one another. Finally Dian broke the silence saying, "I can plow."

"There's the machine," said Alexie.

"Show me the shifts," Dian responded. A little over a year later Alexie told me that "that girl plowed that entire field. The only trouble was that as she finished the last furrow, she hit a rock, and broke the plow. Little did I care. The field was ready for discing, and I had seen a *real* woman!"

Alexie was over here to go to Notre Dame and on that first night he told me he was going to accomplish two things while in the United States: get his degree from Notre Dame and marry Dian Fossey. I had no objection to either objective, but I did tell him that he would have to be some man to win my "British Bulldog."

By the end of his freshman year he must have proven himself some man, for they became engaged. A handsomer couple would be hard to find. Both stood at about six feet, two inches; each was endowed by God with exceptionally good looks; each was magnificently built. However, true love never runs smoothly. Against my advice, they set the date for the wedding for August at the end of his sophomore year. But just before Easter of that year Alexie had second thoughts and decided to postpone the wedding until after his graduation. I do not know exactly how Dian took that, but I do know that Dr. Louis Leakey showed up in

Louisville just about the time Dian got the news of the postponement. He sent for her, and asked her to come to Africa to study gorillas! After some reflection she agreed to go! I told her she was running away, which she denied, and she signed a contract for three years. Leakey is elated. Alexie is distressed. I am appalled. She went first to the Congo. Jane Goodall and Alan Root helped her set up camp just below Mt. Mikeno, and left her there with three Congolese. She said her Swahili was not proficient enough for any socializing, so from one of her earliest letters I saw that she was very lonely. She wrote: "Greetings from the heights of mist, moss and malaria. How's that for a start? Had to write tonight, for today we found a gorilla skeleton. That 'we' refers to Sanwekwe and myself. After digging up half the mountain, we came home with some vital parts missing, but anyway, tonight I stayed in my half of the hut longer than usual cleaning the bones and trying to put them together. Sanwekwe and the two others were in their half of the hut, sitting around their fire, when Sanwekwe started to sing. Would you believe it: He knows all, well, some of the same chants I've heard for lo these many years at Gethsemani. In fact, he knows practically all of them, except the *Salve Regina*, and he knows them in Latin! I just dropped the vertebrae I was working on, and just sat there crying. It was so beautiful. I just closed my eyes and I was back at Gethsemani. I found out later that he learned them all at a Mission in the Congo."

Three weeks later I received this from the "gorilla girl" as I had come to call her. "This is going to be a 'me-letter' just to tell you about the past week, and also because it is a beautiful Sunday afternoon which I want to share with you. This morning Sanwekwe and I decided to take the day off. We have had only one since I've been up here. It was Sunday, further we had spent yesterday climbing for a total of eight hours. We practically climbed to the top of Mikeno, almost 13,000 feet — only to be charged by the adult silverback, male gorilla, so we saw the group for only about twenty-five minutes, after all that climbing. This morning Sanwekwe and I celebrated Mass as well as we could. I know you won't agree, but up on this mountain the absence of the Sacramental Presence lends just that much more meaning to the celebration, gives some keener realization of His Presence. Does that make any sense at all?"

Of course I sat back after that and tried to picture that "Mass" — an American lady-scientist with a lone African man, endeavoring, in their own way, to keep holy the Sabbath Day. He spoke no English, she, only a little Swahili. He, most likely, sang some Latin chant recalled from his boyhood with the Belgian missionaries. She, a convert of only a few years, remembered the rich liturgical celebrations at Gethsemani and the crowded congregations at Sunday Mass in Louisville.

I doubt that she had read Teilhard de Chardin's works. She may have seen his *The Divine Milieu*, for Mrs. Henry had given me a copy, but I felt sure that she had not seen his *Mass Over the Universe*. Yet here she was, in circumstances similar to those which had him doing what she had done, and finally producing that very beautiful and quite poetic book.

She presented me with the age-old problem of what constitutes a violation of the Sabbath. She went on to tell how for two hours, with only a panga, a shovel, and a spoon, she, with her cook-boy and Sanwekwe, had cleared a jungle slope and planted a garden of potatoes, corn, beans, lettuce, tomatoes, parsley, onions, carrots, cabbage and cauliflower. Gardening may not be menial labor but clearing a jungle is that proverbial white horse of a different color. She said the Africans thought it comical when she instructed them on the proper depth of the seeds, and the precise space between them, and concluded, "Of course I don't know whether anything will grow, but for Sanwekwe's sake, I hope something does."

Her next letter told how a herd of elephants came within a few nights after that planting, and trampled the entire garden! "With the entire Congo to frolic in, why did they have to choose my little patch of ground as the one place they would make a freeway? Then, to add insult to injury, those same elephants decided to investigate my tent. I awoke at 1:00 A.M. to the sounds of copious amounts of dung being deposited at my doorstep, belly rumbles, and the motion of my cot and my tent rocking back and forth. At first I thought it was the volcano erupting, and was sincerely sorry I had to go this way. Then I realized I had company in rather large form. Since I didn't relish being buried alive in green canvas and elephant dung, I began to call softly to Sanwekwe. No response from my 'reliable guard.' Then I started to whistle. No response. So, throwing caution to the winds, I began to beat on a pot with the butt of my pistol. That frightened the elephants away, and when I went outside to see what damage had been done to the tent, there stood Sanwekwe huddled in the doorway of the hut. It seems he has one phobia: elephants. He had been standing there all along, too terrified to move."

Before summer had come on, Tshombe and Mobutu were having a bit of a dispute as to just who would run the Congo, as it was then called. That little affair gave Dian, and myself, by proxy, some real experiences. She was taken hostage, and held for three weeks in a Belgian Castle from which she could look out and see a breathtaking view of the volcanoes all around her. At the same time, when she took her eyes off that magnificence, she saw nothing but road blocks, military armed with machine guns and filled not only with "importance" but also with pomle (native beer). She came to have respect only for the "mercs" — the mercenaries — who hired themselves out to either side.

She was extradited at least three times, and forbidden the Congo — why, she never found out. As she claimed, "what could be more innocuous than a lady scientist studying gorilla up on the mountainside?" That brought her over to Rwanda where Dr. Leakey insisted she'd find gorilla. A Madame de Munck, a Belgian lady who had just lost her husband in open-heart surgery in Paris, offered Dian her Shangri-La, which her late husband had just built for her up in the mountains. What a prospect: "Am leaving on a chartered plane tomorrow morning at dawn for Kigali, Rwanda . . . I don't mind telling you I am scared to death. The people who claim to know the area tell me there are no gorilla there but only pygmy head-hunters, poachers, herdsmen, and smugglers. . . . Dr. Leakey convinced the American ambassador here in Nairobi that I was self-reliant enough to do the job. I just wish I had his faith in me! The rest of the embassy staff has forbidden a lone female to go into the area. I just hope I can prove them wrong, find gorilla, and get back to a very rewarding and sane way of life. You'd better pray."

Well, I did, and as the world, at least that part of it which reads *National Geographic* or watches TV, knows, Dian proved them wrong, found her gorilla — and, as far as she is concerned, got back to her rewarding and sane way of life.

Not all in the world would agree that it is either rewarding or sane, but those three years have now stretched to twelve. Dr. Leakey has gone to his reward. Dian is still studying gorilla, and as she once told me, "has the dubious distinction of being the only living human female who has had a living gorilla touch her."

My "kids" as I call them, told me of seeing Dian on TV, and that it was something to see a gorilla take off her wristwatch, look at it, and then hand it back to her. I have not told you about my kids as yet, but I think it was because of them I introduced you to Dian, for she took care of them often. But, no, that was not the prime reason. I wanted you to see God at work again through Joachim, who brought so many different and unusual people into my ambient. Further, I meant to tell you how nature, which Dian always loved, became Nature for her after conversion, and how the universe even, or especially the jungles and mountainsides of Africa, became a "burning bush" for this young lady who always loved animals and who, through a strange set of circumstances met Dr. Leakey — and gorilla!

But she does lead me, quite naturally, into an exposé of my next "vocation," and how I learned more about God as *Our Father*, than I ever managed to learn from years of theological study among books.

13

I Learn That God Is Our Father

†

That title should give everyone who reads it some comfort and hope. For here I am in my seventy-fifth year of life, my fifty-eighth as a religious, and my forty-fifth as a priest, and I am confessing that only now have I come to the realest realization that God *is* our Father! Since Dom James Fox had so much to do with my realizing that truth, we'll begin with him and his last days as my abbot — my father.

He had come to my room one morning in late November, 1967 to tell me some woman, Marion B. Conkling, down in Florida had just died and left me $10,000 in her will — for "my children." I had never met this woman, although we had corresponded. It was after she had read *This Is Your Tomorrow and Today,* the story of my brother Charlie's last years with cancer. She had been a nurse during the First World War and was assigning her insurance, given her during that War, to me for "my children."

Really, it was Dom James who, under God, had given me this paternity. I well recall the day in 1955 when I knelt beside his desk and said, "Reverend Father, it's about time we had a baby." He knew how I liked to startle people, but I could see a light of fear flame in his eyes after that statement. When he asked what I meant, I went on teasing him. "Just what I said: It's about time we had a baby." He smiled and asked what was on my mind. I thanked him for crediting me with having one, then told him that Kay, Charlie's wife, was "in a family way" again, and that Charlie was broke. That did it. Few knew, as well as I, how kind Dom James was. He immediately smiled and said: "Sure. Sure. You get Charlie to send all the pre-natal, the natal, and the post-natal bills to you. We'll pay them." So I became the "financial father" of Christine Marie, the last of Charlie and Kay's seven living children. They had lost their first, Sheila Mae, through leukemia, before she was five years of age.

That was only the beginning of my paternity. A few years later, at Eastertide, I was again kneeling at James' feet. This time it was: "Reverend Father, I just received a total of a little over five hundred dollars as gifts in my Easter mail. (We received our mail only four times a year in those days.) And Charlie tells me he is in debt to the tune of five hundred. Would you mind if I used these gifts for Charlie?"

Without a moment's hesitation there came that usual: "Sure. Sure." But then he added: "From now on whatever you receive in the way of gifts you may keep and use for Charlie and his family." That explains why he was in my room this morning in 1967 to tell me about Marion Conkling's bequest.

But I had more on my mind than Charlie this particular morning. I had been hearing rumors that Dom James was going to resign. I did not believe them, but there is nothing like finding the truth from the one involved, so I asked, "When can a father resign from his family?"

"Never."

"I thought so."

"Come on, Raymond, what are you talking about?"

"You. We call you *Abba* — Father, don't we? Some are saying you are going to resign."

His face changed. He became animated. He did not

deny nor affirm. He asked: "Do you realize I haven't had a moment to myself for twenty-five years?"

"I also realize that from all eternity God decreed that you would not have a moment to yourself these past twenty-five years. So?"

He smiled then, but left me without having confirmed or denied the rumor. He did resign a few weeks later, and to follow him we elected Dom Flavian Burns. Before this good man was in office a month I was kneeling at his feet saying: "Reverend Father, I am a disgrace as a Trappist." When he looked and then questioned why I said such a thing, I began with "I get more mail in a day than you'll get all year." He agreed. "I have more visitors in a month than the rest of the Community has in an entire year." He agreed again. "I see more people in a week than others here will see in their lifetimes."

"Father Raymond, I am convinced that you and Thomas Merton have a vocation within this vocation. God sends these people here. I want you to see them."

I looked at my young abbot; he was born twenty-eight years after me, and entered Gethsemani fifteen years later than I. I smiled and said: "Ok, Father, but if you give me an inch, I may take a mile."

He then made one of the wisest remarks I've ever heard a young man make. "That will be on your conscience."

I don't think I took any mile, but I was forced to take many an inch, for it was just after Vatican II, and religious congregations and orders had to revise their constitutions. I don't know how many different delegations came to Gethsemani asking to see Father Raymond who was supposed to be able to help them with their revisions, but I do know I saw many different nuns those days. Added to that there was the steady influx of college students with their particular problems. I am reminded of Kathy Curran from nearby Nazareth College who, at one of their bull sessions, was asked: "Who is this Uncle Joe you people are always talking

289

about?" (Many of them were calling me "Uncle Joe" at this time.) Kathy answered: "I'll tell you: He is sixty-five, looks forty-five, and acts twenty-five." I was not exactly flattered by that summation, but I did have to admit that she had reason for the statement. I felt very free with these youngsters, and I am sure I did act twenty-five.

This "popularity" did not last too long. For, very soon, it was being noised about that Raymond is a conservative. I never admitted to the label, for when asked whether I was conservative or liberal, I would always answer: "Neither. I'm a Catholic."

I did know something of the history of dogma, and recognized many of the new trends to be nothing but old, old errors wrapped up in new cellophane. The new breed did not impress me as having any real depth, nor any genuine discernment. They were getting the headlines, but I could not discover very much head behind those lines. I could understand the reactions of the young, especially the more or less young nuns, to my brand of preaching and teaching. Age may not bring wisdom, but it does make one wary of innovations. Moreover, I have never been known as diplomatic, as I would call a spade a spade. I have always aimed at being clear, so clear that people cannot fail to get my point.

It is no wonder that one of my confreres said: "The only thing consistent about Raymond was his inconsistency." While I have always held the line in dogma and morals, they could not fail to see me going to the visitors parlor day in and day out, here where I was supposedly secluded from the world. Little did they know what it was that took me to "my hermitage," once the eremitical life began to attract so many young monks. That hermitage was the back room at the gate house where I would be beset with all kinds of problems; marital, sociological, psychological, dogmatic, historical, and many of the present-day changes in the Church. If my confreres only knew, I was envying them for their seclusion.

Getting back to my family, my brother Charlie died in the early summer of 1958. His wife Kay dropped dead a year and a half later, leaving seven orphans ranging in age from nineteen to five. I had to care for those seven children, but how could I, hidden behind these walls, solemnly professed with a vow of stability and a vow of poverty which prevented me from calling so much as one red cent my own? Well it has been done for over twenty-five years, and that is why I learned more real theology from caring for my kids than I ever learned from books.

Charlie's X ray was taken in September of 1956. Early in the following year Dr. Henry B. Asman, a rectal surgeon, had to open me up. Then the real manifestation of God's goodness began. Dom James gave me permission to call Charlie on the phone every time I went into the hospital for a check-up. I had to go in frequently after this surgery, for I kept on bleeding. In early May Henry Asman stood by my bedside to say that he was going to go in again. When I asked him what for, he laughed and said: "This is going to sound strange to you. There is one little area that will not heal. That is why you bleed. I am going to make that larger, hoping that then it will heal."

It did not make too much sense to me, but I had complete confidence in Henry Asman. He made that open wound larger, but I kept on bleeding. Of course, I had to keep on going in to the hospital. I could contact Charlie by phone; hence, the disadvantages were far outweighed by that one advantage as far as I was concerned. Some months later, Henry went in for the third time. I kept on bleeding, and consequently kept in touch with my suffering and slowly dying youngest brother. That went on for over a year and a half. The day Charlie left this world, that bleeding *left me*.

Medically there may be an explanation. But, as far as I was concerned, I was not interested in that medical explanation. I believe in God. I take the theological explanation as making much more sense: God *is* our Father! He used me and my voice to help His other son Charlie face the long-drawn-out Calvary that would lead him to that "passover" which comes before we can live the life of all living.

Kay's financial condition was not improved by Charlie's frequent hospitalizations. But God is a financier as well as father. A great benefactress of Gethsemani heard of my position. I never met her or corresponded with her up to that moment. Nevertheless she wrote and ordered me to send to her all the bills connected with Charlie's funeral.

I had hardly thanked Mrs. Kurtis Froedtert of Milwaukee for the way she had cared for the funeral when a letter came from the mother general of the Daughters of Charity, telling me how a Sister Oliva, who had visited my mother frequently during her last illness, had accosted her on the grounds of the motherhouse in Emmitsburg asking if she had read my latest book about Charlie. Mother General had just finished it. Did she remember Kathy, the second eldest girl of the family, who had been mentioned more than once in the narrative. Mother did. Well, according to Sister Oliva, Kathy was interested in nursing. Mother, therefore, was writing me to say that Kathy could have a full scholarship, room, board, and books for free, if I could manage her transportation from Boston to Emmitsburg.

Whilst I was reading that revelation of generosity and charity I was summoned to the gate house to meet Ed Bleakley. I found him with his wife-to-be. They were on their way to New York to be married by Fulton Sheen in St. Patrick's Cathedral. I brought Mother General's letter down with me, and passed it to Ed saying, "This is why I believe in God." He passed it to Ethel, his wife-to-be. As soon as she had read it, she looked at Ed and asked, "Can't we take care of that transportation?" They did for four full years. No one believes me when I say I passed that letter to the to-be-weds without the slightest idea about that transportation. All I was doing was marveling at God's paternal care for Kathy and her education.

A few months before that happening I was in the hospital for a checkup when in came a Margaret Rogers, whom I had never met before, but who had heard about Charlie's demise and the seven children he had left behind. Margaret was all enthused about her latest purchase: a share in the Colonel Bradley Horse Farm, Idle Hour, and the two three-year-olds whom she claimed were going to win the next Derby. She wanted it to be a dead heat, for if one of them won, the other would be brokenhearted. It was all amusing to me and quite stimulating to find this grown woman so enthusiastic about a horse race.

Then she changed the subject and astounded me. Sister Margaret of surgery had told Mrs. Rogers about my children, so she very directly told me she wanted to do something for them. Was there anything they needed right away? All I could think of at that moment was Kay's last letter, in which she had told me her car was falling apart, and that she'd like to get a secondhand station wagon. I told Margaret Rogers of Kay's plight and plea. After fishing around a bit in her over-sized handbag, she came up with a roll of bills that would have choked both of her three-year-olds!

She moistened her fingers as she said: "People laugh at me for doing this, but it is the only way I can handle bills. You know, Father, if you keep money, it gets moldy." Then she peeled off one-hundred-dollar bills till she had five of them between her fingers. "This will help," says she, and hands the bills over to me. The following summer Kay drove down in a station wagon, with Kathy who was on her way to college, and young Kevin, who was still in grammar school. That was the last time I saw Kay alive.

Kay had another reason besides seeing me for that trip. The January after Charlie's death, she had called me to tell me that the truant officer had just visited her about her eldest son H. Charles, Jr. who, the officer said, "was afraid of neither God nor the devil." It seems that Charles was having difficulty adjusting to his role as man of the house. Psychologically, I could understand his difficulty. He had two sisters who were older than he. What chance did he have to act as head of the house with them around? Sibling rivalry is a fact in any household. But the way Charles was manifesting his manliness and maturity was not too palatable to me. How could the authorities in the school up on Cape Cod be expected to swallow it? I realized that Kay was upset. But when she told me the school the officer suggested for her son, I all but screamed, "Never! That's nothing but a prep school to Sing Sing." I knew that much, for it was what they called a reform school. Little reforming was ever done in any such school. When she anxiously asked what she was to do, I said, "Be as calm as you can be for the night. I'll call you back in the morning."

Just what I had in mind as I said that, I don't know. I called the headmaster of St. Joseph Prep, a boarding school in nearby Bardstown, conducted by the Xaverian Brothers. I got a Brother De Sales on the line. I asked him if he read *This Is Your Tomorrow and Today.* He had just finished it. Did he remember young Charlie in that book? "The youngster who stole home by running right over the catcher?" That was he. Well, it seems that he needs a change of location. The good brother asked only a few questions then astounded me with the words: "Get him down here tomorrow, Father, for our second semester opens the day after."

Charlie made that second semester. When I sent him home to the Cape for the summer his mother could not believe her eyes. She wrote me again and asked, "What did you do to my son? He's an angel-child! I can't believe he's the same boy I sent you last January." Kay wanted to see me, but she wanted to see this "reforming" school even more!

Charlie won't mind if I tell the world that the reformation did not last too long! The following year, just one year from the day of his arrival in Kentucky I had to send for him to tell him his mother had gone to join his daddy. That was one of the most difficult jobs I ever had to handle. The boy took it like a little man. I sent him home with Dian Fossey, for I realized he was only fifteen years of age, and had lost both parents. Dian not only took Charlie home, she went home with him, and ran the entire wake, funeral, and the aftermath. She brought Charlie back to school also. But at the end of that semester, Brother De Sales had to tell me that Charlie would not be welcomed back for his junior year. It seems that Charlie had decided to celebrate his sixteenth birthday by a swim in the school pool after hours. Finding it too well guarded in the cool of that May evening, he and his companion decided to go out on the town. But after only a few blocks they realized that Bardstown is a small town, and that they would readily be recognized as St. Joe boys. The good townsfolk would inform the headmaster, so the two youngsters decided to "borrow" a car. Actually, there was something in their rationalization, for they fully intended to bring the car back, have the same amount of gas in it as it had when they borrowed it, and leave it in the exact spot from which they took it. But, as they drove up to a gas station in Louisville, they found a police car on the same lot. The cops ordered them out, asked for their licenses. Neither of them had one! While the police were frisking his companion, Charlie took off, and actually got away.

At three o'clock in the morning the police called Brother De Sales. When the headmaster offered to go right in to take the one student they had captured off their hands he was told: "Stay where you are, Brother. We're sick and tired of these teenagers. We're going to throw the book at these boys. We haven't got Flanagan. But we'll get him."

Brother called me early that same morning to ask what I wanted him to do. I advised him to wait. I insisted I knew where Charlie was likely to go. I then called Dian Fossey. No, she had not seen Charlie. So I told her to call me if he showed up. The same with the Maginnises. Neither Jimmie nor Mickey had heard from Charlie. They received the same directive. Nothing happened that morning, which, incidentally, was Charlie's sixteenth birthday! After dinner, as I approached my "rat-hole," I saw Brother De Sales standing in the doorway. When I reached him I looked in and espied H. Charles with a tear-stained face.

At first Brother thought he might be able to accept Charlie the following year. His companion, in the meantime, had been bundled on to a plane and sent home to Chicago. The cops had thrown the book at him. To this day they have never laid eyes on Charlie. But we did have to hand him over to Jim Southerland, the county judge, who came to ask me what I wanted done with the boy. I said: "Put the fear of God in him, if you can, Judge. But watch out. The kid is a charmer. Everyone falls in love with him. He'll have you around his little finger in no time." Jim pooh-poohed the very idea. He then told me how he handled juveniles. It was a sound psychological methodology. I admired it and him, wished him well, and awaited the results.

One week later Jim was back to the monastery. When I asked him if he had gotten through to Charlie and put the fear of God in him, the judge very honestly replied: "I really am not sure." Then with seriousness and intensity, he went on. "But, Father, I want to adopt that boy. He's one of the finest little gentlemen I've ever met.

I laughed. "Didn't a mad monk tell you only last week, Jim, to watch out lest this youngster have you around his little finger in no time?"

Jim grew more serious and became more intense. I saw how deeply concerned the judge was, so I dropped my banter and told him the arrangements I had made for Charlie's summer. He was to stay with the Maginnises and to work for Office Equipment Company in Louisville. The judge accepted that arrangement, and handed Charlie over to the custody of James S. Maginnis, who was to report weekly on Charlie's behavior.

In the middle of that same summer I received word

from Brother De Sales that, while he was willing to accept Charlie back, the faculty thought it would be unwise for the morale of the other students. What a position to be in. Here I was in the monastery. There was a sixteen-year-old orphan with high school only half completed. What was my next move? I prayed, as many a parent has prayed, for guidance. I looked into a few military academies, thinking Charlie needed discipline. Their board and tuition were far out of my range. But then Jimmie Maginnis, with his usual resourcefulness came up with the idea of keeping Charlie in his house, and getting him into St. Xavier's High in Louisville. When I pointed out that it was conducted by the same Xaverian Brothers who had just refused to accept Charlie back, Jim responded, "No problem, Joe. Leave it to me." Jim got him into Xavier, and Mickey kept after Charlie in such a fashion that he graduated without further mishap.

If you believe in God as Our Father the way I do, you can see every link in His paternal plan: my cancer; meeting Dr. Henry; being adopted into that family — which held Jimmie Maginnis and another orphan as a member; Jimmie marrying Mickey Lawlor; Jim's association with the brothers since his early days as a boarder in St. Joseph Prep, and his relationship, by marriage, to Bill Kelley, President of Office Equipment where I had obtained a summer job for H. Charles, Jr.

The Maginnises made quite a man of Charlie. Recently, while talking to Mickey, after she had asked about Charlie, who has his own construction business now, I told her that that young man had picked up every trait her husband has as a businessman, and that she had rightly "christened" him Charlie "Flanaginnis."

I must not get too far ahead of my story about how I learned that God *is* our Father. After her mother's death in late January, Kathy stayed home from college to care for Kevin and the three little girls. Maureen, you see, was already married and stationed, with her air force husband, in

Florida. I did not know it at the time, but Kathy had balked about going back to St. Joseph College for her second semester as a freshman. Actually, she was happy to have a real excuse to stay at home. But in mid-March, she called me to say that she knew that God had given her a brain, and that she feared that she might become a vegetable there on the Cape. Hence, she'd like to go back to college the following semester. When I asked her where, she told me how Boston University would be opening a branch down on the Cape. When I asked what would be her major, she touched off my ever-short fuse by saying something about business and secretarial work. I think I said, "If you ever go back to college, it will be St. Joe's College in Emmitsburg." She can voice her opinions rather pointedly at times, and this was one of them. So I said, "Kathy, pack your bag. Get down here tomorrow. Mrs. Henry will drive you out. We'll talk it over." After that, I, most likely, slammed down the phone.

She came. As she was getting out of the car I overheard her saying to Mrs. Henry, "No one but Uncle Al can tell me what I am to do." Uncle Al, her maternal uncle, I had named as legal guardian, since I, as a religious, could not accept that position. But Al knew the situation. He was a retiree from some office in the New England Telephone Company, was older than I, and had a severe cardiac condition. I saw then and there that I had a rebel on my hands, and that I would have to walk on egg-shells while dealing with this aroused young lady.

It was March 25, Feast of the Annunciation. I had held my Mass for Kathy's arrival. After thanking Mrs. Henry, and seeing her off, I turned to Kathy and said: "Let's have Mass, then we can discuss the situation." She agreed.

What she did not know was that I had reread a letter I had received from a Mrs. Henry V. Ratke, wife of a surgeon in Williamsport, Pennsylvania, who had eight children of her own, two of whom, twins, had entered St. Joseph College with Kathy, and one of whom was Kathy's first room-

mate. Mrs. Ratke was President of St. Joseph Alumnae that
year. As soon as she heard of Kay's death, she had written
me to say that she would be happy to take in the four
youngest Flanagans so that Kathy could complete her studies.

The silent music of that low Mass changed Kathy. She
still had a chip on her shoulder, but she was in no way as
dogmatic as she had been with Mrs. Henry. When we got
seated I said: "Kathy, you just heard the most important
word in any language. What was it?" It took some probing,
but I finally got her around to *fiat*. I then showed her how
on the lips of God, that brought about Creation, for God
had said: *Fiat lux, et lux facta est.* Mother Mary had said
Fiat mihi, and we had the Incarnation. We heard it from
the lips of Jesus in the Garden of Gethsemani, *Fiat voluntas
tua* and we got Redemption. Once that point was made, I
proceeded to tell her I had her come down to learn God's
will for her — not mine, not her own, but God's — so that
she could say, *fiat*, and thus glorify her Father, sanctify herself, and help Christ save mankind.

I heard no more about Uncle Al being the only one
who could command her, nor anything about that branch
Boston University was about to open on Cape Cod. I told
her about Mrs. Ratke's offer.

I told Kathy my prime purpose was to keep the family
together and never let them be placed in any institution
such as an orphan asylum. She seemed to follow my theme.
I then oriented her on the legal restrictions on religious, and
informed her why I had her Uncle Al put down as legal
guardian. It was an informative and quiet session. Since the
Easter vacation was coming up, I suggested that she and
Charlie go to Williamsport and look over the possibilities.
They came back enthusiastic. What wonderful parents!
What a marvelous home! What a glorious family!

I then wrote Doctor and Mrs. Ratke and showed the
difficulties and the burden they would be assuming. They
had eight children of their own. To take four little Flana- ·

gans would swell that number to a round dozen. I also told them that the Flanagans were Flanagans — and explained just what that meant. Their reply showed me that God has some very generous humans on His earth, and some genuinely Catholic couples.

The following September saw the Flanagans en route to Williamsport with Dian Fossey the lead driver. All went gloriously until the end of May. Early in that month, my brother Fr. Jack went to the Ratke home to be present at Christy's First Holy Communion. His report subsequent to that visit was a paean — a hymn of praise for the Ratkes, a song of joy for the young Flanagans, and balm to my heart and mind. But my own hymn of thanksgiving was not fully sung when I received a telegram stating that he, Dr. Ratke, would be down to Gethsemani the following day with Kevin, and that other arrangements would have to be made.

They arrived and found a monk who was curious, uneasy, and a bit bewildered. The doctor and I sent Kevin and a Ratke daughter off for a walk, while we sat down to discuss the situation. I soon saw that paradise was lost to the Flanagan youngsters. So Doc and his daughter were sent off with profound thanks for all that had been done, while Kevin remained with me.

We are allowed to have our visitors stay here for three days. Kathy was still in college. Charlie was in Louisville. The three younger girls were still up at Ratkes until the end of the school year. Nobody was at home on the Cape. Well, the very next day Brother De Sales visited me. I introduced him to Charlie's brother, Kevin, who would be entering St. Joseph Prep the coming September, if Brother would have him. Brother asked a few questions about his schooling and his grades. No trouble there. Kevin would be welcomed at St. Joe's. Then Brother asked: "What are you going to do with him for the summer?"

"I wish I knew," was all I could answer, then gave him the situation of the scattered family.

"Listen, Father, I'll be opening camp in two weeks. I could use Kevin to help me set up. In fact, I could use him all summer long at the camp. His help would pay his keep."

What could I say to that offer? I can tell you what I said in my heart: God *is* our Father.

So June not only brought the roses, it brought me some momentary relief. Charlie had his job in Louisville and his home with the Maginnises. Kevin had his summer camp, and was having a ball. Kathy was at home with the three young girls on the Cape, and all were enjoying their familyness and the sunshine of Cape Cod. But I had to think of the next school year for those three young girls.

Out of the clear blue of a July day came a telegram from a Sister Benedict, in Buffalo, telling me that one Gen Jacobs "would like to help me with the education of the Flanagan girls. Would I allow her to send them to the Madames of the Sacred Heart Academy in Albany."

Who was Sister Benedict? Who was Gen Jacobs? I already knew about the Madames of the Sacred Heart and the exceptionally fine schools they conducted. But I also knew those schools were almost exclusively for the very well-to-do. My kids were practically penniless orphans!

I contacted Sister Benedict, and she had me in touch with Gen Jacobs. Gen told me how she had read *This Is Your Tomorrow and Today*, and how her heart went out to those little children. Then she went on to extol the Madames as teachers. Her final words were, "Can you have the three little girls meet me in the Essex House in New York City next week? I have some business there, and would like to meet the children."

I felt like the Chosen People in the desert. I was saying, as did they that first morning when they found the ground covered with what looked like hoar frost: "*Manhu*-what is this?" Indeed I recognized manna from heaven!

The three little orphans went to New York. They were put up in the Essex House in suites worthy of, and often

301

reserved for, royalty! Gen Jacobs came to Gethsemani to meet me. You already know my estimate of Mother Betty Henry — a perfect Southern lady. Gen Jacobs was a replica! What a lady! I learned that she had married Lou Jacobs, owner of Sports, Inc. Lou would tell you he was a peanut vendor, and without any false humility tell you he had once been a poor newsboy. At this time Lou did not know exactly how much he was worth and didn't seem to care. Gen had been his secretary. He married her and she made him the proud father of three boys and three girls, who were grown now. The Jacobs' home, which anyone else would call a mansion, had plenty of room for the three little orphans.

There was no need to twist my arm. The three girls went to Buffalo and into that mansion of a home. Patti and Mary were sent to the Madames in Albany. Christy was too young, so she stayed home with Gen, and was sent to Sister Benedict's special school. In the summer, Gen sent the girls to day camp, hoping to make them bilingual.

My brother, Father Eddie, was stationed in Buffalo at that time. He was a frequent visitor at the Jacobs, and showed the little orphans all around the town. Kathy and the boys also visited them in Buffalo. So my objective was being maintained: The family was *not* in any institution, and were, more or less, together.

But trouble entered that paradise, too. It came from Christy's tantrums. They so upset the usually imperturbable Gen that, one snowy day in February, after the children had been up there for three years and more, I received a telegram, again from Sister Benedict, saying that other arrangements will have to be made. Life is undulant, isn't it?

I was soon on the phone with Gen. I learned the difficulty. She was adamant. Other arrangements would have to be made. The cloister can be confining at times! I was learning to be like Job. I had certainly learned that the Lord gives, and the Lord takes away. I had to really learn to say: blessed be the name of the Lord.

By this time Kathy had graduated, passed her state boards, and was employed in Boston. She came down to talk things over. She had grown up quite a bit from the little girl who told Mrs. Henry that no one but Uncle Al could give her directions, so much so that she very maturely said, "Uncle Joe, these kids will accept no one in the place of their parents, not even you." I could only reply that I admired them for that. But her next statement opened my eyes. "Let me come to Louisville and take care of all of them." I not only opened my eyes in amazement, I opened my mouth in consternation. "How old are you, Kathy?" She told me. "Are you married?" Of course not. "Would you like to get married?" Of course she would. "Who on earth is going to consider you with three children on your hands?"

That did not faze her. "Look," she said. "These kids will obey me. They won't obey anyone else. I think I can handle it."

Talk about bravery. Talk about unselfishness. Talk about love. I always admired this little girl, and knew she had substance to her character. I really believe I was temporizing when I said, "Why Louisville? Practically all your friends are up in Boston. All your relatives are there. You have a splendid job. You have your own apartment. Whom do you know in Louisville?" She knew no one, practically speaking, but she reminded me that I knew a lot of people here. I sent her home saying that we both would have to think over it, and more especially, pray over it.

Well, it never rains but it pours. Before summer was on I learned that Patti would not be allowed back with the Madames. She broke one of their rules. She crossed the street while she was "campused." That was enough for the Madames, and she was out! Buffalo closed. Albany closed. And about the same time St. Joe's Prep closed to Kevin!

You can see why I allowed them to come to Louisville. But I was still uneasy about the schooling for the three little girls as well as the burden on young Kathy.

Watch Our Father at work! A Frank McCarthy had acted as my lawyer in the Penney case. Frank was a great benefactor to Cardome, a Visitandine convent and academy in Georgetown, Kentucky. He was also a very close friend to Mother Jane Frances Blakely. I had to go to Lexington, Kentucky, for a check-up at St. Joseph Hospital. Well, Mother Jane Frances contacted me at the hospital, and again it was out of the clear blue. She identified herself, and located me by a reference to Frank McCarthy. Then she offered me full scholarships for the girls at Cardome!

I immediately contacted my abbot and obtained permission to visit Cardome after my check-up. I fell in love with the place and with the Visitandines. Like St. Joe's Prep in Bardstown, it had once been *the* boarding school of the South. Again like St. Joe's, it had fallen on meaner days. The enrollment was small, but, to me, that was an advantage. The upshot of that visit was that Patti and Mary were enrolled at Cardome for the fall semester, and Mother Jane Frances insisted that they house Christy while she could attend classes in the nearby parochial school.

Thus it was done. So I had Kathy in a large enough apartment in Louisville, which is only an hour and fifteen minute drive from Cardome, Charlie attending Bellarmine College in Louisville, Kevin about to graduate from Boys Town, Nebraska, after which he, too, would go to Bellarmine. Things were looking up again for the orphans, and for their Uncle Joe, for Kathy had an excellent position teaching pediatrics at a Catholic school for nurses. The family was still together.

That paradisal situation lasted less than three years! To make a really long story short, I think I have given enough evidence to quiet those who might ask: "What does a priest know about parental difficulties?" I might be able to give them lessons on how to handle everything from dropouts, to drugs, from adolescent rebellion to runaways, from childish pranks to actual refusal to accept authority, from premarital to post marital problems, not to omit the intermittent ones. I could write an interesting book on each of my children. I have three with college degrees, and another with the equivalent. I have also two who refused to complete their college careers, but, all in all, it is not too bad. All are married save Kevin, the professional gemologist, and even he told me he would be married before long. I have fourteen, I guess you might call them, great-nieces and nephews. So for a mad monk, who had to raise a family from within the confines of a monastery, I must only look up and say: "Thank You, God; You have been a truly paternal Love!" Yes, He *is* our Father!

Would you think me cruel for one day having said to the assembled family of mine: "Kids, you cannot thank God enough for His fathering of the lot of you. Now I don't mean this in any disparaging sense, but the fact is that you are better off sociologically, scholastically, financially, and I dare add, psychologically, than if your parents had not been called home by God. I know no human can ever take the place of your parents, but I want you to know that God has shown Himself a providing, loving, nurturing, and nourishing Father to each and all of you."

To give you a last example of how God works, I must tell you about Emmett J. Culligan. Of course he could have gone into that chapter in which I told you about the great men who have met me, for if ever there was a character amongst my friends, Dodo, as I came to call Emmett J., was certainly that.

Like so many of my friends, and God's instruments, he came to me out of the clear blue. He had a manuscript; oh, how many of those I have seen! It was about *The Last World War*. That did not refer to World War II. Nor was it about that often mentioned World War III. This was about what it was named: The *last* world war — Armageddon. Dodo collated all the apparitions of Our Lady and pondered long over the messages she had delivered. Then he went into the Apocalypse and the fascinating number 666. I read his manuscript, and enjoyed it, for you already know my "sonship of Mary," and my never-dying interest in all of her appearances, revelations, and warnings. As for the number 666, I must say I always had difficulties with the passage. I had never been able to figure out what John was trying to tell us. Exegetes were no great help. Dodo's explanation proved arresting and very interesting. But when I found him setting down the actual date for the end of the world, I objected.

"Dodo," I said, "you'll never get an imprimatur for this if you dare to insist on that specific date. Christ Himself stressed the fact that 'not even the Son of Man, but only the Father knew that day and hour.' Yet you give us both. No, Dodo, it won't go."

That led to a long discussion. I could not fault his mathematics. I could not question his interpretations of Mary's messages. I did, however, object to the date he gave. We parted the warmest of friends, and that warmth came not from the arguments but from the nationalities. Dodo was even more Irish than I, and that is saying something! He went back to San Bernardino. He did not get an imprimatur, but he did publish his book, and it enjoyed a very fine sale. That brought Dodo back to Gethsemani for the sake of sharing his joy over the accomplishment. He liked Gethsemani, so much so that he sent his young sons for a visit, and brought his wife Anna here, too.

Two visits stand out with rare vividness for me right now. One was for the occasion of the *dies irae* that Dodo had predicted. He told me the circumstances which surrounded it himself. He had to be in Northbrook, Illinois, for a meeting with the officers of his Culligan Soft Water Co. It was a Saturday in the fall, and Notre Dame was playing one of her arch-rivals — has she any other kind? After chairing the meeting, Dodo stood up and asked if any of his men would like tickets for the game. With characteristic flair,

Culligan threw a good-sized bundle of those unobtainable tickets on the table, saying: "Help yourself. I'm going to Gethsemani for the 'crack of doom.'"

He was convinced, but to me, he was not fully convincing. Prior to this, Dodo had given me the astounding story of his life, He was a farmer in Iowa when the bottom fell out of the corn market. His sixth child was due, and Dodo tells me he went out in the corn field, knelt down, dug his fists into the soil and prayed: "God, you will have to help me and my growing family." Then he said: "Now Father, I won't say this actually happened, but I felt God's hand on my shoulder, and heard Him saying: 'Of course, Culligan. Why didn't you talk to me this way before!'" Dodo went to the hospital to see his wife, whom I always called Lady Anna. While there he came across an old chum from high schools days, and asked him what he was doing for a living. He responded, "I'm selling green sand." When Dodo expressed his disbelief, he was told to go down to the basement of that hospital to see for himself. He did. He saw a good sized mound of green sand. When he came up, he asked his chum what it was all about. He was told to take some of that sand home with him, put it in a can, perforate the bottom, and put it under his tap, allow the water to run through it, then use that water for washing, etc. He did. Dodo then told me he had a lot of washing to do those days with the new baby! The water was soft, and saved him soap. He was curious, and called his chum and asked him who his distributor was in Culligan's part of the state. He was told the whole southwest was his if he wanted to take it. That's how the Culligan Soft Water business began.

Of course, Dodo was a genius, an inventor, a dreamer as all inventors are, an innovator, and very truly an individual. We became very close friends, and he became a very great benefactor to my family. When he met young Kevin Flanagan he took a very paternal interest in the boy. After Dian Fossey, who had Kevin for some weeks in the summer, took the youngster with her to California and visited the Culligans in their home in San Bernardino, that paternal interest deepened to such a depth that Dodo wrote me saying that he and Lady Anna had talked it over and decided that they would pay Kevin's way through college. He said he would send me a monthly check to care for the boy. From that day until his death on the anniversary of Our Lady's Apparition at Fatima, May 13, a long envelope with a good-sized check would arrive each month without a single word of correspondence. Dodo stole a line from G. K. Chesterton and stated, "I never write letters to those I love." That was his apologia for the check without another word!

Never will I forget one of my feast days, February 6, Feast of St. Raymond of Fitero, founder of the Knights of Calatrava. It was raining, snowing, sleeting — a truly miserable day — and I thought that Dodo would never make it. He did, however, and as I was escorting him to the guest house, he put his arm around me saying, "I won't tell you now, but neither the Culligans nor the Flanagans will ever have to worry again." Before we reached his room he was telling me why. "My accountant came to my office a few days ago and asked me if I was not supposed to get a royalty on every replacement of equipment for soft water. I told him I was. He then told me that my company, from which I retired some time ago, had been withholding royalties to the tune of millions of dollars. I am going to split that money between the Culligans and the Flanagans. So, Father Raymond, you'll never have to worry again."

The company felt themselves free from any obligation to pay any royalty, so I never saw any of that "back-pay." Whether the Culligans did or not, I never found out, but money never bothered Dodo. He claimed that if he ever hoarded it, God would take it away from him. He considered himself God's almoner, and he lived up to the title. Truly, Dodo Culligan could be called an eschatological man. From his interest in the eschaton, he was keenly con-

308

scious of and even expectant of the final days. Catholic to the core, he could be called a truly Faith-full individual, a keenly God-conscious man.

God, of course, was always conscious of Dodo. I will never forget the time he went to the solemn profession of his son in Wisconsin. He had to leave his hideaway which he had built somewhere in Montana in expectation of the cataclysm. He told me that the devil couldn't even find him. He had flown in all the lumber and other materials necessary for the building of the lodge up in the mountains. He had episcopal permission for perpetual adoration of the Blessed Sacrament, and had some bishops and priests as semi-permanent members of his family. The very day he was watching his son pronounce his vows in the presence of the entire Culligan family, there was an earthquake in Montana which split that lodge in two! No one of the Culligans was injured in the slightest.

I could go on and on about Dodo, but I believe I have given you enough evidence to prove that God is our Father, and I am a disgrace as a Trappist, but made so by God, for I do believe that He was the one who made me Father in more than the usual meaning of that title. I have raised a family from within these walls.

I have mentioned many names in this narrative, but I have failed to mention many, many more. Allow me to say with the beloved disciple: There are many other things that "— God did to show that He is our Father (and very many other things that "my kids" did) — if all were written down, the world itself, I suppose, would not hold all the books that would have to be written," especially were I to mention all those others who could, and, in a way, should be mentioned who helped me father these fatherless ones. But there are at least two other families I must mention to show you why I say that God's name must be Murphy.

14

God's Name Must Be Murphy

✝

I have had a lot of fun writing these memoirs. I hope I
have shared a few laughs with you as I have recalled some
of the more interesting and, I hope, character-forming and
soul-shaping happenings during my forty years behind the
wall. I wished to dispel some wrong notions about the cloistered life entertained by those within, as well as without,
the cloister.

I have been flippant often in these pages, because that
is the way I am. But, please God, behind all my flippancy
there is always depth, and especially deep faith. Without
faith no man can really live. He may exist, but he will not
live. Surely you see that no man could even exist in this
monastery for any length of time without a lively, even a
flaming faith. The one purpose of this life is to seek and find
God! That takes a faith that is fire. As St. Paul so honestly
stated, "we see in a dark manner." But let me insist we see!

My last chapter on my paternity seems sketchy. In a
sense, it had to be, for countless have been the laughs my
kids have given me, even as they gave me many a headache
and heartache. But it has been a deeply religious experience. Never once was I unconscious of the fact that to deal
with humans is a very serious affair, for it is to live amongst
possible gods or goddesses. I have always been mindful of

the truth that the dullest and most uninteresting person you deal with may one day be a creature whom, if we saw him or her clearly now, we would be strongly tempted to worship. All day long we are actually helping each other, in some degree, to one or other of these final destinations. That is the frightening, and the thrilling fact. My kids have helped me. I hope I've helped them.

None of us should ever consider any human as ordinary, nor look upon any as merely mortal. *Things* are mortal. Yes, even nations, cultures, civilizations, though made up of humans, are truly mortal. They pass away. But those with whom we joke, work, play, snub, or exploit are immortal. Hence, when I was entertaining Charlie or Kevin, arguing with Kathy or Patti, cajoling Mary or Christy, or writing to Maureen, I knew I was dealing with *possible* everlasting splendors. So, while I played with them much, I prayed for them much more.

As a priest I had been blessed with a passionate love for Christ in the Mass, and especially blessed with a veritable passion for the truth of the Mystical Body. Hence, it was practically inevitable that I should come to look upon all humans as, next to the Blessed Sacrament, the holiest objects presented to my senses. When I knew them to be baptized humans, I knew they were, or at least could be, as holy almost as the Blessed Sacrament. I could say of them exactly what I sing about the Eucharist: *in his Christus vere latitat.* Yes, in them Christ, the glorifier and the glorified, is *truly hidden.* So, while I railed at my kids now and then, I always reverenced them. Better, I reverenced Christ in them, and them in Christ. So you see how what could have distracted me beyond measure, actually made me ever more and more God-conscious. That is one of the reasons why I say God's name must be Murphy.

That blasphemous-sounding sentence came to me one morning last fall as I sat in the dentist chair in our clinic here at Gethsemani. Dr. Jim Dorso was working on the drill,

311

endeavoring to change heads, when he said something to the effect that Murphy's Law is working today, and he went on working on that drill. "Murphy's Law," thought I. Because of my education, I have become acquainted with many, many laws. But never had I heard of Murphy's Law. I had to ask: "What in world is that, Doc?"

"You never heard of Murphy's Law?"

"Never. What is it?"

He then went on to tell me that someone by the name of Murphy, while down around Cape Kennedy (or Canaveral) during our space program came up with the idea that if anything can go wrong, it will. That explains why we had two, and at times, three back-up systems in our space vehicles. Then Doc told me he always adds to Murphy's dictum, ". . . and at the wrong time."

Well, if you know your philosophy, you know that every truth can be reductively brought back to Him who is Truth — God. So with every good law, it can be brought back to Him who is the only Lawgiver! Again I say — to God! So I rephrase Murphy's Law to say: "Expect the unexpected!" The life I have led behind these walls shows how that law has been operative in my life for forty years. Since we know that God is behind all happenings, you can see why I say God's name must be Murphy!

Lacordaire, the great French preacher once described the life of a priest in these terrifyingly true terms: "To live in the midst of the world, without wishing its pleasures; to be a member of each family, yet belonging to none; to share all sufferings; to penetrate all secrets; to heal all wounds; to go from men to God and offer Him their prayers; to return from God to men to bring pardon and hope; to have a heart of fire for charity; and a heart of bronze for chastity; to teach and to pardon; console and bless always. . . ." Then he exclaims: "My God, what a life! And it is yours, O Priest of Jesus Christ!"

What he meant by that last exclamation, I don't know,

but I do know that I have striven to live up to the description he gave, and take it as an exclamation of joy! From the time I was ordained in 1933, to this moment, I have had a joy-filled existence. Oh, no one knows better than I how often I failed to live up to the ideal perfectly. But never once did I lower the ideal, no matter how far below it the real turned out to be. I am nearing the particular judgment, with some shame, but without an iota of fear. For I know who my judge will be, and I know Him as merciful, even in His justice.

But just look at that description of the life of any and every priest, and look at the way Murphy's Law has operated in my days, nights, and years. Indeed, I have to expect the unexpected.

I left the world, but have lived in the midst of the world. I left my family, and that was not easy, but look at the families that have adopted me! There is hardly a state in the union wherein I do not have a family. But I must tell you about one extended family in nearby Bardstown.

One day while I was out in my salad patch, a car stopped. A young man got out from behind the wheel, approached, and introduced himself as Pike Conway. "Father," said he, "will you come over to the car and bless my dad?" I did. Shortly after meeting Mr. Jim Conway, who had been mayor of Bardstown for two terms at least, I met Pike's wife Marie or as I came to call her, "Ma Belle," whose father had been mayor of Bardstown for two terms at least. Then I met Pike's sister Kitty, whose husband Gus Wilson is now on his fourth term as mayor of the same town. I learned that Gus' father Frank had been mayor of Bardstown for a few terms. You see how we have kept the mayorality all in the family for about thirty years. Hence, I call Bardstown our town. I was adopted by them all right — so much so that when misinterpretations of Vatican II had priests leaving to marry I was jokingly asked by little Ann Conway, who was then about ten or twelve, when I was going to get married. I told her I would marry her. From that day to this she calls me "hubby," and I humor her enough to call her "my wife." Recently I told Pike that I was going to seek an annulment if Ann, who is now a junior in Transylvania University, did not come to see "her husband" when she was home for her spring break.

What a family! What an extended family! The parents have gone to God, but the two sons and two daughters are closer than ever. Jody and Kitty see one another almost daily. Pike and Jim are in constant contact. The in-laws are all in the same business — auto dealerships. The Conways have the Ford; the Wilsons the Chevrolet; the Sympsons the Dodge. While people think it makes no difference from whom you buy, or what you buy, for it is all in the family, let me tell you it is friendly, but sometimes fierce competition.

I left one family, the Flanagans, with some sadness, but just look at the countless families God has given me since. From the two Americas to Africa and Australia I have families into which I have been adopted. That's Murphy's Law in operation for it all has been unexpected.

I came to be silent. Forty years ago I was told to write. This is my twenty-second book. There are twenty-three booklets from my pen. So I, who came to "share all secrets, bear all sufferings" have been constantly endeavoring to open the secrets of God to you, even as I tried to bear His sufferings for you. I was to go from men to God, and I have been commissioned to really come from God to you. I came to be cut off from the world. Daily that world comes into me by mail, and I must average three thousand letters a year answering not all my mail, but all that seems needing some reply. I was to be a solitary. I could not count the number of people who have come to me in this solitude, from every walk in life, from every country, even from behind the Curtains, and I do believe God sent them.

I came here to lead a life of seclusion. What did God do? He gave me a very select carcinoma, which carried me

314

to the hospital where I became reacquainted with the world, with a wide, wide world. Yes, I have to expect the unexpected. I expected to die from that cancer, yet here I am quite alive almost thirty years after that first surgery. My surgeon Doctor M. J. Henry was a vigorous man when he excised that carcinoma. Yet on the first Friday in June, just a few years after his marvelous work, he dropped dead in St. Agnes Church, in Louisville, just as he started to go up to the altar to receive the Sacred Heart beating in that transubstantiated Host.

Doctor Mickey Maguire then took over my case. He was years and years younger than Joe Henry, and to me, he appeared like a boy. But what a surgeon Mickey was! One day, only a few years after taking over my case, he was doing a vein-ligation on our mutual friend, the surgical nurse, Maxine Wheat. Mickey never finished that ligation. In the middle of that surgery, he rose on his toes, then fell back on the floor, and died right there in that surgical suite. Expect the unexpected. I doubt that Mickey even suspected his heart was not right.

Small wonder then that Hallie Asman, Dr. Henry's beautiful wife, came to my hospital room to say: "I don't know as I'm very happy, Father Raymond, that you have selected Henry as your surgeon."

"Why, Hallie! What's eating you?"

"What happened to your first surgeon?"

"He dropped dead from a heart attack."

"What happened to your second surgeon?"

"He dropped dead, and from a heart attack."

"Well, Father, I'd like to keep my husband for some time."

She did for quite some time, but just a year or so ago Henry B. Asman died suddenly. So my latest surgeons, Dr. Jack Hemmer and Dr. Lewis Bosworth, had better expect the unexpected.

I was not back long from my second cancer excision

before Bill Bruce, President of the Bruce Publishing Company, was asking me to write something to reassure the many Catholics who had been upset by the upheaval that followed in the wake of Vatican II. I dashed off *Relax and Rejoice — for the Hand on the Tiller is Firm.* The effort was readily accepted and expertly edited by Bernard Wirth. He handed it over to the head of the Literary Foundation, who claimed it was "the best thing Raymond has written," and selected it for the Book-of-the-Month for October, 1967.

Then Murphy came in under the guise of a very well-written letter which told me that a new policy had been introduced at Bruce, according to which no manuscript could be accepted on the word of one editor. It would have to be submitted to the entire board.

Not long after, I received a second letter saying that the board had decided not to accept *Relax and Rejoice.* I was not surprised. I suspected a "liberal" had come to Milwaukee. But Murphy came in again, this time under the guise of my old friend Dodo Culligan. When I told him the story, he asked if he could read the manuscript. He did, and with his usual enthusiasm exclaimed, "Give it to me, Father. I'm in the publishing business now. I'll show them what one man can do from his home in San Bernardino."

That was not my last book however, for one day, a year or so later, as I was coming down the lane which leads to the gate house, a man with wavy, white hair accosted me with, "Are you Father Raymond?" When I nodded affirmatively, he went on: "I am Doctor Russinovich, a psychiatrist. Can I have a few minutes of your time?" I took him to a room in the men's guest house and there listened to one of the most engrossing life-stories I had ever heard.

Dr. Nicholas Russinovich told me he was a Croatian. I had never heard of such a country, nor of such a race. Then he informed me that he had been his country's ambassador to the Vatican when he was thirty-two years old. Next, when Tito took over his homeland, Dr. Nick landed in

Dachau! There he stayed for over two years. Since he was a medical man, he got a bit more food than the other prisoners, but how he ever managed to survive while under constant captivity and incessant interrogation, is still a bit beyond me. It appears that he was born in the United States, but was taken back to Croatia, which, by this time, was part of Yugoslavia, when he was a year old. Hence, he could answer the question "Are you a Croatian?" with his constantly repeated, "I am an American citizen. I am also a Croatian patriot." That angered his interrogators, but it also gave them pause, for America was winning the war at that time, and had the USSR as an "ally."

It was the Americans who liberated Dr. Nick from Dachau. Then the even more fascinating part of his narrative began. He was whisked to Vienna and put up in a very plush hotel. He was convinced this was but a prelude to his execution. Next morning they brought him a luscious breakfast. He took it to be the last meal they served people about to be shot. He could not touch it. Instead of taking him out and standing him up against a wall, they placed him in a limousine and drove him to the Italian border. All the time he had been in Dachau his wife and two children were back in Croatia. He did not know how they had been faring, nor did they know whether he was alive or not. At the border a French colonel approached the doctor and said: "I want you to take good care of this poor widow and her two children," then winked as he pointed to Maria, Nick's wife, to young Yolanda and Nick Junior, their children. Then to the wide-eyed and open-mouthed doctor the colonel said, "*Bon Voyage!*"

It was one of those happy, yet nervous reunions, for Nick had developed what is now a deathless distrust of the Communists. The family was being transported to Italy. When Nick learned they were to be housed in a huge Italian villa, he told Maria to go ahead with the children, and he would contact them later. He then managed to board a ship for South America. Once in Chile, I believe it was, he began practicing his medicine. When fairly well established, he sent for his wife and family. They joined him. But one day Nick startled Maria by saying, "I'm going back to my country." Back he went and had to go through all the usual steps of examinations, internship, etc., before he got his license. Somehow or other he ended up in Glasgow, Kentucky, as head of a hospital for TB patients.

One bright morning while making his rounds he came upon one patient whose TB was arrested, but who was deeply depressed. Nick, with customary impulsiveness, exclaimed: "I can minister to their bodies, but not to their minds. I'm going to become a psychiatrist." He was then fifty-three years of age. But today Dr. Nicholas Russinovich is chief of staff in psychiatry at the V.A. Hospital in Louisville, professor of psychiatry at the University of Louisville, consultant at Norton Childrens Hospital, internationally known as one of the leading psychiatrists of the day.

Yet he had not come to Gethsemani to tell me his story, but to get me to write the story of Cardinal Stepinac. Nick had been baptized by the cardinal, and married by him, too, if memory serves me aright. I was interested, for Stepinac was to Croatia and Yugoslavia what Mindszenty was to Hungary, and I had always admired real heroes. I wrote the book. I titled it *The Man for This Moment* and paralleled Stepinac to that other great man and real martyr, the man for all seasons, Thomas More. That book was published in 1971. Since then I have been rather silent.

I have shown you much sunshine that has fallen on me during these forty years, but I would not have you think there have been no shadows. There have, deep ones at times. As you well know, the rose must have the darkness and the dew. I have had both. God, obviously, likes wave-motion; for life is undulant.

I have told you of the veritable deluge of mail that comes to me. In letters requesting advice and direction, not only for their spiritual or marital lives, but even for their social, scholastic, and, occasionally, economic lives. In that I see normality. For didn't Lacordaire, in his excellent description of a priest, say that he should have a heart of charity, and didn't Christ Himself commission us all to teach? When other correspondents presented their difficulties, I accepted such representations and revelations as part of my priestly vocation. Lacordaire tells how a priest is called "to share all sufferings, penetrate all secrets." I accepted all that as normal so long as it came by mail. The rub came when, to my very face, many would tell me I was "a very spiritual man," and some would go so far as to use the word "saintly." That is when I knew something had to be done quickly. That is when I decided on my tactic.

In the silly, rambunctious, and occasionally dangerous sixties, I had a number of college girls call on me, especially groups from Nazareth College. They would show me that they were with it by their T-shirts, slacks, and whatnot. Some of them would go a step further and use words they thought had real shock value. I heard them out with a smile. I think I read them right when I saw them as endeavoring to show this poor cloistered monk, who really knew nothing about life, as it was being lived these days, this famed writer of spirituality, which was so anachronistic, this saintly priest, who had no idea whatsoever of what reality was like, that they could not only take him out of his ivy tower, but bring the tower down. It was amusing, and a bit puzzling. I well knew if I showed them that I not only saw them, but actually saw through them, then told them how unladylike their talk, dress, and some of their actions were, they'd only act tougher. So I let them rave.

When they began to try to shock me by talking about marriage, citing some names of priests who had made the news by getting married, I laughed and said, "Why should I even consider it, girls, when I already have a harem?"

So much for the women, single, married, divorced, or

319

widowed. But then came the nuns. Many very wrongly concluded that because a man wrote on spirituality, he was, therefore, a very spiritual man. I must make a distinction. The less young among them actually canonize Fr. Raymond. The young, however, really tease the same individual. They tell me to get with it, don't be so old-fashioned, and remind me that there has been a Second Vatican Council, etc. I have found these even more amusing than the college girls. I have been really embarrassed by "canonization" and may have made a mistake by the tactic I used to show many of them that I'm no angel. I succeeded — only too well! I do not know how I stand, spiritually, before God. Who does? I know that, habitually, I have tried to live up to the idea and ideal of a priest as given by Lacordaire.

But God's work was not yet completed. There came requests to write on the Holy Spirit. Then assignments to preach on Pentecost, give conferences on His place in Sacred Scripture. Finally, after Vatican II, there came the Catholic Charismatic movement. I had to look more deeply into Him whom I had called the neglected Person of the Trinity — the Holy Spirit.

Now, please understand that last statement, which is both an understatement and an overstatement. We had always ended each prayer, psalm, and hymn with a doxology, wherein the Holy Spirit is mentioned, and mentioned personally. Yet we old-timers have to concede that there was little popular devotion to the Holy Spirit in our earlier days, In that sense He was neglected. Now, however, we have the opposite happening. It does seem as though action and reaction are equal even in the spiritual life, doesn't it? Hence, there is real danger of excess.

Being Jesuit-trained, I am not cynical, not skeptical, but I am cautious and, please God, a bit prudent. In the early days of the Pentecostal movement I was embarrassed more than once — by myself, though, not by those in the movement. I was too quick on the trigger. When one would ask me what I thought of the movement, I would immediately say, "Not much." Should they persist and pursue that matter with the query: "Why do you say that?" I would expatiate on feelings, sentiments, emotions and their place in the spiritual life and show that they are not to hold a very high place. I might even add a caution about exaggerated enthusiasm, and add the profound truth expressed by the ancients in their axiom of *Violenta non durant*, which means that a tornado, or a tidal wave does not last long. After going on in this strain, the questioner might softly say, "I'm a Pentecostal," and my visage would take on the hue of a blood-red rose! That happened more than once in those early days of that movement.

Today, I am still cautious about the whole thing, and am simply waiting and watching. The Gospel measure is still a very sound measure: "By their fruits you shall know them." I consider it still a bit early for truly mature, actually mellow fruit. But that does not mean that I do not see the Holy Spirit working. He is, always has been, and always will be. When Christ said "I am with you all days," He was talking about the Triune God, and in that One God there are Three Persons! Further, how could I doubt the Holy Spirit's presence and His workings, when I hold so firmly to my doctrine of the Mystical Body? The Third Person of the Trinity is the soul of that Body, and you know the soul is the vital principle of any and every body. It would appear that today the Holy Spirit is being more clearly recognized in His activities. For that I am keenly grateful and actually enthusiastic. Yet I still shy from feelings, sentiments, and emotions in the spiritual life. I do concede they do function in that life, but I also insist they are a very poor barometer to read and follow!

Yet "Murphy" has brought me to a true devotion to the Third Person, and that is really new for me. Actually, it is a Trinitarian spirituality I now cultivate, and that, as I now see it, is the culmination of the contemplative life.

I have had to laugh many a time when our younger men returned from their studies in Europe and told how they met me, by name, in Italy, Spain, Portugal, Germany, France, and in England. One of our men told me how he almost jumped out of his shoes when in London. He had been sauntering along the street, when he happened to look into the window of a book shop and there, in front of him, staring out at him was a picture of his former abbot Dom Mary Frederic Dunne. Bruce had used it on the frontispiece of *The Less Travelled Road*.

How does it feel to be internationally known after hiding oneself behind these walls? I am amazed, and amused! But it also has one, who has but a modicum of common-sense, saying and praying with Louise Imogen Guiney:

> *Delight* is a menace, if Thou brood not by;
>   *Power*, a quicksand; *Fame,* a gathering jeer
> Oft as the morn (though none of earth deny
>   these things are dear),
> *Wash me of them!*
>   That I may be renewed, and wander free —
> And wander free amid my new-born *joys!*
>   Close Thou my hand on BEATITUDE —
> Not on her *TOYS*.

Let me be inconsistent in my consistency. I say that a wise Trappist scorns toys such as delight, power, and fame; yet, when I wrote of Dom Frederic, I depicted him as a child who was always playing with blocks, and insisted that Dom Frederic always had those blocks spelling GOD — and He is Beatitude!

Then how dare I call Him who is our All-Holy God, our Holy Almighty One, our Holy Immortal One, Murphy? I say it with all reverence, and have to say it in the face of reality. Allow me just one last example of this unexpected in all my expectancies. I'll take it from my own family.

322

In 1935 I was out on the Olympic Peninsula at Port Townsend, making my tertianship. A telegram came saying my Dad had been found with cancer. I flew back to Boston, and saw Dad and his doctors. I told them of my heavy Lenten schedule and that I wouldn't be free until June. They assured me Dad would last that long, and I got deeply into the schedule. I had just finished a mission at Corvallis, in Oregon, and was about to begin my morning Mass when Fr. Jack Mitchell, the pastor, handed me a telegram. Before I bent over for the Confiteor, I read, "Dad died this morning." It was April 16. Unexpected? You had better believe it!

In 1949 I was back from my surgery for my first cancer. My mother was in Boston after her surgery, and not doing so well. Yet she told all the family that she was going to Gethsemani for our Centenary. Knowing the determination that was Mother's. I shook my head in some doubt, yet with some conviction that her determination would carry her down. I stood in my choir-stall, awaiting the beginning of the conventual Mass, when Dom James Fox came up to me, and squeezed a telegram into my hand. From the eloquence of the squeeze, I knew the message. "Mother went to God early this morning." It was dated June 9, 1949. So much for expecting the unexpected, as far as my parents were concerned.

As for Charlie, my baby brother, even there was an element of the unexpected, for Fr. Jack, Sister Mary Clare, and Fr. Eddie, along with my married sister, Peg Collins, as well as her youngest son, my namesake, Joe-Ray, were all set to come down to Gethsemani June 22nd, to celebrate my silver jubilee as a priest, and the anniversary of my first Mass, June 23rd. Arrangements had been completed, airline tickets purchased, and reservations of rooms made here. I was all anticipation. But then, God stepped in, and called Charlie home June 23rd, 1958. Yes, in its way, it was unexpected, and another proof that no matter how long and lingering the illness, death is always sudden.

Now we come to my youngest sister, Betty. I was allowed to go up to Boston to assist her in her last days with cancer. My abbot was away on a visitation, and when he returned on May 24th, instead of sending me to Boston, as he intended, he tried to condole with me over Betty's sudden passing-over on May 21st, 1976. I told him he should be congratulating me, for Fr. Jack had been on hand to give Betty Christ just before she went to meet Him Face-to-face.

The following month of that same year, Dom Timothy Kelley had some business to be transacted in New York City. He deputed me to discharge that business for him and added that I was to go on to Boston to visit Fr. Eddie, who was hospitalized from a severe stroke which had left him paralyzed on his entire left side. I was elated. But Murphy had a surprise for me! The evening before I was to set out, Dom Timothy came to my room with the news that a friendly Carmelite priest had discharged the business he had for me in New York City. My heart sank, but it quickly rose up again when Dom Timothy told me I was to fly directly to Boston to visit Fr. Eddie and to celebrate Fr. Jack's 82nd birthday with him!

I had no sooner landed in Boston when Fr. Eddie had a massive bleeding ulcer, and had to be transferred immediately to the intensive care unit of St. John's Hospital in Lowell. You can readily surmise what kind of a celebration we had, for not two months had passed since Betty had gone to God. I was on the road continuously between Boston and Lowell. Fr. Ed survived that bleeding ulcer, though he is still paralyzed, and still hospitalized.

The following June I was talking to Fr. Jack on the phone for his 83rd birthday. Fr. Ed and I had always kidded Fr. Jack saying, "You'll never die, Bozo; we'll have to take you out and shoot you." Yet this day, in my usual flippant, yet truly serious, manner, I said: "Hey, Flanagan, isn't it high time you got off this earth, and went home where you belong?"

His reply was unexpected. "I'd like to live another year, Joe.

"In God's Name, why?"

"To celebrate my golden jubilee as priest of God in the Society of Jesus," he said.

There are not many Jesuits who do celebrate their golden sacerdotal jubilee. But early fall of that same year found Fr. Jack in the hospital. He had been as healthy as a horse all his life, so this was a bit unexpected. Then, what a series of blunders took place! First they diagnosed his trouble as lumbar inflammation. Some months later, after the medication brought no improvement, they changed the diagnosis to diverticulitis. Again, there was no improvement. Finally, they found what they should have looked for first, given the Flanagan family medical history. They found cancer of the colon. That actually raised my hopes for Fr. Jack.

Still, the blundering went on. They operated on Halloween. They got it all, but four days later Fr. Jack distended, and his abdomen became as hard as rock. They allowed days to pass, and it was not until 9:30 P.M. on November 7th that they got him back to surgery for a caecostomy. After that surgery, Fr. Jack was put in intensive care. He never left it alive.

But Murphy was not letting me down. He had me in Boston for my birthday, November 29th, and with Fr. Jack, who recognized me immediately. I had a week of daily visits with him, which lasted but a few minutes each time. Actually, despite his position and his condition, I had an expectation, because of his robust physical frame and lifelong healthiness, that he would yet fool the doctors. But on December 6th, 2:30 in the morning, I was aroused from sleep to be told that the grand old warrior had gone to his King.

On December 10th, Murphy, had this cloistered Gethsemani monk standing in the old sodality chapel of Fr. Jack's and my own alma mater, Boston College High saying:

My first word to you must be relax, for Father Joe is at the rostrom, and he has never been known as the soul of wit; that is, for brevity. Then, not to make it a commercial exactly, I do add: rejoice. Daily, we monks sing: "I rejoiced when I heard them say: Let us go to God's House. And now our feet are standing within your gates, O Jerusalem."

The learned fathers on each side of me will recognize that as the song King David sang in that long advent for the people of God centuries before Christ Himself sang it with Mary and Joseph, as they made their way up to Jerusalem annually. This morning all you, chosen people of God, should sing it; for you are in the burning bush as truly as was Moses the day he saw that bush "which was burning, but not being consumed," and whence we first heard God tell us His Name: "I am who am." Yes, God is here! He is here by His Omnipresence, his Omniscience, and His Omnipotence. Christ is here; for "wherever two or three are gathered in My Name, there am I in the midst of them." Shortly, He will be here in His Glorified Body — substantially. So why shouldn't we be glad?

But, really, my first word is a shout of *thanks*. Thank You, God, for all you did in, through, and to Fr. Jack. Thank you, people of God, for coming here to rejoice with me and the family. Thank you, relatives of mine. Thank you, ever-gracious and ever-generous Fr. Rector — and you good Jesuits, Oblates, and others. Thank you, family of mine, given me by God and in Christ. But, above all, thank you, Jack, for all you have been, and ever will be to me personally, and to all the family, not only the Flanagan family, but to the entire family of God and mankind!

Yes, this is Thanksgiving Day. We are gathered in this beautiful chapel for one purpose only: to thank, and thank, and thank! And we are about to do it in the most efficacious manner possible to man; for the Sacrifice left us, and commanded each and everyone of us to offer — for we are all priest: you out there are offering priests, made so by baptism and confirmation; we, here in the sanctuary, are consecrating priest, made so by holy orders. Hence, I say, we have all been commanded by Christ to "Do this . . ." And what are we about to do? Offer a Thanksgiving Sacrifice; for Eucharist, you do know, means Thanksgiving. Therefore, this is to be a *joyous* and even a *joy-filled* celebration!

"But," you may ask, "how can you Flanagans be glad and rejoice when Jack, the eldest of the family, is not in your midst physically? How can you be joyous and joy-filled when he, who was a shining light to you all, no longer so much as glows? When he, who was your leader, your mentor, your model, no longer leads, directs, molds, or models? And how can you, Joe, whose mind and heart he shaped, how can you rejoice and be glad?"

A legitimate query. A solid objection. For if ever it could be said about two brothers that they were *cor unum et anima una* — of *one* mind and *one* heart — it could, and must be said of Jack and Joe. But, friends, I do rejoice with exceeding great joy, and so does my family, for what lies before us is but the "envelope" which held that letter written by God, as St. Paul puts it, and believe me it was a love-letter! Only the envelope lies here; the letter has been returned to its Sender. Isn't that reason enough to rejoice?

When Fr. Rector so graciously offered me the opportunity to speak, and I had so greedily grasped it, I wondered just what text I would use as most apt for this great brother of mine. A whole tessera of them tumbled through my mind, any one of which was apt. But I wanted the *most* apt. It was something of a struggle.

Many of you, knowing Jack's great love for Shakespeare, and his towering, though undeserved, love for me, might suppose I would quote the Bard of Avon, and say: "My heart is in the coffin there with Caesar . . ." for how often did I call him Little Caesar. There would have been aptness in the quote, for when I requested this extraordinary permission to come north from my abbot, I did say: "Remember, Reverend Father, Jack is the diastole of my heart." I could have added: "And the systole, as well," and been factual. But Shakespeare will not do, for how could I ever go on with "I have come to bury Caesar, not to praise him" when I am standing before you expressly to eulogize this great priest of God?

The Holy Spirit, through John the Beloved will do much better. Early on, in this other great love of Fr. Jack, I found the line which tells the truth, the whole truth, and tells it truthfully. For St. John writes: *Fuit homo, missus a Deo, cui nomen erat Joannes.* Yes, there was a man — and what a man — sent by God, and his name was John! That line was first written about John the Baptist. Oh, what parallels ran through my head as I was thinking: *Cui assimilabe te; aut cui comparabo te?* For the Baptist was something of a model for my brother. The Baptist was forthright — so was Jack. The Baptist was fearless — so was Jack. The Baptist was sent by God to point out the Truth — Jack considered his life as having that one same mission, and how he fulfilled it! The Baptist would never compromise, even though it cost him his life — neither would my brother Jack! The Baptist ever and always spoke the truth, and from earliest youth, Jack dedicated himself to truth — objective truth! Some laughed at him for such a dedication. But, Jack, now that you have met Him, who is Truth, you and I know who will have the last laugh, and who will laugh the loudest!

On and on I could go with such parallels. But parallel lines never meet, and Jack has already met God. Further, *omnis comparatio claudicat* — every comparison limps — and if there is one day I must not limp, this is the day! So away with parallels and all comparisons. I will simply say of you what I must say of Christ, whom you ever strove to reproduce, the New Law's only High Priest, and I will take as my text: *Ecce Sacerdos Magnus!* — Behold a great priest!

Oh, I know, Jack, as you well knew, there are those who are asking, "What is a priest?" God forgive them, and God help them! You knew *ab initio et usque ad finem;* yes, from the very beginning and to your last breath that, a priest is Christ, since Christ is *the* Priest! To that silly, un-called for, and, if you will pardon the word, stupid query, there is no other answer that is adequate, no other answer that is true! You knew that answer, Jack, and you lived it! From the very beginning you knew. In those days, to that foolish query: 'What is a priest?', we used to say, He is an *alter-Christus* — another Christ. But, thanks to the true de-velopment of dogma, especially to the doctrine of the Mys-tical Body, we refine our reply today. We drop the *alter* and state simply, a priest is Christ! For we are His members, and we act *in Persona Christi* — yes, in, and as the very Per-son of Christ. For, when at the altar, we do not say, "This is *His* Body," but "This is *My* Body," and we well know that it is not our flesh and blood under the appearances of tran-substantiated bread and wine. We all know that only God can forgive sins, yet, in the Sacrament of Reconciliation, we always say, "*I* forgive." The same is true of all the other Sacraments; we act in the very Person of Christ! What His human nature was for Redemption: an *instrumentum con-junctum Deo,* we are for salvation: a conjoined instrument, and we are conjoined to God! We are not mere ambassadors for Christ, for an ambassador will say, '*My* country wants this . . .' or '*My* country thinks thus. . . .' We always say 'I,' and that 'I' speaks truth, for we *are* Christ!

I served your first Mass, Jack, almost fifty years ago. I heard what you said and I knew what God effected by your words! It was the mystery, the marvel, the miracle of tran-substantiation. I served your Mass many times adown the years. It was my great privilege to be with you as you of-fered your last Mass, offered in the intensive care unit in

Sancta Maria Hospital, when I saw you, body and blood, soul and humanity, on the corporal of white hospital sheets, while on the paten of your ever-generous hands lay your very self, and you were saying: "This is your Body, Lord; this, your Blood. You gave them to me — now I give them back to you. Take them; for they are yours; Take them, but transubstantiate me!" He heard you. He took you at your word. He kept his promise to come as a thief in the night, and commit His grand larceny! He did it to set the Triune God rejoicing, Our Lady-Mother's eyes sparkling with glad welcome, the angelic choirs singing, Ignatius and the whole Society of Jesus standing proud — and that really means the entire court of heaven, for there, we will all be Jesuits, for we will live forever in the *Society of Jesus!*

But you know, Jack, how I always labor, and even belabor, the specific difference, for, as I insist, it makes all the difference in the world. Since this leopard will never change his spots, I stress now the specific difference in your God-given vocation. He not only called you to be a priest, but He called you to be a religious priest, even more specifically, a Jesuit religious priest. And those modifiers and specifiers modified and specified your life and all your living.

Ab initio — ab ineunte aetate — as a Jesuit novice, Ignatius put you through the ropes and even through the wringer. He gave you the ropes which enabled you to climb the very mountain of God, and never once in your long life of almost sixty-four years as a Jesuit, did you ever lose your grasp on those ropes. I am sure there are those in this audience who have heard you tell of the epitaph Swiss mountain-climbers craved for themselves: "Died while climbing." Many of them won that epitaph by accidentally falling while they climbed. You won it by climbing until you reached the summit, where you were clasped by God, and heard that welcome of all welcomes: "Well done, my good, and faithful servant. . . . Come, you blessed of my Father — possess the kingdom prepared for you!"

330

Ignatius placed those ropes in your hands the first time you made his inspired and inspiring Spiritual Exercises in the long, long ago, as a first-year novice. Unlike so many of us, Jack, you not only made those Exercises, you *lived* them, and allowed them to *make* you!

As for putting you through the wringer, Ignatius did that by the very first words of his Exercises wherein he taught you what true humility is, as well as teaching you what a glory it is to be truly humble. He states apodictably: *Homo creatus est.* . . . That is telling precisely what a human *is*. Dust! And even less than dust. A creature is *nothing!* For creation is the production of something from nothing. . . . We remind the people of God of this fact at the beginning of every Lent as we place ashes on their foreheads and say: "Remember man that thou art dust, . . ." but because that is not the entire truth about creation, I always add: Remember dust that thou art *splendor!* For the complete definition of creation is the production of something from nothing, by an *act of God*. Only God can create. Therefore, every creature, from the highest to the lowest, is an act of God. You are an act of the Omnipotent, Omniscient, Omnipresent, All-Beautiful God!

You knew that, Jack, and, as I say, you lived that truth. You lived the entire Exercises, and they made you what Ignatius hoped his Exercises would make every Exercitant. They made you Who you were: Christ. They made you what you were called to be: a Jesuit priest. They made you JESUS!

Unlike so many of us, when you heard the call of the King, you answered with all the love and loyalty of your being. For whenever you took a text from Scripture, or even from your beloved Shakespeare, you not only translated it with your lips, you translated it with your life. When you saw the two standards, there was no hesitancy in your choice. Nor would you be anything less than an *insignis* in His service. The *unice* of the foundation enabled you to be what you set out to be under His standard. You said, and you meant, and you achieved what you meant and said: "Master, go on. And I will follow Thee, to the last gasp with love and loyalty!" The three modes of humility you recognized as three ways of loving, and you loved in the third and highest mode. The three classes of men made an interesting study, but you were interested only in the third class, the *best*. When you made your election, it was your first and final. When you ended your colloquy with Christ after that election, you made it pure prayer. Your *Summe et Suscipe* rang and was registered in heaven:

> Take and receive, O Lord, my liberty;
> Take all my will, my mind, my memory;
> All things I own, and all I have are Thine;
> Thine was the gift — to Thee I all resign . . .

That was your *kenosis* — your emptying self of self. The *pleroma* followed as you added: "Only Thy Grace and Love on me bestow; Possessing these, all riches I forego!"

That, in its own way, was your first Mass, even as a novice, unordained by holy orders, for it was your uncompromising dedication and commitment to follow the Master, whose only purpose on earth was to offer His Mass, to be priest and victim in the one great Sacrifice. Like Him you made your life a Mass, even as you made His Mass your life!

Ignatius showed you that the call of the King was *fact*, not fiction, as he took you through the rest of the second week of the Exercises, on into the bloody third week, which led to the glory of the fourth week, with his contemplations of the Risen Christ. On and on until you reached that climax of all climaxes, that *Contemplatio ad Amorem*, that contemplation to acquire more and more love for God!

You laughed at me often, Jack, when I told you that you were a true contemplative. You laughed louder and longer, and at me, when I insisted in my ever simplistic way that contemplation is naught but looking and loving. Yes, my brother was a contemplative, for he had his gaze fixed unfalteringly on Christ, his leader, and, looking at Him, he loved Him, and loving Him, he served Him! Since love gives, and since Jack's life was one long giving, I say my brother's life was one long act of *love*.

To put it another way, I say, he was a priest through and through, which means that he was Christ day in and day out, year after year, *usque and finem*, right to the end! So, if you want a summary, a sentence that is both epitome and epitaph, an epitaph every priest should strive to earn, and which Jack merited fully, take what I gave a moment ago: He made the Mass his life, and his life a Mass. In parenthesis let me tell you that my young nephews, who knew and loved Jack well, suggested I use one of Jack's favorite quotes from Shakespeare as summary. They suggested: "He was a man, take him for all in all . . ." and that is apt. But you priests, and you people of God know that I cannot go on and say "we shall not look upon his like again." You well know that all of us must pray and pray that we shall look upon his like again and again! For every priest should make his life what Jack made his: an act of love! That is what the Mass was for Christ. He told us so Himself: 'Greater love than this no man has: that he lay down his life for his friend.' Christ did that for us when we were His enemies. And Jack was . . . Christ!

Am I exaggerating? Am I hyperbolic? Am I allowing my brotherly admiration and my fraternal affection to cloud my judgment? Look! Christ, in His Glorified Body is in heaven. Oh, of course as God He is everywhere. As God-Man He is in our midst under the guise of wheat and wine. But, how could He go about doing good in New England, in parish after parish, from the tip of Maine to the lowest extremity of these New England states, unless Jack loaned Him his feet? How could Christ say that He had nowhere to

333

lay His head, unless Jack lived out of a suitcase for over forty years? How could other Magdalenes hear, 'Thy sins are forgiven thee," unless Jack gave Christ his breath to say those words of comfort? How could eyes spiritually blind, ears spiritually deaf, be opened, unless Jack, in the very Person of Christ said: *Epheta?* How could the feet of the spiritually lame be set dancing, the skin of spiritual lepers be made clean? How could Christ be amongst us, even Sacramentally, unless Jack gave and gave and gave himself to Christ, to *be* Christ?

For most of his fifty years, Jack was a worker-priest, not in the style of the French, but a worker-priest in the Ignatian manner, a tireless Jesuit working for God. Even after the mission band was no more, after giving his long life of over forty years to that band, Jack continued to be a worker-priest; for, out to Milton he went week after week unto this last month of September. Ask any who offered Mass with Jack out there, and listened to his homilies, if Jack was a worker-priest. My brother never belonged to the *dabitur vobis* group. No, he prepared his every homily. Despite his lifetime at preaching, he would not rely on his habitual knowledge, but week after week, studied the texts for the day, prayed over them, then wrote out, by hand the thoughts the Holy Spirit had given him. That was not enough. Even in his eighty-third year, he would memorize what he had written. Think of that! When I remonstrated with him, insisting that there was no necessity for him to subject himself to such labor, he smiled and said: "Joe, you do it your way. I'll do it mine. I'm handling the word of God, and giving it to the people of God." Was that work? Ask any who have tried it!

But, as yet, Jack had not lived his priesthood to the hilt, to borrow another of his favorite phrases — worker-priest though he had been, holy priest as he ever was, there was still one other facet. In the New Law the priest is also the victim. In the Old Law the priest offered bullocks and goats, lambs and other beasts, often slain by others. In the New Law, the One High Priest, Jesus Christ, was also Lamb of God who offered Himself, and offered Himself for slaughter! That is why, two months ago, almost to this day and this hour, Jack was asked by God to live his priesthood to the hilt, show himself a thorough priest by dropping all his work, and allowing himself to be worked upon.

Over to Sancta Maria Hospital — what a lovely name: Holy Mary — he went not to offer Christ the victim, but to be Christ's victim, "to fill up what is wanting to His Passion, for His Body, which is the Church." With that piercing intellect, with which he was endowed, he knew. Yes, he knew what God was about. With that will of steel that was his, he said: *Fiat*, and became a lamb for God, silent under his shearers, not opening his mouth. Days went into weeks, weeks mounted into months, and still his only word was the one word Christ uttered in Gethsemani: *Fiat!* Ask the nuns, ask the nurses, ask any of the doctors, if they ever heard a complaint from this priest of God who was then God's lamb for Sacrifice. Early in the morning of December 6th, came, if not from his lips, then surely from his heart, that triumphant cry: *Consummatum est!* or, if you prefer: *Ite, Missa Est!* Then the heart of this great priest, this *sacerdos magnus*, stopped, and the soul of this *sacerdos magnus* flew to his two Fathers — God Almighty and Patrick J. Flanagan; to his two Mothers, Mary — to her who was maid in Nazareth, and to her who was one time maid in Limerick; to his brothers: Jesus, Jim, Lawrence, and Charlie; to his sisters: Sister Leo Stanislaus and Betty — to hear that: Welcome home! Indeed I rejoiced when I heard them say, Let us go to God's house — and now, Jack, your feet are standing — and there they will stand forever within Thy courts, the courts of the heavenly Jerusalem, to live forever in the Society of *Jesus!*

Lest you think I have been carried away by my admiration and affection for this great priest, who was my brother

Jack, to you in the legal profession I will recall what is said about the testimony of two, and ask your indulgence to quote from Jack's last letter to me. It is dated September 8th, the sixty-second anniversary of his entrance into the Society. He wrote: "I am in my 84th year of life, my 63rd in the Society, and my 50th as a priest — and am getting ready for the particular judgment. I am indeed a fortunate man, being in robust physical health (this was before his hospitalization). I have the love of my dear ones, and opportunities to do some good for others. I have habitually tried to live up to my obligations. I am conscious of my lapses, but I have an all-abiding trust and hope in the mercy of Christ, who will judge me. Hence, I go along with the challenge of each day, beginning it with my great privilege of offering Christ to the Father in the Holy Sacrifice of the Mass. All the while I strive to accept and use the means of grace given me — both actual and sanctifying — and I lift my mind and heart to God continually. I know what Christ said about 'Not he who says: "Lord, Lord" . . . 'but he who does the Will of My Father will enter Heaven.' Now love is the fulfilling of the law, and love is, as you know, union of wills." With that quote, I rest my case. Have I not the right to rejoice and be glad and to exclaim: *Ecce sacerdos magnus?* Thank you, Jack, for all you were, and ever have been, and for what you'll continue to be: My *big* brother, Christ's great priest!"

I end with Lacordaire's exclamation: "My God, what a life!" and I add: "What a glorious life! What a joy-filled life! — and it has been mine — A Priest of Jesus Christ. *Alleluia!*"

Now let me use my priestly power on you, my reader, and say: May Almighty God bless you — The Father, who made you; The Son, who redeemed you; and the Holy Spirit, who sanctifies you. Amen."

Now we both can say: "*Thanks be to God!*"